Drums of the
Birkenhead

First edition 1972
Second enlarged edition 1989

By the same author

Non-Fiction
A Guide to Collecting English Banknotes

Fiction
Sangrento

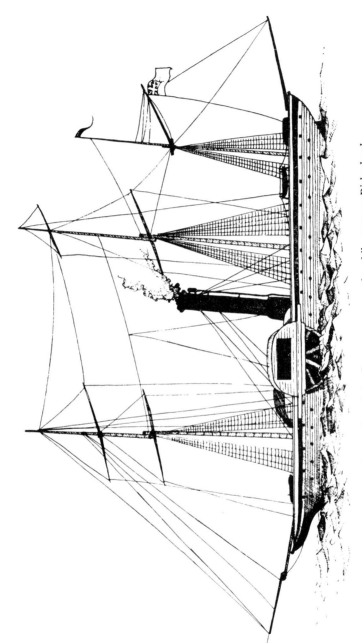

An artist's impression of the Government-owned paddle-steamer *Birkenhead*, illustrated prior to her conversion to a troopship.

Drums of the
Birkenhead

DAVID BEVAN
F.R.G.S., F.B.S.C.

The London Stamp Exchange

Published 1989 by
THE LONDON STAMP EXCHANGE LTD.
The Military & Naval Book Specialists
5 Buckingham Street
Strand
London WC2N 6BS

Copyright © David Bevan 1972, 1989

ISBN 0 948130

Additional material laserset by
Langlands Edition Ltd
Loughborough

Printed by
Antony Rowe Ltd
Chippenham

DEDICATED TO

The memory of those brave men of the Birkenhead.
Their discipline was steady and unbroken
and their heroism steadfast and resolute.
Our heritage has been enriched by these men
who established the tradition of
'women and children first'
which is now accepted in times of tragedy
on the sea.

Dedicated also to Karen,
who lost her courageous fight for life,
aged 14 years.

Contents

Author's Notes
and Acknowledgements

When I first heard of the *Birkenhead* story roughly twelve months ago, quite honestly I didn't really believe it. 'Two-hundred-odd men, on the deck of a troop-ship,' I mused, 'standing to attention to a roll of drums while the ship went down.' 'It's not on,' I thought, 'it's just not on.'

Nevertheless, the story did intrigue me and I went ahead with a little research to discover there *had* been a troopship named the *Birkenhead*, and she *had* gone down under rather unique circumstances. After having laboriously thumbed my way through countless books and endless records I eventually emerged, bleary-eyed, and convinced that not only was the story true but there was far more to it than I ever imagined. Every spare moment was spent delving deeper and deeper into the subject and, bit by bit as the details unfolded, I was so absorbed that it became something of an obsession. I visited all the museums of the ten *Birkenhead* regiments, including the three in Scotland, and I practically lived in libraries, as far apart as Portsmouth in Hampshire and Birkenhead in Cheshire. I spoke to a great number of interesting people connected in one way or another with the incident, some of whom, like Mrs. E. Russell in Somerset, are actually related to men who were on the *Birkenhead*.

It was a fantastic story I had stumbled on, magnificent in deed, and rich in value. A lot of men had died, most of them taken in the prime of their lives. A needless waste of human life? I think not. Through the heritage we are left with, provided we learn the lesson, those men did not die in vain.

The facts I gathered went down on paper and were gradually formed into the book I have proudly entitled, *Drums of the Birkenhead*, and now, one year later, apart from the enormous sense of satisfaction in completing this account of the tremendously moving and inspiring display of courage, I can look back at several months of stimulating and rewarding work. And during those months as I wrote the story, to me the men who sailed on that last voyage of the ill-fated *Birkenhead* were more than just names from a roll-call out of history, they came to life and were real people. Every night too, as I relived the event while piecing together all the state-ments and reports of the survivors, I almost literally walked the deck where those men stood, and then went down with her.

It was impossible to make this a 'technical' book in the sense of trying to establish exactly what happened prior to the disaster, particularly in relation to the position of the ship, bearing in mind a possible compass error. Too much time has passed and there are insufficient records available. And what evidence there is, tends to contradict itself. The facts as known, however, have been presented in as intelligible and interesting manner at possible and it is not my intention to offer any conclusions on the cause of the disaster. The reader himself must decide where error, if error there was, was made, and where blame, if blame there is to be, must lie. All I wish to do within the pages of this book is to give a general background to the disaster and then throw the 'spotlight', as it were, on to those last few incredible moments on deck when the men, in answer to the call made, defied any easy explanation, and to a man 'stood firm'.

Finally, I would like to acknowledge the help and assistance given by so many people, not the least of whom has been my long suffering and patient wife, Pauline, who has lived and died the *Birkenhead* story from the outset. Apart from the material help she so willingly gave, her moral support, much needed at times, was always there.

I wish too, to sincerely thank the following persons and concerns, without whose assistance this book could never have been written: Her Majesty's Stationery Office, London; Historical Library, Ministry of Defence; Imperial War Museum; National Library of Scotland, Edinburgh; National Maritime Museum; Public Records Office; *Radio Times* Hulton Picture Library; Reference Library, *Cape Times* newspaper South Africa; Williamson Art Gallery, Birkenhead; Cammell Laird & Co. (Shipbuilders & Engineers) Ltd.; John Cashmore Ltd., Newport; The Illustrated London News & Sketch Ltd.; British Museum Newspaper Library, London; 'Swordsman' Antiques, Redbourne, Herts.

Various editions of the following newspapers and magazines: *The Times, Morning Post, Morning Herald, Daily News, The Scotsman, Chronicle, Examiner, United Services Gazette*.

Macmillan & Co. Ltd., publishers, London and Basingstoke; Dr. W. Findlay, A.R.P.S., A.B.F.P., Perth; R. W. Hallock, Esq., Cape Town; Mrs. J. Martin, Mounie Castle, Scotland; Michael Presswell, London; Mrs. E. Russell, Somerset; Captain J. Russell, Basingstoke; James E. Macmillan, Esq., F.S.A. (Scot.) Perth.

The regimental museums of the following regiments: the Royal Regiment of Fusiliers (Royal Warwickshire Regimental Museum, Warwick); 9th/12th Royal Lancers (Prince of Wales's), Wigston, Leicestershire; Suffolk Regiment, Bury St. Edmunds; the Royal Greenjackets (Oxfordshire and Buckinghamshire Light Infantry Regimental Museum, Winchester): the Worcestershire and Sherwood Foresters Regiment; the Black Watch, Regimental Museum, Perth; the Royal Highland Fusiliers (Highland Light Infantry Regimental Museum, Glasgow); the Argyll and Sutherland Highlanders, Stirling.

The following public libraries: Birkenhead, Portsmouth, New Malden, Westminster.

The following books to whom acknowledgement is made to the author and publisher:

Major M. Barnes, *A History of the Regiments and Uniforms of the British Army*;
The Revd. Thomas Thomson, *Biographical Dictionary of Eminent Scotsmen*;
Agnes Strickland, *The Queens of England*;
J. Lennox Kerr, *The Unfortunate Ship*;
Jock Haswell, *Queen's Royal Regiment*;
David Seton, *Wreck of the Birkenhead*;
Catharine Sinclair, *Hill and Valley*;
Douglas Sutherland, *The Argyll and Sutherland Highlanders*;
Guthrie Moir, *The Suffolk Regiment*;
L. B. Oates, *Highland Light Infantry*;
A. H. Peters, *Ship Disasters and their Possible Causes*;
A. C. Addison and W. H. Matthews, *A Deathless Story*.

Illustrations at the head of Chapters 1 to 7
by Michael Presswell.
Illustration at head of Chapter 8
by Michelle Castle
Sketch of 1852 diving suit by Cilla Bateman.

Foreword

by

Brigadier G. R. P. Roupell, V.C., C.B., D.L. Last Colonel of The East Surrey Regiment, now part of The Queen's Regiment.

It is interesting to realise that those qualities which are so essential for a soldier to possess on the battlefield, namely loyalty, courage, comradeship and self-control, may be, and often are, equally essential at sea, either in combat with the enemy or in facing a natural disaster.

Mr. Bevan has in this book given us a graphic and inspiring account of the loss of H.M. Troopship *Birkenhead*; graphic in that he gives us a clear picture of the circumstances leading up to and attending this tragedy, and inspiring in that he recounts the splendid behaviour of all ranks on the doomed vessel; behaviour which appears to have been up to the finest traditions of the British Army.

A number of our County Regiments were originally Marines and then, early in the 18th century, when their services at sea were no longer required, they became Regiments of the Line; their histories and those of other Line Regiments record many experiences of soldiers at sea, and I will quote two examples, one of fighting an aggressive enemy, the other of dealing with a natural disaster.

In 1793 at the outbreak of the Napoleonic War with France, The Queen's Regiment was split up into detachments to serve with the fleet as Marines, and it was then that the Regiment's close and happy association with the Royal Navy began.

That Regiment still celebrates annually 'The Glorious First of June' to commemorate the gallant part played by their predecessors on board the battleships of Lord Howe in the successful action against the French in 1794, when they acted as boarding parties against the French ships or in beating off the attempted capture of our own vessels.

The other example, that of dealing with a natural disaster, is, in many respects, not unlike the *Birkenhead* incident.

In 1825 the 31st Foot, later to become The East Surrey Regiment, embarked for India with Bn. H.Q. and the Right Wing in The Honourable East India Company's Ship the *Kent*.

As in the case of the *Birkenhead* there was a number of women and children on board. The ship caught fire in the Bay of Biscay and became a total loss, but thanks to the splendid discipline and the courageous behaviour of all ranks of the 31st Foot, comparatively few lives were lost, particularly amongst the women and children, and eventually the brig *Cambria* picked up the survivors.

Recent events, for example the exemplary behaviour of our troops in Northern Ireland, remind one that the spirit which has permeated our armed forces in the past still lives in the Army today.

Mr. Bevan has done good service in recording this story of the *Birkenhead* as an inspiration for this and for future generations.

Introduction

DRUMS OF THE *BIRKENHEAD*

Toll of the brave
The brave who are no more
Gone beneath the waves
Far from their native shore

The toll of bravery, the price of courage . . .

Discipline, which is often the foundation stone for courage, and courage itself, are two qualities we all possess. For most of the time they lie dormant within us, needing only a particular sequence of circumstances to bring them out, and as has been proved time and time again, in any emergency or moment of sudden crisis, discipline, and the ability that comes with it of being ready to face, and having the capacity to endure, adverse conditions including fear and great danger, can save lives. But even if the ultimate result is death, no one can deny the supreme importance of that state of mind and body that produces clear thinking and self-control when events are such that the human body's system would otherwise collapse.

It is not possible to give a clear and precise definition of courage, as this, to each individual person, is something quite different that shows itself in a variety of ways. Nor is it possible to answer with any certainty why, with some men under specific conditions, the instinct of discipline and consequently courage, is greater even than the instinct of life itself.

Courage is displayed in degrees. It is something that can develop over a long period of time and can be seen in ordinary people in all walks of life. People on whom tragedy has fallen, but who bear up to their responsibilities and are able to live their lives to the full, and give of their best, as if nothing at all had happened.

Or, courage can be spontaneous, as is frequently the case with soldiers in battle. The illustrious story of the British Army has a thousand and one examples of this type of courage, in events which have inspired authors, painters, and poets alike.

But does it really matter though, what the initial cause that triggers off the reaction we call courage? Situations in history, and closer to home in people we know and love, have shown us that the end result is worthy indeed of the virtue which lifts mankind to a level higher than the dimensions we normally accept in our day-to-day lives.

It is with the discipline and courage shown by our soldiers that this book is concerned. Anyone who has served in the Forces will appreciate that discipline is a
basic ingredient of service life and without it the whole system of military co-ordina-
tion would fall in shreds. It is the first thing a soldier learns. His opportunity for
courage comes later.

Whose imagination at some time or another has not been stirred a little, and
whose heart has not beaten a little faster, as thoughts come to mind of epic battles
and great deeds of courage from the past. Who cannot fail to be moved at the men
of the 17th/21st Lancers who, together with five other regiments numbering 600
men in all, charged to immortality in the 'Valley of Death' at Balaclava. When
the Russian guns opened fire and the tragic error of their famous charge became
obvious, not one lancer faltered or wavered. They rode on, heroically charging the
guns and were cut to pieces. And who cannot fail to marvel at the Argyll and
Sutherland Highlanders who formed the 'Thin Red Line' and not only withstood
a full charge of crack Russian Cossacks, but drove them off in utter confusion
and with great losses. Or the inspiring and almost unbelievable defence of Rorke's
Drift, in South Africa, by one company of the South Wales Borderers against
thousands of Zulu warriors. Their courage and devotion to duty, in an action
that aroused the wonder and admiration of the entire world, was of the highest
degree.

The British Army can trace its history and traditions back over four centuries
and during this time its splendid achievements have remained unsurpassed by any
other army. The roll-call of name places from the battle honours of the regiments
of the line is endless, and there is hardly a portion of the globe where British soldiers
have not set new heights of courage and discipline which have carved for themselves,
their regiments, and for England herself, a distinguished and honoured place in the
annals of military history. And these men who served England so well in her finest
hours were the pioneers who helped in creating and maintaining the greatest empire
the world had ever known.

Prior to the turn of the century discipline in the British Army was strict, even
ruthless, and the punishments for insubordination and lack of proper conduct were
extremely severe. Disobeying orders, particularly while on active service abroad,
could mean first a whipping, and then the guilty soldier being spreadeagled across
the wheels of a gun carriage for a taste of the hot sun. There were other inhuman
sentences too, that were carried out as a matter of disciplinary routine, even execution for certain offences, and these perhaps will prompt people to say that to a
large extent discipline, and consequent acts of courage, were motivated by fear. But
on the other hand, it is an undisputed fact that soldiers had a tremendous pride in
their regiments, and patriotism to Queen and country at this time was at its highest.
The colours, too, the very heart of a regiment and its rallying point in battle, which

were taken into action and displayed prominently, were treasured symbols of a glorious past that men would fight and die to defend.

So what is it that makes men stand up and face overwhelming odds? Fear, or pride? Or perhaps it's a little of each, who can really tell? Even men who have lived through an experience which has brought them face to face with death, who have shown immense courage and fortitude throughout, find it difficult, almost impossible, to describe afterwards exactly what their innermost feelings were at the time.

No-one wants to die. Life is very precious. And in almost every situation, no matter how bad, there is always the chance that death will pass by. In even the most bitter of battles, to each man involved there is always the possibility of survival. The thought that, although men all around are being hit, '. . . it won't happen to me, I'm going to make it'. Perhaps it is this small glimmer of hope that makes men go unflinchingly forward.

But what of the men who display the most noble brand of courage of all, that of deliberately laying down their lives so that others will live? For men who do this, there is no chance and no hope. They have time to think and they are perfectly aware of the deed they are doing. This is heroism that is impossible to equal. Heroism whose shining light wears the years with undiminished brightness.

The story contained within the pages of this book offers us this sort of heroism. It is one of the most magnificent stories of iron discipline and meritorious self-sacrifice ever recorded and one that deserves to be told, and told again.

It took place 120 years ago, not in some epic battle as one might imagine, but on the sea, on board a troopship, during a quiet and peaceful voyage to South Africa.

The story was carried by all major newspapers and magazines throughout the world and it so impressed the King of Prussia, Frederick Wilhelm IV, that he ordered a full account of the conduct of the British soldiers to be brought to the attention of all his troops. Accordingly, a record of the event was read out at the head of every single regiment in the Prussian Army.

England had every right to be proud of her sons, and what was done that day remained deeply impregnated in the mind of the nation for a long time. About the turn of the century memories gradually became hazy and events such as the First World War grimly overshadowed the past. But it has not been completely forgotten, particularly by the regiments involved who, with every justification, place an unparalleled pride on the event and give to it the same honour and respect they show to their greatest battle honour.

This supreme test of valour, enacted in the very jaws of death, touched the hearts and inspired the strength of people everywhere, and has, throughout the years, become known as, 'The Drums of the *Birkenhead*'.

So much of value has been learned from this incident, and whilst we must not live nor revel in past glories, it is only right that they should be mentioned, not just to enable us to sing our praises but so that they might act as a spur to us and ensure that, like the men of the *Birkenhead*, we give of our best when called upon to do so.

1. Prelude to disaster

First just a tremor was felt as the engines started to turn and, amidst a chorus of shouts, orders, and ringing of bells, the capstans began to groan and creak their way round, slowly winching in the ropes and chains that raised the anchors. Then a more definite and rhythmic vibration ran through the vessel as the gap between the ship and the shore widened, and Her Majesty's Troopship *Birkenhead*, under the command of Captain Robert Salmond, R.N., gradually pulled away towards the open sea.

Serving under Captain Salmond, his executive officers included Mr. William Brodie the Master of the *Birkenhead*, Mr. Whyham the Chief Engineer, Mr. R. Speer and Mr. Jeremiah O'Davis the two Second Masters, and Mr. R. Richards and Mr. C. Hare the Master's Assistants. Mr. John T. Archbold, a seaman typical of the 'hearts of oak' type, was the Master Gunner of the ship, and Mr. C. Renwick and Mr. Benjamin Barber were the First-Class and Third-Class Engineers, respectively.

Mr. Brodie who was originally of the Mercantile Marine had joined the Navy in 1843 and was appointed to the *Birkenhead* in June 1851, having previously served as second master on the 120-gun flagship, H.M.S. *Vincent*. Mr. Barber, another highly experienced and efficient seaman had entered the Navy ten years previously, in 1842, and after his apprenticeship was made third-class assistant engineer in 1847, joining Captain Salmond on the *Birkenhead* in 1851.

All the officers worked well together, as did the crew, who were content and glad to be aboard a ship such as the *Birkenhead*, which, as an iron vessel, had an easier routine than the wooden warships. It was a well-disciplined ship and one that its captain was justly proud of.

It was raining and blowing hard on that fateful day in January 1852 when the *Birkenhead* left the port of Cork, Southern Ireland, and on the open seas the ship pitched and rolled violently, with the bad weather continuing for nearly two weeks until well past the Bay of Biscay.

At this time England was engaged in the Kaffir War in South Africa and the task of the *Birkenhead* on this particular voyage was to convey troop reinforcements to the aid of Lieutenant General Sir Harry Smith, the Governor and Military Commander at the Cape. Of the 693 personnel on board the ship, the military persons were made up of the following drafts for the various regiments serving on the frontier:

> 2nd Foot (The Queen's, Royal West Surrey Regiment). Ensign Boylan, 1 sergeant, 50 men.
> 6th Foot (Royal Warwickshire Regiment). Ensign Metford, 1 sergeant, 60 men.
> 12th Lancers (9th/12th Royal Lancers). Cornets Sheldon-Bond and Rolt, 1 sergeant, 5 men.
> 12th Foot (Suffolk Regiment). Lieutenant Fairclough, 1 sergeant, 68 men.
> 43rd Light Infantry (1st Battalion Oxfordshire and Buckinghamshire Light Infantry). Lieutenant Girardot, 1 sergeant, 40 men.
> 45th Foot (1st Battalion Nottinghamshire and Derby Regiment). One warrant officer, 1 sergeant, 15 men.
> 73rd Foot (2nd Battalion Royal Highland Regiment). Lieutenants Robinson and Booth, Ensign Lucas, 1 sergeant, 70 men.
> 74th Foot (2nd Battalion Highland Light Infantry). Lieutenant-Colonel A. Seton, Ensign Russell, 1 warrant officer, 60 men.
> 91st Foot (1st Battalion Argyll and Sutherland Highlanders). Captain E. Wright, 2 sergeants, 100 men.[1, 2]

Some families also accompanied the troops and the ship's total contingent consisted of 31 children, 25 women, 1 naval surgeon (Dr. William Culhane), 17 ship's officers, 125 crew, 3 military surgeons (Staff Surgeon Laing and Staff Assistant

1. The numbers shown for the 91st include a detachment of 1 sergeant and 40 men of the 60th Rifles, which were temporarily attached to the 91st.
2. Due to changes in the British Army, reductions and amalgamations between regiments, some of the following names may now be different:
   2nd Foot, now known as the Queen's Regiment.
   6th Foot, now known as Royal Regiment of Fusiliers.
   12th Lancers, now known as 9th/12th Royal Lancers.
   12th Foot, now known as Suffolk Regiment.
   43rd Light Infantry, now known as Royal Greenjackets.
   45th Foot, now known as the Worcestershire and Sherwood Foresters Regiment.
   73rd Foot, now known as the Black Watch.
   74th Foot, now known as Royal Highland Fusiliers.
   91st Foot, now known as Argyll and Sutherland Highlanders.

Surgeons Robertson and Bowen), 12 military officers, and 479 soldiers of other ranks.

Lieutenant-Colonel Alexander Seton, a tall, distinguished 38-year-old Scotsman, was the senior military officer on board. Coming from a noble line of ancestors, whose family seat at Mounie Castle, Aberdeen, had held connections with Mary Queen of Scots, there could not have been a better man to command the troops on the *Birkenhead*. He showed a degree of strictness and fairness which produced the right combination of authority necessary to command such a wide variety of men from the different regiments on the ship. Entering the Army in November 1832 at the age of 18 years he served initially as a second lieutenant in the 21st Royal North British Fusiliers, seeing service in Australia, Germany, and India. He was a gifted man with a brilliant mind, and among his numerous qualifications he spoke fifteen languages, including Hindustani and Persian, and was recognized as an expert authority on natural philosophy, mathematics, mechanics, and surveying. He was also a lover of music and his tastes in this field were yet further proof of his great strength of character and his immense personality. His first love, however, was the Army, and this point is noted quite definitely in the reference to him which may be found in the *Biographical Dictionary of Eminent Scotsmen*: '. . . but his prevailing bias was towards the Military profession, which he studied as a science, and to which all his acquirements were made subservient'.

In 1847, having attained the rank of captain, he joined the 74th Highlanders, then stationed in Ireland. After four years' service with the 74th he was promoted to lieutenant-colonel and instructed to proceed to South Africa to take over as commanding officer of the regiment which, apart from a small number of men, had already been despatched to the Cape several months earlier.

The second senior military officer on board the *Birkenhead* was Captain Edward Wright who, in later years, was to rise to the rank of full colonel and who, in 1870 one year prior to his death in Chelsea, was to receive by the grace of Her Majesty the Queen an appointment to the Most Honourable Order of the Bath. Captain Wright's military service was exemplary, being mentioned in general orders and dispatches on more than one occasion for conspicuous conduct and successful operations against the enemy in the two Kaffir wars. For two years he commanded the 91st Regiment, which served in the Fort Beaufort area, and his exploits in the field of battle and his military leadership earned the respect and admiration of all who knew him, and made his name a legend amongst the troops on the frontier.

During the voyage both the Lieutenant-Colonel and Captain Wright were kept occupied with military matters, as, despite the fact that the troops were on board ship and on the high seas, military life with its musters, roll-calls, defaulters' parades, and other procedures, still went on.

Most of the soldiers on board had only been in uniform for just a matter of weeks

Lieutenant-Colonel Alexander Seton as a young
second lieutenant in the Royal North British
Fusiliers. From a family portrait.

and a good number of these men, although wearing the scarlet and blue of England or the tartan of Scottish regiments, were young Irishmen who had joined to escape the poverty and destitution that faced the population of Ireland at that time. The disastrous potato blight of the 1840s had left in its wake a country stripped almost to the bone by famine, and hundreds of thousands of people died under the most horrible conditions from disease and starvation. Of those that survived, but who chose to remain existing pitifully in Ireland instead of joining the mass emigration to England or America, thousands of young boys, and what able-bodied men there were left, only too gladly answered the call to arms and enlisted in the British Army. Although the pay wasn't good, even for those days, more often than not it was regular. A shilling a day for a private soldier in the infantry, or 1s. 3d. per day for a trooper in a cavalry regiment. And at least it meant clothes on their backs, boots on their feet, and, most important of all, food in their hungry bellies.

Even so, in spite of this swelling of their ranks, the Army was still continuously short of men and often there was no time, nor were there the facilities available, to train them properly. They were put straight into uniform, handed a musket, and sent off to war, most of them being drafted into regiments on active service in South Africa, as this war, at that time, was the biggest drain on the Army's resources.

The *Birkenhead* had arrived in Ireland during early January with two detachments already on board, the 12th Foot, under the command of Lieutenant Fairclough, and a small number of the 12th Lancers, under two young cornets, John Rolt and the dashing and debonair 23-year-old Ralph Sheldon-Bond. They had embarked at Portsmouth where the *Birkenhead*, fully crewed, had lain at anchor since early December, awaiting the orders which eventually came. She was stocked with fuel and provisions, and included in the supplies was a large quantity of wine destined for the officers' mess in the garrisons on the front line. Also loaded on board were 350 double-barrelled rifle carbines of a new pattern for the use of the 12th Lancers and, although there is no direct evidence such as written military or naval records to support the theory, there is a strong probability that a shipment of gold, to the value of £250,000 was put aboard to be used for payment to the troops on active service.

On 3 January the *Birkenhead* got under way and headed out of the Solent, around the south-west coast of England and into the Irish Sea. She docked off Queenstown in the precincts of Cork Harbour on 5 January and for the next two days was a hive of activity preparing for the long voyage ahead. Her supplies of fresh water, meat, and coal for the boilers were topped up, and the troop accommodation immediately made ready for the remaining 416 soldiers, and the women and children.

The embarkation of the troops was carried out as swiftly as possible and was watched by many of the townsfolk. Women and girls lining the route from the barracks to the quayside sobbed, and called out as they saw boys they knew and loved going bravely away, perhaps even for ever. They reached forward to familiar faces and tried to touch the arms of the soldiers as they marched along to the stirring music of the garrison drum and fife band down the narrow twisting streets of the town. Small boys, ragged and dirty-faced and grinning from ear to ear, kept up with the columns of men, copying their marching steps in exaggerated movements as small boys everywhere do when soldiers go marching by. It was exciting and it was sad. But the sight of soldiers, some mere boys really, going to war always is.

As they reached the quay the women and girls who had followed behind their menfolk huddled together in little groups, pulling their shawls closer around their shoulders, and sheltering each other as best they could from the bitter wind that came in from the open sea and bit into their faces, and while the small boys still jumped about and cheered wildly, everyone who had gathered to watch waved grimly as the troops clambered clumsily into the boats which would take them out to where the black and white painted troopship lay anchored at her moorings.

On the *Birkenhead* the troops were rapidly assembled into some sort of order by their officers and non-commissioned officers, who were also shivering from the cold and stamping their feet, and with much hustle and bustle, and shouting by the sergeants, the men were quickly split into small groups to be led by seamen to the quarters allotted to them. And for the majority of these inexperienced recruits, some of whom had never before been in any form of boat or ship in their entire lives, the alarming prospect of descending through the narrow hatchways and down into the dim, lantern-lit decks below, gave rise to a sudden feeling of fear and apprehension in a good many stomachs.

However, urged on by the incessant pushing and bellowing of the bull-like sergeants they struggled through the hatches which, a few moments earlier, for a man with all his equipment on his back and a musket in his hands had seemed almost an impossibility. But worse was to come. Once through the tiny openings they then had to feel out blindly with their feet for the precarious rungs of the ladders which led downwards. Gripping the side of the ladders tightly with one hand, they clutched their muskets hard to their bodies with the other, and with much muttering and occasional swearing they made the descent.

Short, sharp, jerky movements brought them rapidly down the ladders, literally falling off the last rung on to the men in front who had clustered together at the bottom. As they jostled against each other with their knapsacks, which stuck out behind them, slowly their eyes became accustomed to the gloom, and snatching quick frightened glances they took in the strange new surroundings that would be their home for the next few weeks. They became aware, too, of the weird smells and peculiar creaking noises which are unique to iron ships. Some of the older troops though, who had been on the earlier rat-infested and airless wooden sailing ships, were in a far happier and relaxed state as the *Birkenhead*, by comparison, was luxurious. She was spacious and dry inside, and the iron hull plates were clean and fresh-looking with paint. In the large troop sections, where the men would live, eat, and sleep, long scrubbed wooden tables ranged out on each side of the compartments, leaving a narrow gangway down the centre, and overhead there were adequate racks for the men's equipment. Oh yes, thought the older soldiers smugly, this is a good ship.

The whole of the lower deck, except for a portion at the stern occupied by wives and children, was taken up by the soldiers, as was part of the main deck forward of the engine-room. The military officers, including Lieutenant-Colonel Seton, and the ship's junior officers, together with two of the officer's wives, had cabins at the stern end of the main deck, while the ship's senior officers, including the captain, were in the cabins in the raised poop. These cabins, on both decks, were built around the sides and stern of the ship, the ones on the main deck opening out into the messes. The sleeping arrangements for the officers and all the women and children consisted of bunks, but the troops, as with the ship's crew, had hammocks. These hammocks, when in use, were slung the regulation 18 in. apart on hooks in the overhead beams. During the day they were packed and stored around the covered base of the funnel, between the paddle-boxes on the upper deck.

There were various ship's regulations to be observed by the troops and these were read out, together with a list of duties for those soldiers detailed to assist the crew in tasks on board.

By 7 January, two days after embarkation, the troops were properly quartered and had more or less settled in, although in such a short space of time, and through not having yet sailed and tasted the sea proper, the transformation from landlubbers to seamen was far from complete. On the ship generally the paraphernalia of pre-paration had finished, and the scheduled time of departure had come. Men were positioned at their stations on the upper deck, and down below in the cavern-like engine-room the engineers were poised ready at their controls. But before the Captain's awaited orders that would bring the engines, first hissing, and then roaring into life, a final check was made by Mr. Brodie, the ship's Master, and his assistants to ensure the capstans were fully manned in readiness for bringing up the anchors, and that all movable objects on the open upper deck were securely lashed. After which, Mr. Brodie returned swiftly to the poop and reported to Captain Salmond that all was well.

The Captain instructed the anchors to be raised and while this order was being carried out satisfied himself the ship's two compasses were operational and function-ing accurately.

Both compasses were on the poop; the 'standard compass', located near the mizzen mast, was the more accurate of the two and was the one used for all naviga-tional work and for taking bearings. It was also the compass referred to in all entries on the ship's log. The 'binnacle compass' was fixed in an illuminated lantern-shaped binnacle that was just in front of the wheel, and this was the compass used for steering the ship.

Moving to the fore end of the poop, Captain Salmond faced down the ship and took one last searching look around the upper deck, acknowledging with his hand the signal from the forecastle that the anchors were now aweigh. His order to steam ahead came loud and clear, and in a fanfare of noise the *Birkenhead* moved slowly forward. Her voyage into the pages of history had begun.

As the ship cleared the harbour and steamed out into the open sea the earlier fears and apprehensions of the soldiers, in their first hours on board, were nothing compared to the blind terror that now gripped them as the *Birkenhead* fought its way through the heavy seas; seas that threatened, with each downward plunge of the vessel, to swallow up the iron trespasser and deliver it to eternity. Everybody was on the lower decks, except for the seamen at the helm, who fought and strained with every ounce of strength in their bodies to keep the wheel straight, and those men on watch duty, including the Captain on the poop, who sheltered as best they could, holding firmly on to the nearest solid fixture to prevent themselves being torn from the deck and flung helplessly aside like toys. Down below the packed troop decks were a shambles. Loose bits and pieces of equipment clattered back and forth across the floor with the rolling of the ship, and white-faced men sat tightly on the heavy benches or lay huddled about in corners, holding on to whatever they could. Most of them, apart from the older hardened ones, were ill and violently seasick, and some were so bad and so utterly exhausted, that they prayed for the death they were convinced would surely come. The hatches on the upper deck were closed down and secured, and the small amount of air that came down the ventilation shafts was nowhere near enough to clear the awful smells of sweating human bodies and the stench of vomit thrown up from stomachs, heaved to their limits, that lay in pools everywhere.

The ship was taking a tremendous pounding, and with each downward thrust of the front end into the valley of water created by the shape of the mountainous waves, the stern would lift high in the air, bringing the huge rudder right out of the water, and the vessel would remain in that suspended position, poised and helpless, for what, to the men trapped inside, seemed like a lifetime. And while the angry sea momentarily held its breath, as if to summon up an even greater effort, the ship would judder from stem to stern, seemingly in defiance of the forces of nature that wished to destroy it, before crashing down with an immense impact through the waves sweeping in fury across the length of the deck. Again and again, with no relent and no mercy, the berserk sea tossed its opponent at will, but the *Birkenhead*, with thick black smoke belching from its funnel, refused to submit.

For ten nerve-shattering days there was no let-up from the mighty Atlantic. Then, gradually, as the tired ship battled its way south the gale began to blow itself out, and the violence and turmoil of the sea ceased. That the *Birkenhead* survived the frenzy of the storm for so many days is a reflection not just of the ship, but of the skill and endurance of the sailors who crewed her, and is indeed a triumph of man's ingenuity over the elements.

To the poor soldiers, and the women and children who had been no less tortured and terrified, sanity seemed to return as the ship slowly adopted a more even movement in the calmer seas. And for Dr. Culhane, the ship's surgeon, and his military colleagues, Laing, Robertson, and Bowen, the lull in the weather meant they could finally get some rest. Since the day the ship had left port they had been on duty almost continuously, attending to the women and children and doing what they could for the worst cases amongst the soldiers. To add to their burden the tremendous buffeting the ship had undergone resulted in no less than six of the women, who were pregnant, giving birth prematurely. Some of the older more hardened ones who managed to remain on their feet, like Mrs. Darkin travelling out with her 4-year-old daughter Marian to join her husband Drum-Major Darkin of the Queen's, were towers of strength and gladly gave what help they could to the tired surgeons. Bandmaster Zwyker's wife, travelling out with her husband, was another who assisted. They sat with the young terror-stricken mothers who could not remember, nor cared, when it all started but simply longed for it to end. They held their trembling hands tightly, talking and comforting them while wiping their sweating brows, and supplying their parched throats liberally with gin and rum which helped a little to ease the pain. After hours of suffering the shrill cries of newborn babies meant, for three of the women at least, that the agonizing ordeal was finally over and they lay back exhausted, but content at last, fingering gently the tiny new faces beside them. But for the other three, the unequal struggle was to prove too great and as their long-drawn-out labours continued, their screams gradually diminished to become soft pathetic moans and sobs. The deep, dark shadows which had formed under their eyes were made more noticeable now that their straining and tossing had stopped, and they lay still. That death was a relief was shown by the look of final peace that formed on their pale young faces.

Another woman was to die horribly, of consumption, and within the following few days, in a simple but moving ceremony on deck, the four canvas-shrouded bodies were buried at sea.

After the havoc of the storms the *Birkenhead* became a hive of working activity. Fortunately only superficial repairs were needed to be carried out, as structurally the ship had not suffered any damage, and while these were being attended to by some of the crew members others, with soldiers helping, got on with the job of cleaning up the mess everywhere. On the upper deck, equipment, coal bags, and other articles which had broken loose, were fastened back in position and a pump swilled water over the deck after it had been scoured by soldiers and sailors working on their knees. Ropes were re-coiled and laid neatly down and the ship's brass fittings were polished until they gleamed. There was a lot to do and the men worked hard.

Although the troops were beginning to recover from the after effects of what they had endured, to Seton, they presented an appalling sight when they were paraded on deck for the first time for a muster call. Dirty, unshaven, and unkempt, they emerged from below weak and listless. Their uniforms were torn and stained and their unwashed bodies still smelled of sickness.

Seeing their dreadful state and slovenly bearing gave Seton, the professional military man and perfectionist, a determination to turn these raw country lads, not only into well-trained soldiers, but also into men who would take an interest in themselves and their appearance, who would wear their uniform with pride and give only of their best to their respective regiments.

First they were put to work in their own quarters, cleaning up the troop decks and putting them into order. The wooden tables and benches were scrubbed vigorously and their equipment, which had been stewn across the floor, was sorted out, cleaned, and restacked on the racks. And then, when Seton was satisfied with the results, he skilfully directed the men's attention to their own cleanliness and smartness.

It was not an easy task that Seton had set himself, but it was the sort of challenge that a man of his calibre and nature relished, and it was during this initial period that his real brilliance and qualities of leadership shone through. His success was reflected in the change in the troops which, in the days that followed, was truly remarkable. He had in any case, already earned a great deal of trust and respect from the soldiers by his interest in them and his behaviour during the storms when, always immaculately dressed and completely composed he had made a daily tour of the troop decks to talk to, and reassure them. And by his firm and confident manner had managed to instil in the soldiers some measure of the immense strength that radiated from him. In doing so he alleviated a little of the terror which, as strangers to such a violent world as an angry sea, they had suffered.

A daily training routine was soon established, in which drills and inspections played a prominent part, and Seton was fortunate in that he could rely to a very large extent on the value of his subordinate officers, and the experienced and able non-commissioned officers, under his command on the ship. Captain Wright in particular, whose military standards approached those of his senior officer, proved to be a tremendous asset, and so did the younger officers like Alexander Russell, fresh from Glenadmond, Scotland, the 19-year-old ensign in Seton's own regiment; young Arthur Lucas of the 73rd whose ambitions lay outside the Army and who looked upon his military service as merely a short phase in his career; 23-year-old Frank Girardot of the 43rd Light Infantry, a vicar's son from Nottinghamshire; and the well-born and wealthy John Rolt of 19 years. They showed that now they too were back on their feet, they had enough keenness to learn and eagerness to succeed, to make up for any lack of experience. Throughout the training programme the right degree of discipline was enforced by Seton on to the troops who, instinctively, sensed that here in this unique Scottish colonel was a sincere man, a man from whom they could learn only what was good and right, a man they could look up to who consistently set an example they felt compelled to copy, and who could, were it ever to become necessary, lead them safely through even the most direful adversity.

The weather had now changed completely and as the days went by the *Birkenhead* made good steady progress, gaining some of the time lost earlier during the storms. The days became much warmer and life on board, particularly amongst the passengers, was considerably brighter.

Stops were made at Madeira, Sierra Leone, and, finally, on 9 February after crossing the Equator a few days earlier, with the troops sweltering under the hottest sun they had ever known, the *Birkenhead* docked at the island of St. Helena, in the South Atlantic. Some of the officers went ashore at these ports of call, but the soldiers had to remain on board to assist the crew in loading the coal and fresh provisions. The *Birkenhead* stayed in port no longer than was absolutely necessary, and after being replenished at St. Helena, she resumed her journey down the West Coast of Africa.

The ship was still dwarfed by the immensity of the ocean round her, but now, in the tranquillity of a sea at rest, and caught in the intense heat of the day, the scene on board was so different to that of the first two weeks of the voyage. The sky was blue from one horizon to the other, and the only movement in the still green surround was the churning of the water each side of the ship as its huge paddles turned and fell with lazy monotony.

Children were running about, eagerly exploring and then hiding behind the stacks of equipment on those parts of the deck on which they were allowed, before being found by their mothers and lightly scolded. And on the deck of the forecastle and the forward part of the upper deck, to which the troops were restricted, groups of men stood or sat about in between their duties, smiling and chatting, and enjoying the calm sea and hot sun. Some were reading while others, perhaps more conscientiously, were cleaning and polishing their equipment. They were now mixing more with the sailors, and often a good hour or so could be passed talking with new friends and exchanging favourite yarns. The women, in gay sun bonnets, were there too, arms linked in those of their husbands. If their menfolk happened to be on duty, they would sit in the sun busy mending and sewing uniforms.

The officers, as was to be expected, were at the other end of the ship, Seton having obtained permission from Captain Salmond for them to have recreational facilities on the poop deck and away from the men, thus ensuring the two groups would not have to mingle during their leisure hours. The officers were not permitted on the fore end of the poop however, as that was where the ship's officer of the watch paced back and fore.

Seton and Wright would often talk together on the poop, and whilst standing close to the bulwarks at the stern discussing, perhaps, daily affairs or the Kaffir War they were about to join, they would glance down at the water and allow for a few moments their eyes to follow the white froth that formed a continual and ever-widening triangle in the ship's wake.

Although both men got on well together and shared a mutual respect for one another, each in fact came from an entirely different social background and whereas Seton's entry into the British Army had been by the purchase of a commission, the tall, well-built Edward Wright had risen through the ranks and earned his commission at a military collage.[3] Both men however, were excellent officers and experienced commanders and as they grew to know each other better they found they had many common interests. Each too, had been on foreign service. Seton though, in contrast to Wright who had seen action, had never fired a gun in anger.

On the other hand, Seton's relationship with Captain Salmond, until they came to understand each other better, was somewhat strained. The young Lieutenant-Colonel often found it difficult to accept the authority of a man who, although a master commander and captain of the ship, was not a commissioned officer. His rank, and this applied to all the *Birkenhead*'s officers, was that of warrant officer. They did not hold the Queen's Commission, but this did not in any way indicate a lack of intelligence or experience. In fact it was quite the contrary. In those days the Royal Navy possessed many high-ranking officers who attained their positions more often than not by whom they knew, rather than what they knew, but men like Robert Salmond (described by *The Scotsman*, '. . . as a navigator Mr. Salmond ranked among the most skilful of the Royal Navy') who, although only of warrant rank rose to command ships on sheer merit and the strength of their own capabilities.

The *Birkenhead* continued to make good progress. The days were perfect and the troops in high spirits. They still had their training periods, but the whole atmosphere of life on board had changed. By no stretch of the imagination though

3. Seton's promotion was as follows:
   November 1832: second-lieutenant by purchase, Royal North British Fusiliers.
   March 1838: first-lieutenant by purchase.
   January 1842: captain without purchase, 74th Highlanders.
   May 1850: major by purchase.
His final promotion to lieutenant-colonel was without purchase.
   Captain Wright's second-lieutenancy was without purchase. His promotion to first-lieutenant, then captain, was by purchase.

Purely as a matter of interest the following purchase table applied during the period 1844–59.

	Lieutenant-colonel	Major	Captain	Lieutenant	Cornet
Dragoons (£)	6,175	4,575	3,725	1,190	840
Infantry (£)	4,540	3,200	1,800	700	450

The ranks of cornet and ensign were equivalent

were the men in any way pampered; and they still suffered the discomforts of the troop decks. The food, served up three times a day, was grim too and usually consisted of a mug of greasy cocoa and a rock-hard biscuit for breakfast; for their lunch at noon, beef or pork, which had been soaked in brine and which many thought could be put to better use on the soles of their boots; and finally, cocoa and the same rock-hard biscuits again in the evening.

But all this was forgotten, as were the two weeks of misery at the start of their journey, as they relaxed on the open decks in the warm soft evenings, laughing and joking, against a musical background provided by the pipes of Scottish soldiers. All thoughts of the war ahead went from their minds, and they joined heartily in the lusty strains of 'Highland Laddie' and renderings of other Scottish and Irish melodies which contributed in no small way to the pleasure and liveliness that generated through the *Birkenhead* and prevailed on her as she steamed further south for the remainder of the forty-seven-day voyage to the Cape. And for two young people especially, the trip had a particularly wonderful meaning. Young Ensign Metford of the 6th Foot had chosen the Christmas period, only a few days before embarkation, to marry a pretty, fresh-faced Irish girl named Maria Falkiner from Newagh, so for this blissful couple the journey to South Africa was a honeymoon voyage and to them the *Birkenhead* was more than just a troopship.

★   ★   ★   ★

Launched in December 1845, the iron paddle-steamer *Birkenhead*, originally intended to be a warship for the Royal Navy, was constructed by Laird's of Birkenhead and named after the city in which she was built. And for John Laird, the man who designed her, standing with his guests as the launching ceremony was performed by the elegant Marchioness of Westminster, this was the realization of a dream. But underneath the proud look in his eyes as the huge hull slid majestically down the greased slipway to cut a trough in the waters of Wallasey Pool, was deep disappointment, anger, and frustration. For he knew that the *Birkenhead*, the finest ship he had ever designed and built, had become no more than a political scapegoat.

In 1828 John Laird joined the firm founded eighteen years previously by his father William Laird, and from that moment on, shipbuilding and the development of the city of Birkenhead became his life. Up to about 1830 the growth of the firm as shipbuilders had been slow, and the previous years had seen William Laird's original plans to establish Birkenhead as a major port collapse. However, his

John Laird. By courtesy
of Cammell Laird &
Co. (Shipbuilders &
Engineers) Ltd., Birken-
head.

industrial grip on the area was secure and his was the force which laid the foundations for the gigantic complex the city of Birkenhead was to eventually become.

During the mid-nineteenth century the evolution of ships made new and far-
reaching progress, involving the change from sail to steam, and from wood to iron,
and although they proceeded together slowly, steam in place of sail had been
accepted more readily than iron in place of wood. There were still a great number
of prominent persons who argued on three main points, firstly that ships built of
iron would be too heavy to float; secondly that they were more easily damaged
in any collision and in this event it would need skilled labour and elaborate
equipment to repair any such damage, and this might not be available in foreign
ports, whereas wooden ships were easily repaired, even by crew members; and
thirdly, that the magnetic attraction of the iron could cause errors in the compass
readings.

But wooden ships, too, had much to condemn them, and there were many con-
siderations here to be taken into account. For instance, home-grown timber was
very scarce as the farmers, finding more profit in crops, were not replanting the
forests which had already been stripped of trees. Consequently timber, often of a
poor quality, had to be imported and this only added to the costs of building. And
the thickness of the timbers in the ship took up valuable space, and each joint in the
short lengths of wood was a weakness that could prove disastrous under stress. As

sail gave way to steam, this last point was particularly noticeable. In many cases the wood was not strong enough to bear the weight of the boilers and engines of steam-ships.

Iron, on the other hand, which was far stronger, was plentiful in England and to men like John Laird and his father it seemed the obvious choice as an alternative to wood. Watertight bulkheads could be incorporated in the structure of these iron ships, which meant even if they were badly holed the remaining compartments would give them enough buoyancy to float. And fire was a hazard that could vir-tually be forgotten as iron would not burn. These were just two of the claims that the iron shipbuilders voiced to support their contention. In various parts of England iron ships were being built in the yards which were pioneering iron construction, including, from the Laird yards, the *John Randolph* that went to America in 1834; the warship *Guadaloupe* in 1836; and in 1837 the then largest iron ship the *Rainbow*, for the General Steam Navigation Company. There were also a number of 'com-posite type' ships in use during this period, these being vessels built with wooden planking on iron frames.

However, the opposition to all iron ships and the scientific approach to shipping that came with them, was incredibly strong. The main weapon in the hands of those that refused to accept them was the effect of iron on the ship's compasses, and unfortunately the number of iron ships that were wrecked as a result of compass inaccuracies was sadly impressive, thus giving the advocates of wooden ships plenty of ammunition. The Lairds knew that if iron was to become generally accepted for shipbuilding, then the problem of the dangerous effect of the iron on the compasses must be overcome. Accordingly, after many abortive experiments, John Laird in 1837 finally enlisted the services of Professor Airey the distinguished Astronomer Royal, and under this eminent scientist tests, which gave the first glimmer of hope, were carried out on board the *Rainbow*.

Airey discovered that an 'all-iron' ship did not have the same effect on a compass as that of a moveable iron object on board a wooden ship. It pulled the compass off course, that was true, but the deviation was constant, and when the difference was calculated an allowance could be made to correct it. The corrections were made by counter-attractions, such as boxes of iron chains and magnets, secured near the compass and positioned so that they would attract the needle to point to its correct indication. It was found essential that the compass be corrected when the ship was actually moving, and for every course, and then a list compiled of deviations for every point on the compass.

All the calculations which were now involved in the navigation of a ship were not readily accepted by the seamen, and particularly the older ones who, set in their ways as it were, resented having to learn new methods they were suspicious of. Neverthe-less, iron ships did gradually gain ground, but it was not until 1841 that any headway was made with the Admiralty who had remained firmly and adamantly against the innovation of iron warships.

In 1836 John Laird, in desperation one would imagine, due to the attitude of those in control of the Royal Navy for their continued refusal to support iron ships, speculated with his own money and ordered that the keel be laid for an iron warship

The iron gunboat *Nemesis* in action in the China Seas. Her success in these operations played a large part in creating the opportunity for the *Birkenhead* and ships like her to be built. Photographed from a print in the author's possession.

with which he was determined to prove to the Admiralty, once and for all, that fighting ships made of iron were the thing of the future and that the days of wooden ships were numbered. The ship that Laird built was a 183-ft.-long ocean-going vessel with an armament equal to that of a naval frigate. She was rigged as a sailing vessel and although originally designed for screw propulsion, paddles were ultimately fitted. It was a fine ship, but the Admiralty, abundant with admirals of the 'old-school' type who, clinging to their positions and not wishing to see any change in the Navy they understood and believed in, true to form said no. Opportunity came

in the unexpected shape of the Mexican Government who, apart from merely showing an interest in Laird's new ship, gave her the name *Guadaloupe* and bought her virtually on the spot.

She sailed for Vera Cruz, crossing the Atlantic in record time, and was soon in action against Mexico's enemies which at that time included Texas. She was under the command of a Captain Charleswood, an ex-officer of the Royal Navy. Charleswood handled his ship magnificently and in return the *Guadaloupe* gave a tremendous performance which, in the fighting she was engaged in, was second to none. On his return to England, Captain Charleswood had nothing but high praise for the iron warship and he added his weight enthusiastically to the innovators.

In 1840 John Laird had another outstanding success, this time with an iron gunboat nemed *Nemesis*, which, in the service of the East India Company in the first of the opium wars in the China Seas, earned through its successful operation the respect of the Chinese who opposed it and the nick-name the 'Devil Ship'. Its performance was superb in every way and it left nothing to be desired. The Chinese even offered a reward of $50,000 for its destruction. And British captains, who were serving in that area on conventional wooden warships and witnessed the 'Devil Ship' in action, were surprised and impressed. Full of envy and admiration, they were soon pressing the Admiralty for similar warships.

Many of the younger and more progressive officers in the Royal Navy were now feeling more and more favourable towards iron fighting ships and they were uneasy about the Admiralty's stubborn stand. And in May 1840 one of the most noted and respected naval architects of the time, Mr. Augustine Creuze, came out strongly in favour of iron warships. After following closely the controversy which raged back and forth, and carefully studying tests and reports of both sides, he was able to witness repair work being carried out on an iron ship that had been damaged by a gash in her hull. Creuze was so amazed at the cheapness, speed, and efficiency of the repair that he was prompted to write a lengthy article strongly in favour of iron ships. This was published in the *United Services Journal* soon afterwards and what he wrote swayed a lot of people.

The year 1841 saw a new Conservative Government in power, under Sir Robert Peel, now Prime Minister for the second time. The Earl of Haddington was appointed First Lord of the Admiralty and Admiral Sir George Cockburn, a keen supporter of iron warships, became First Sea Lord. Cockburn was an intelligent and far-sighted officer, who took to heart the lessons of the *Nemesis* and the *Guadaloupe*. He had been quick to appreciate the value of iron warships and now that foreign navies were beginning to use them, he had no wish to see England lag behind and jeopardize her supremacy on the oceans of the world. He approved a programme of iron ships, and shipbuilders were invited to submit plans to the Admiralty.

This was what John Laird and others like him had strived for, for many years, and he wasted no time in getting his plans and designs, for what was to be the *Birkenhead*, laid before their Lordships of the Admiralty.

As he later wrote:

> The designs I submitted and which were finally approved, were of a vessel 210 feet long (being about 20 feet longer than any vessel of her class had been built), and 37·6 beam, with a displacement of 1,918 tons on the load water line of 15·9. The only change made by the authorities at the Admiralty in these designs was in the position of the paddle shaft, which was ordered to be moved several feet more forward. The change was unfortunate, as it makes the vessel, unless due care is taken in stowing the hold, trim by the head. With this exception I am answerable for the model, specification, displacement, and general arrangement of the hull of the vessel.

Eventually the building programme, involving Laird and other shipbuilders, got under way. Nearly forty iron auxiliary vessels and warships, including four more similar to the one Laird had designed, were to be built. But the sum involved in this huge project was £2,000,000 and when this amount was made public it raised a clamour of protest from the critics. Even Captain Charles Napier (later Admiral Sir Charles Napier), who had been a staunch supporter of iron, turned about and declared his surprise at '. . . the madness to spend such a sum without further and more searching tests'. And Sir William Symonds, the Royal Navy's Chief Constructor of Ships, referred to these '. . . monstrous iron vessels'. The same admirals, who had resisted iron warships for so long, now shouted even louder, and it was not long before the issue became a political weapon in the hands of the Government Opposition who were only too delighted to join the diehards and take up the cry. Every incident, however small, was used as a lever to sway feeling against iron ships.

Numerous tests had been carried out under Admiralty supervision at the Royal Arsenal, Woolwich, and at Portsmouth, to prove the strength and reliance, or otherwise, of iron-built ships in battle, but these had not all been conducted under the fairest of conditions. In particular, the results of one test at Portsmouth early in 1845 were later found to have been completely misleading, and parts of the report favourable to iron, suppressed. In this test a small iron ship, the *Ruby*, had been moored in the Solent and used as a target for Her Majesty's Warship *Excellent*. The idea was to show how an iron-built ship would stand up to shot. But to use a ship like the *Ruby* was ridiculous. She was one of the earliest iron ships and her iron plates, originally very thin, were now even thinner through years of wear. She was normally used as a harbour boat between Portsmouth and Gosport and by no stretch of the imagination was she really representative of the frigates under construction. When the guns of H.M.S. *Excellent* opened fire on their tiny little target, the *Ruby* might just as well have been made of cardboard. After just a few hours of pounding she was reduced to a heap of scrap.

The outcome for iron ships was damning. A fierce demand both in Parliament and in the press was made in no uncertain terms for a cancellation of Cockburn's building programme, and Peel's Government, on its last legs anyway, in an attempt to appease brought work on the iron ships to a halt.

Laird's ship, the first to be started, was almost ready, so a decision was taken to have her completed, not as the frigate she should have been, but in the new role of troopship.

As a warship, the *Birkenhead*'s armament was to have included two 96-pounder pivot guns, one fore and the other aft, and four 68-pounders, two each broadside. She was to have had a maximum speed of 11 knots, and all in all would have been one of the largest and fastest iron steamers in the Navy, and most certainly as a warship would have proved a formidable opponent on the high seas.

Made entirely of iron, except for the wooden planking of her decks and the paddle-boxes, her hull was $\frac{5}{8}$ in. thick below the water line, the plates overlapping with double rows of rivets (clencher built). Above the waterline she was carvel built with $\frac{9}{16}$-in. thick plates, the levelled edges held by internal iron straps, and rivets. The iron bulwarks which surrounded the ship's sides were 5 ft. high surmounted with lengths of polished teak, and of the guns she would have carried only four were in fact fitted for the purpose of self-defence.

She was a pleasing vessel to look at, being rigged as a brigantine with a foremast and a fore and aft mainmast, and one funnel at centre. She had a round stern and her bow terminated in a large figure of Vulcan the mythical god of fire and patron of those who work in iron.

After the launching ceremony in December 1845 the Birkenhead was towed to the berth where her 350-h.p. engines were to be installed by George Forester and Company. The increased accommodation for the troops came later. This was achieved by the addition of a poop deck, the highest deck on the stern of a ship, and a forecastle, and in trials carried out after final completion she was found to be fast and comfortable with sufficient space for 500 troops and their kit.

However, before the additions were actually made in 1847, the *Birkenhead* was used for a variety of tasks around the coast of England, Scotland, and Ireland, including, in August 1847, towing the S.S. *Great Britain* from Dundrum Bay, where she had run aground eleven months earlier, to Liverpool.

Isambard Kingdom Brunel's 322-ft.-long iron masterpiece, the largest and most splendid ship in the world, had left Liverpool on 22 September 1846, with 180 passengers bound for New York. The weather had deteriorated rapidly that night and as she crossed the Irish Sea she encountered fierce rain squalls, and missed the Chicken Rock Light on the Isle of Man. She carried on too far before making her turn up the Irish coast and consequently ran aground in Dundrum Bay on the coast of County Down. Nobody was injured and there was no panic, in fact, everyone returned calmly to their beds for the remainder of the night and were disembarked safely the following morning.

However, the *Great Britain* was in a perilous position. She was holed in two places and lay fully exposed to the crippling southerly gales that came regularly and relentlessly. Efforts to move her were unsuccessful and she remained firmly embedded until August 1847.

The S.S. *Great Britain* aground in Dundrum Bay and the arrival of H.M.S. *Birkenhead* and H.M.S. *Scourge*. Reproduced by courtesy of the *Radio Times*, Hulton Picture Library.

James Bremner, a Scottish expert on ship salvage, was called in and under his ingenious but unconventional methods the *Great Britain* was eventually refloated, and the *Birkenhead*, under the command of Captain A. H. Ingram, arrived on the scene in time to tow her roughly 150 yards out into deeper water. Although the holes in the hull of the *Great Britain* had been temporarily patched with iron plates, she still leaked, so it was decided not to risk a direct tow to Liverpool, instead the *Birkenhead* towed her to Belfast for further repair work, and after this had been carried out, across the Irish Sea to Liverpool. The weather was not good and their progress was sluggish, with some 300 bluejackets, many from the *Birkenhead*, toiling on the *Great Britain*'s pumps to maintain her buoyancy. But, despite all the setbacks, Captain Ingram succeeded in bringing the iron monster safely to the Merseyside.

The accomplishment of this tremendous feat should have provided the critics of iron ships with sufficient proof of their worth, and superiority over wooden vessels. The *Great Britain* had withstood her exposure to the weather, through two extremely bad winters, and had emerged with remarkably little damage, and

BREMNER'S PLAN TO REFLOAT
THE S.S. *GREAT BRITAIN*

When James Bremner restarted operations in the Spring of 1847 the problem was how to lift the ship from the pit which she had steadily burrowed for herself in the sand, and remove the rocks which impaled her. Bremner, from long experience, had devised methods of his own for wreck-raising and when he arrived on the scene of any disaster with his home-made devices he usually inspired a great deal of derisive laughter. On this occasion he drove huge logs into the sand on either side of the vessel; at the top of the logs he had twenty boxes of sand each weighing some fifty tons. A rope ran from each box over the top of its log in a groove and down to the vessel; as the boxes descended so the ship would come up.

Then long, stout timbers were driven under the *Great Britain* and rocks and anchors—anything heavy, even two of the ship's iron lifeboats filled with sand—were piled on their outer ends. As the action of the levers and the sand boxes lifted the hull, so tons of stones were poured down shutes into the cavity beneath the ship. Thus at each tide she gradually came up a little higher; then huge wedges were driven under her. On July 29th a team of boilermakers from Portsmouth were able to patch up the holes ripped in her bottom.

In August 1847 a series of high tides led to a change in technique: the boxes were emptied of their sand and were used instead to give extra buoyancy to the iron hull. Two naval ships arrived, *HMS Birkenhead* and *HMS Scourge*, to provide extra manpower plus towing power; their crews using ground tackle managed to move the *Great Britain* eighteen feet further out to sea.

Success came at last on August 27th when the *Birkenhead* managed to tow the *Great Britain* another 160 yards out to sea where she was anchored. She was still leaking, so a direct tow to Liverpool would have been too risky; instead the ship was taken to Belfast, cleared of water, and then towed sluggishly across the Irish Sea to Liverpool.

The ingenious arrangements of weights and levers devised by James Bremner to refloat the ship in 1847.

Text by courtesy of Macmillan & Co. Ltd., from *The SS Great Britain Official Guide*. Illustration by courtesy of *Radio Times*, Hulton Picture Library.

the *Birkenhead*, by her fantastic performance and manoeuvrability in freeing, and then towing, the *Great Britain* had shown what a powerful and able ship she was.

But their Lordships at the Admiralty did not appear to be over-impressed and the wooden ship supporters simply overlooked the incident.

Later in the year work on the *Birkenhead*'s conversion to a troopship started, but before the additions were finished she was taken out of service and placed in reserve early in 1848. For almost two years she lay idle at her moorings in Portsmouth, with the Admiralty seemingly not knowing what to do with this ship they had on their hands. Eventually, late in 1850, she was recalled back into service. Work on the increased troop accommodation was restarted and finally completed, and in February 1851, under the command of Captain Robert Salmond, she steamed through the Solent in her new role as troopship. Her first runs were comparatively short, carrying troops to the Channel Islands and Lisbon, and on these journeys she was acclaimed entirely satisfactory in all respects. Later in the year she conveyed a regiment of troops to the Cape in only 45 days, as against 64 days in some cases by other ships. Even the Lords of the Admiralty were pleased with her function and capabilities. And many months later, on 20 April 1852, a correspondent in *The Times* newspaper, looking back at the ship's performances, supported the apparently excellent sea-going qualities of the *Birkenhead* by the following article:

on the whole her performances prove her to have been the fastest most carrying and comfortable vessel in Her Majesty's service as a troopship, and one that could be fully relied on both in hull and machinery. The Admiralty appear to have taken every precaution to keep her in efficient condition, as she was docked on her return from the Cape in October 1851, and her hull examined and reported in perfect order, her machinery was improved with the view of economising fuel, and in her trial at Spithead after this refit she made, with 40 tons of coal, 60 tons of water, and four months stores on board, fully 10 knots per hour.

As events were to prove so tragically however, the 'efficient condition' of certain parts of the ship, in particular the equipment securing the lifeboats, was far from satisfactory. Also, during her conversion to a troopship, while the interior space was being modified to enable as many troops as possible to be carried, it was thought that the movement of so many men about the ship would be far easier if doors were cut into some of the watertight iron bulkheads that divided the compartments.

The science of iron ships and their arrangement of watertight compartments was in its infancy at this time, and this is the only excuse that can be suggested for such a foolhardy and tragic decision.

A profile of the *Birkenhead* is shown on page 28 and the positions are marked where it is imagined the watertight bulkheads would have been constructed.

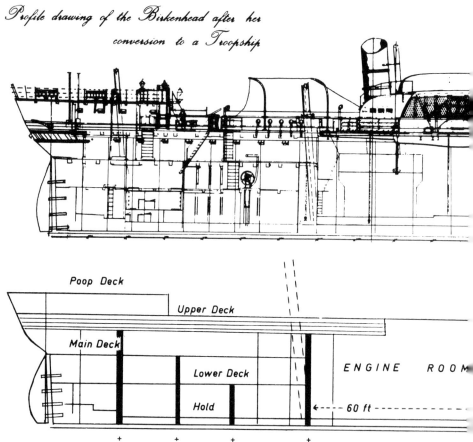

Profile drawing of the Birkenhead after her conversion to a Troopship

Poop Deck

Upper Deck

Main Deck

Lower Deck

ENGINE ROOM

Hold

60 ft

Probable positions of the iron bulkheads - marked thus +

THE *BIRKENHEAD* IRON STEAM FRIGATE.

This fine steam frigate has recently been built by Mr. John Laird at his shipyard at North Birkenhead and was launched towards the close of last month, the Marchioness of Westminster naming the vessel.

The *Birkenhead* will be one of the largest iron steamers belonging to the Government. The following are her dimensions:

Length between perpendiculars	210 feet	Ditto outside ditto about	60½ feet
Breadth between Paddle Wheels	37½ feet	Depth of hold	23 feet

Tonnage, carpenters measurement   1400 tons.

She is to be propelled by paddle wheels, and the engines by Messrs. George Forrester & Co, will be collectively of 560 horse power. The model was by Mr. Laird himself and approved of by the Admiralty. She is in fact all that can be desired by the most critical judges in naval architecture, sharpe at both extremeties, yet with that fulness and rotundity of bottom and bearings which will enable her to do her work well, 'Blow high, or blow low'.

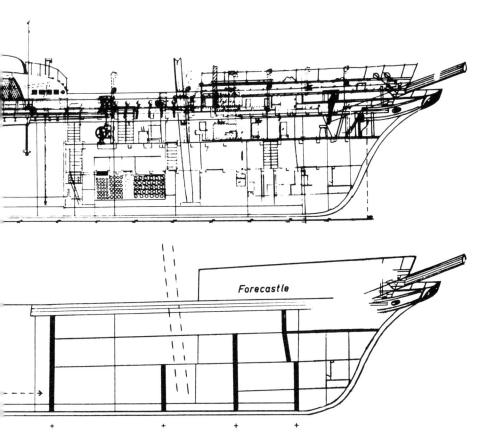

Forecastle

Text from *Illustrated London News*, Saturday, 24 January 1846.

Unfortunately there are no records available to give an accurate indication, neither is it possible to state exactly where the doors were cut and which compartments would have been effected. Nevertheless, it is on record that a number of the bulkheads were pierced in this manner and consequently this weakening of the ship's watertight capacity was later to contribute, possibly to a large extent, to its very rapid destruction.

★   ★   ★   ★

On 23 February 1852, the *Birkenhead* docked in Simon's Bay, near Cape Town, her voyage almost over. She had been scrubbed clean in preparation for her arrival and she made an impressive sight as she steamed slowly into harbour. Literally spotless from fore to aft, her brass fittings, caught by the rays of the sun, glistened like pieces of gold in sharp contrast to the smooth matt finish of her painted sides.

Captain Salmond, in frock coat and high hat, stood majestically on the poop issuing the orders that would manoeuvre his ship into port, while Lieutenant-Colonel Seton, in full-dress uniform and sword at his side, proudly paced up and down the ranks of the soldiers paraded on deck. To the people on the quayside who watched it represented all the pomp and splendour of England at her most glorious.

Here at Simon's Bay she was now within two days' sailing time of her final destination of Port Elizabeth in Algoa Bay on the south-east coast of Africa. Everyone continued to be in the best of spirits, with morale amongst the troops still very high. There were some cases of minor illness on board and these people were disembarked at Simon's Bay, together with those of the women and children who were not going on to Algoa Bay. Lieutenant Fairclough of the 12th Foot, and Mr. Freshfield, a clerk on the ship, were also landed through ill-health.

For Mrs. Metford, the young bride of just a few weeks, this was the end of her honeymoon for she too was required to disembark, while her husband went on to join his regiment. It was a particularly sad and tearful parting for these young lovers, neither knowing for certain when they would see each other again.

Seven additional passengers bound for Port Elizabeth joined the ship, these being Mrs. Nesbit with her two children, going to join her husband on the frontier, Mr. Andrew White who was a civilian servant to an army colonel, and three soldiers of the 91st Regiment, Corporal O'Neil and two men, who were returning to their unit.

Before proceeding, the *Birkenhead* took on fresh supplies of water and provisions and restocked with 350 tons of coal. This took the best part of the two days the ship remained at Simon's Bay and was done by soldiers and sailors toiling together. Horses for the Army officers were taken aboard and a large quantity of straw, wired tightly into bales, was loaded for their fodder. The bales, which took up quite a lot of room, were stacked on an already crowded upper deck. Eventually, all the formalities of a ship in transit were complete and, on receipt of orders from Commodore Wyvill of H.M.S. *Castor*, the Naval Commander at the Cape, to put to sea at once and make all possible speed with the troop reinforcements, the *Birkenhead* accordingly resumed her voyage.

Captain Robert Salmond, R.N. From an old print.

2. 'Stand fast'

The *Birkenhead*, with her decks far more crowded than usual, steamed out of Simon's Bay at 6 p.m. in the late afternoon of 25 February, carrying a total complement now of 638 persons on the final stage of her journey. It was a fine and clear evening. The weather was perfect and the sky cloudless as the *Birkenhead* ploughed leisurely through a calm sea at a speed of $8\frac{1}{2}$ knots.

The British regiments on the frontier were not at full strength due to heavy losses having been sustained in the first campaign in South Africa and Captain Salmond's instructions had been to use all possible haste in getting to his destination with the much-needed reinforcements, and, to quicken the journey to Algoa Bay he maintained a course that almost continually kept the ship within approximately three miles of the coast.

To hug the shore so closely was not by any means the action of a reckless and incompetent officer but more the decision of a man, anxious to carry out orders to the best of his ability, who possessed complete and absolute confidence in his own judgement, his ship, and the crew who served under him. Although in a hurry to reach his destination, he was an experienced seaman, not unaware of his responsibilities and of the safety of his passengers at all times. He felt quite relaxed and at ease that evening, and particularly pleased with the progress so far, feeling an added sense of satisfaction that there would be no delay in Algoa Bay and that within two months he would be home again in Gosport with his dear wife and family.

Coming from a long and distinguished line of naval officers, dating back to Elizabethan days, the Salmonds could indeed lay claim to a truly illustrious, yet tragic, record of service to Queen and country. Captain Salmond's four brothers, like their father before them, all died heroes' deaths on active service at sea, one brother, John, having been killed at Copenhagen whilst serving under the great Lord Nelson. Tragically also, of Robert Salmond's two sons, one died at sea before he was even 15 years of age. The Captain's own career commenced in August 1838 when he qualified as Master in the Royal Navy, and from the small steamer to which he was first attached, he saw service in the Mediterranean, America, and Africa, first on H.M.S. *Retribution* and then H.M.S. *Vengeance* under the command of the Rt. Hon. Earl of Hardwicke. His commission to the *Birkenhead* as Master Commander was in February 1851, twelve months previously, and now in February 1852 he stood on the poop of that same ship, hands firmly clasped behind his back and gaze affixed over the fore and out to sea, only hours from the incident that was to arouse world acclaim.

At almost midnight all was still and quiet aboard the *Birkenhead*. Only the steady throbbing of the engines disturbed the silence of the night as she crossed False Bay on her set sourse of S.S.E. $\frac{1}{2}$ E. And like a baby being tenderly rocked to sleep, she rolled gently in the swell which had now begun to set in on the nearby shore.

The passengers had settled down for the night, and the soldiers and seamen, with their hammocks creaking and swaying in unison, were peacefully asleep. The ship was behaving normally and to the Duty Officer and the crew on watch everything appeared to be in order and running to routine. Small clusters of lights visible inland gave an added sense of security to those on duty and there was no premonition of danger to themselves or the ship, nor any awareness that the cold hands of fate now firmly gripped the wheel, steering the *Birkenhead* into a collision course with disaster and death. They were not to know that the destiny of the ship, its crew, and passengers, had already been decided.

The following morning at about 1.45 in the early hours, and only 60 miles from the port she had left less than eight hours earlier, she steamed serenely into the area off Danger Point. And there, just ahead of the ship and directly in its path, everwatching and ever-waiting for its chosen victim, lay the last resting place of Her Majesty's Troopship *Birkenhead*.

Appropriately named, due to the chains of rocks and treacherous reefs that lay hidden beneath shallow depths of water, Danger Point was one of the most notorious and dangerous stretches of the South African coastline. Captain Salmond had now retired for the night leaving Mr. Davies, Second Master, in charge of the ship, and the Duty Officer, fully aware of the hazards predominant on this part of the coastline, ensured all necessary precautions had been taken. Apart from strict observances of the navigational charts and regular bearings being noted, two men kept

Both photographs were taken many years after the disaster.

Colour-Sergeant John Drake, Royal Marines.

Captain (later Colonel) Edward Wright.

According to the records of the Argyll and Sutherland Highlanders, Captain Wright's military career progressed thus:

Ensign   21 Dec. 1832
Lieutenant   13 Nov. 1835
Captain   2 July 1841
Major   1852
Half Pay Brevet Lt Col   6 Jan. 1854

Served in Kaffir War 1846-47 as A.D.C. to Major-General Hare. Served with Reserve Battalion in the latter part of Kaffir War 1852-53.

Before his death in 1871, at 25, Walpole Street, Chelsea, he attained the rank of full Colonel.

sharp look-out from the bows of the vessel, Thomas Daly on one side and John Butcher on the other, and a leadsman, Ordinary Seaman Abel Stone, casting his weight from the paddle-box took constant soundings of the depth of the water which varied between 12 and 14 fathoms.

On the forecastle Colour-Sergeant John Drake of the Royal Marines detachment on board stood talking quietly to his old friend James Jeffrey, one of the stewards. John Drake was a man of intelligence and impeccable character, and one of those men to whom military service fits like a glove. Tall, strong and robust, he looked and behaved as one would imagine, and expect, a sergeant of Marines would, and his calmness and lack of terror, or panic, under even the most adverse of conditions inspired the confidence of all about him. Coming from Dorset, he gave up his job as keeper on a nobleman's estate and enlisted in the Royal Marines at Portsmouth in 1843. He was soon on active service and wherever there was danger or fighting, there too was John Drake.

Of his many exploits perhaps his greatest, and the one for which he was promoted corporal, was the one in which he was first involved. The ship on which he was stationed at the time was H.M.S. *Waterwitch*, and whilst engaged off the coast of Africa they captured a Brazilian slave ship, a brigantine named *Romeo Primero*. It was naturally a good prize to take back to England and a small crew was selected from the *Waterwitch* to perform that task. A Lieutenant Mansfield was put in command and three sailors, one marine and six of the captured Spanish seamen from the *Romeo Primero* made up his crew. The marine chosen being John Drake.

Apart from the duties of sailing the ship, the armed British sailors also had to keep a sharp eye on the prisoners who, under the pretext of carrying out orders, were in fact secretly planning to recapture the *Romeo Primero*. Their chance came after a few days' sailing. Three Spaniards and two English sailors were on deck on duty while Drake, the other Englishman and the remaining three prisoners were resting below. The two sailors were ordered by Lieutenant Mansfield to shorten the sail and as they slowly climbed higher and higher up the rigging the three Spaniards, and the three from below who had crept up, suddenly turned on the officer. Mansfield, although taken completely by surprise and unarmed at the time, fought back grimly but the odds were too great and he was finally beaten senseless and left for dead. The Spaniards then made their way below to the two men still sleeping in their hammocks. They entered the cabin and one of them, creeping forward stealthily, made a sudden lunge towards the defenceless sailor lying beneath him and plunged a knife into the unfortunate man's throat. His only protest was a brief gurgling sound. Two of the other Spaniards simultaneously attacked Drake who was still asleep. One gave him a crushing blow on the side of the head with a handspike while the other, who had drawn a long knife, opened a 6-in. gash under his chin. The cut was deep but by a miracle it missed the jugular vein.

The Spaniards, however, had not reckoned on Drake's amazing strength and courage and their murderous actions did not have the effect they anticipated. Drake staggered to his feet. He was stunned and badly wounded, with blood streaming down his face and chest, but using his bare fists he waded into the Spaniards and was able to wrest the handspike from one of them. Armed with this weapon he made short work of his opponents. The Spaniards were no match for this wounded English tiger. Two were killed outright and the remaining four were battered unconscious. With his shirt and trousers torn to shreds and covered in blood, Drake somehow managed to reach the deck, to be met by the two astonished sailors. They tended his wounds and after securing the Spaniards they saw to Lieutenant Mansfield who was just alive.

The *Romeo Primero* was eventually got safely to England, and Drake who had saved the ship and three lives, apart from a scar on his neck, made a complete recovery. In July 1848 he was further promoted to sergeant and nine months after that to colour-sergeant, his rank on joining the *Birkenhead*.

As John Drake chatted with his friend he could hear in the background the footsteps of one of the sentries pacing back and forth, and he heard him call out to the Officer of the Watch, 'Four bells, sir.' The officer's reply came back instantly, his voice carrying in the still air, 'Strike them, sentry.'

But neither Drake, nor anyone else for that matter, were to hear the ship's bells, for at that precise moment, suddenly, and with no warning whatsoever, a deafening crash shattered the silence of the night and the *Birkenhead* came shuddering violently to a stop. Jeffrey the steward spun back against the rails and Drake was thrown on to the deck as every part of the ship crashed and shook.

Impaled helplessly on the apex of an uncharted rock, her mast swinging back and forth and high in the air, and her rigging banging and rattling, the *Birkenhead*, grotesquely silhouetted against the dark night sky, slowly began her grim and macabre dance of death. Never was destruction more sudden or complete. Fifteen minutes after the vessel struck, the bow broke off. Five more minutes and the hull snapped in two and the *Birkenhead* was no more. And yet, 20 ft. or so on either side of her course she would have sailed safely by.

The rock which had penetrated the ship sliced into the hull just behind the foremast, like a razor through flesh, and ripped open the compartment between the engine-room and forepeak. The inrush of water was so great that the forward compartment of the lower troopdeck filled instantly and a hundred or more soldiers were drowned, almost literally in their hammocks as they slept.

Captain Salmond, wearing a dressing-gown fastened tightly round him, and other officers, including Lieutenant-Colonel Seton and Captain Wright who were also only partially clothed, came running to the top deck within two or three minutes of the impact. They were quickly joined by a breathless Lieutenant Girardot and

South Africa

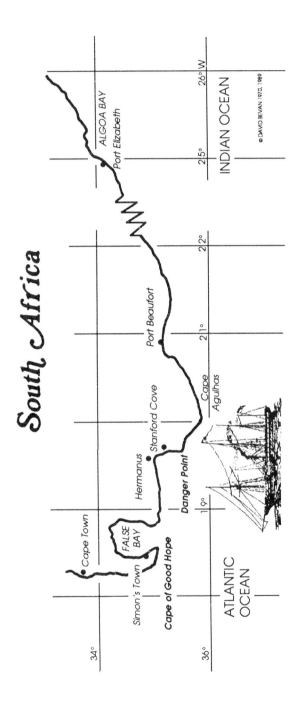

ATLANTIC OCEAN

Cape Town

Simon's Town

FALSE BAY

Cape of Good Hope

Hermanus

Stanford Cove

Danger Point

Cape Agulhas

Port Beaufort

INDIAN OCEAN

ALGOA BAY

Port Elizabeth

© DAVID BEVAN, 1970, 1989

34°

36°

19°

21°

22°

25°

26° W

Location of places named in the story. Not drawn to scale.
The *Birkenhead* sank within two miles off shore, approx. lat. 34° 48′ S., long. 19° 16′ E.

Ensign Lucas who had been on watch duty, and to all of them, that the *Birkenhead* was in a perilous position there was no doubt, but the full extent of the damage and the nearness of death was not immediately apparent.

On the poop deck Seaman Thomas Cuffin at the helm for the middle watch from 12 until 2, fought frantically to hold the wheel steady while Mr. Davies, who a few moments earlier had taken the ship's bearings, reeled backwards from the jolt, striking his head on a beam. The Captain, who had come up on to the poop, took hold of Davies and shook him by the shoulders, asking, 'Are you all right, man? Where are we and what have we hit?'

Davies, drawing his hand across his forehead, murmured with a tremble, 'I don't know, sir. We're steering S.S.E. ½ E. as instructed and our bearings are correct.'

Captain Salmond then inquired of the time and was told it was just before 2 a.m. Only minutes had passed since the initial impact and he was still not completely aware of exactly how much damage the *Birkenhead* had suffered nor how many of the compartments were flooding. Men were now running about below the poop, calling out to one another, and some of the things they were shouting could be heard quite clearly by those on the poop. Salmond, with a sudden sickening feeling in the pit of his stomach, heard someone scream out that a score of soldiers were dead in the lower troopdeck and that more were trapped and drowning at this very moment. He could also make out from the raised and excited voices that water was pouring into the side of the ship and rising quickly. He clenched his fists tightly, his finger-nails biting hard into the palms of his hands and breathing deeply he sensed, rather than knew, that the moment had come when all his years of experience were now to be put to their greatest test.

There was no time to discuss the situation and no time to sit quietly working out the best course of action. His officers had followed him on to the poop and were now standing behind him waiting for his decision. Salmond turned quickly to face them, and in a calm and clear manner, with no outward sign at all of the dead shock he felt, he issued precise orders and instructions which were promptly carried out. In the hope the ship could be prevented from slipping off the rock and into deeper waters, thus giving the men below more time to reach the comparative safety of the upper deck, he ordered the engines to be stopped at once and the small-bower anchor to be lowered. He also dispatched some of the officers to ascertain the damage, emphasizing the need for accuracy and urgency.

Meanwhile, on the upper deck, Lieutenant-Colonel Seton was instructing Captain Wright to have the military officers and men brought up without delay and assembled on deck. A number of the soldiers had already reached the open deck. Others were struggling through the hatchways one after another and then stumbling, dazed and bewildered, across the planking. They were in various states of dress, some in night-shirts, others with perhaps just trousers on, and a few who had

managed to grab tunics were frantically trying to put them on. All of them were bare-footed and most of them were still half asleep and not really sure of what had happened. No lights had been on in the troop decks when the ship struck and the pitch-black darkness, together with the shouts of seamen that the vessel was sinking, had added to the confusion and terror of the soldiers below. Several had panicked and had reached the open deck only by rushing blindly for the ladders and shoving and knocking others out of the way. But once on the upper deck the sight of Seton standing there, calmly giving orders and directing his officers, had a sobering effect on the men, and showing a fantastic response to leadership they answered the summoning roll of drums and drew themselves up in ranks on both sides of the quarterdeck.

Lieutenant-Colonel Seton, hatless, tunic on but unbuttoned, and with his left arm resting on the hilt of his sword, beckoned his officers nearer and as they gathered around him, he addressed them in a voice and manner more befitting an after-dinner speech in the officers' mess, rather than a sinking ship.

'Gentlemen,' he said, slowly and deliberately, and pausing long enough to look at them, each in turn. 'Would you please be kind enough to preserve order and silence amongst the men and ensure that any orders given by Captain Salmond are instantly obeyed.'

The officers answered in the affirmative, gave the customary salute to their senior officer and dispersed, apart from Captain Wright who remained with Seton.

Neither Captain Salmond, nor Lieutenant-Colonel Seton, had been through anything at all like this before, but whatever their inward feelings were, they continued to show nothing but complete composure and self-confidence. And their courage and calmness in those early moments of the disaster set a pattern for the events to come and for the countless acts of heroism that were to be enacted later that night.

Salmond had remained on the poop, and from the reports he was receiving from the officers who had been sent below was now far more acutely aware of the seriousness of the situaion. He turned to Colour-Sergeant Drake, who had come across from the forecastle a few minutes earlier, and ordered him to find Mr. Brodie and have him bring up the women and children. He also gave instructions for the ship's boats to be lowered and to lie alongside, despite the fact he knew them to be hopelessly inadequate for the number of passengers carried. In all, the *Birken-*

One of the Hemy oil paintings depicting a scene on the deck of the stricken troopship. The original of this painting hangs in the Regimental Museum of the Black Watch at Balhousie Castle, Perth, Scotland, by whose courtesy it is reproduced here.

head was equipped with only eight boats. These being one large boat on each of the paddle-boxes, two eight-oared cutters slung on davits on the quarter-deck, one dinghy on davits hung over the stern, two four-oared gigs on the fore part of the ship, and one 30 ft.-long pinnace amidships between the paddle-boxes.

Drake climbed quickly down from the poop and after locating Mr. Brodie and conveying the orders, turned and ran back to the Captain for further instructions. Brodie wasted no time in detailing a party of men to go below to fetch the women and children and then moved smartly around the deck, jumping over bits of equipment and packing that had come loose, directing all the available men he could see to go to the various boat stations. He then went back amidships and climbed on to the port paddle-box to take charge of the lowering of that boat.

The sailors who had gone down for the women and children stumbled along the gangway of the lower deck towards the cabins aft, as fast as they could, passing stragglers amongst the soldiers still coming up until, suddenly and somewhat unexpectedly, the light thrown forward from their lanterns caught the shadowy shapes of the terrified women standing shivering and huddled together. They were sobbing and calling out their husbands' names, trying to comfort each other and their frightened little ones. Few of them had managed to get clothes on after being flung from their bunks when the ship first struck, and except for one or two with shawls or blankets wrapped round their shoulders, they were wearing only nightgowns. They were scared, not only by the frantic motions of the ship and the awful noises of screeching metal, but also by the darkness. Seeing the sailors approaching, they cried out thankfully and moved forward into the strong arms that came towards them. There was no time to gather clothes or other possessions, they had to get out as fast as they could. Some of the seamen took the children in their arms and with reassuring words and firm gestures the pathetic figures of the women were ushered back along the gangway and up the ladders to the open top deck. Once through the last hatchway, they were moved across a few yards of tilting deck to be left sheltered under the poop while the boats were got ready.

Meanwhile Salmond, still on the poop deck, had come to the conclusion the ship was taking too much of a hammering on the rock and he realized that unless she was freed there was an immediate danger of her breaking up. He was also aware now that only one compartment had been holed and he quickly estimated there would be sufficient air in the undamaged compartments to give the ship buoyancy to float, at least for long enough to have the boats lowered and the passengers evacuated under less critical circumstances.

His voice full of urgency, he ordered a turn astern to the engine-room, but within minutes of the order being carried out it proved to have been a tragic decision for when the ship moved she struck again, this time near the engines, tearing a gash several feet long in the side of the hull and ripping open the bottom. The engine-room, the second largest compartment in the ship, flooded immediately, drowning the fires and stopping the engines.

Minutes beforehand, both Mr. Renwick and Mr. Barber, who had been off duty and asleep, came running into the engine-room. Mr. Kitchingman, the Engineer of the Watch, and Mr. Whyham, the Chief Engineer, were already there. Mr. Whyham had just ordered the safety valves of the three boilers to be opened to ease the steam pressure, when the command came through to reverse engines. This was carried out straight away and the ship shuddered and jolted as it changed position, but before the engines had done more than about twenty revolutions the harrowing sound of tearing metal stopped everyone from what they were doing and they stared in horror at the starboard bilge plates as they rose upward, and buckled like cardboard. And then the sea came in. Just a trickle at first, then before anyone had time to say, or even think anything, the flow of water changed almost instantly to an avalanche of death that nothing could stop.

Above the hissing noise of water swishing into the ash-pits of the boilers, Mr. Whyham's calls for all hands to get out fast sent all the stokers and engineers racing for the ladders. Some, like Renwick and Barber, were lucky and escaped the swallowing sea, but many of the poor men who had been working in the engine-room perished as they screamed and tried to claw their way out.

As Renwick finally climbed through the last hatchway and out on to the open deck he coughed and choked, and shook away the hell he had left below, then moving quickly he went straight to the poop to let Captain Salmond know what had happened in the engine-room, adding that nothing further could be done.

The *Birkenhead*, fighting for its life, ground and screeched on the rock on which it lay ensnared. Its bulkheads, the iron partitions dividing the twelve watertight compartments, were no match for the merciless greed of the sea and they twisted and broke with every movement. It was their eventual concession of defeat that finally sealed the fate of the gallant but doomed ship.

The decks were now a scene of complete upheaval. The ship was rolling heavily and wreckage and debris was sliding about everywhere, but despite all this the main body of troops maintained their positions on the quarter-deck. A group of soldiers, about fifty in all, had been ordered to assist the seamen in lowering the boats and while some went to help the sailors who were hauling desperately on the tackles of the two big paddle-box boats trying to get them down to the water, other troops went to the remaining boat stations. Another party of soldiers, under the command of Lieutenant Giradot, had been dispatched to the lower after-deck and were working the chain pumps that scooped the water from the ship's hold and poured it back into the sea. Ralph Sheldon-Bond and about half a dozen men had been ordered to put the horses over the side and they were doing this as expeditiously and as humanely as possible under the nightmarish circumstances. The horses were wild-eyed and frightened. They resisted and struggled madly, making ghastly screeching noises as they were dragged to the gangway and pushed blindfolded over the side to go plummeting into the sea.

There was other, more sinister movement too, in the dark waters below. Killer sharks that had sensed blood were gathered menacingly around the ship and were soon tearing into the poor horses thrashing about helplessly. But the sharks were not satisfied and their black fins still cut silently through the water close to the ship, waiting for the human flesh they seemed to know would come later.

The soldiers and crew engaged in the lowering of the boats were finding this an almost impossible task. Most of the tackle was rotten through lack of use and repair, and on one of the paddle-box boats the davits were actually rusted to an extent that prevented the bolts being released. These boats on the paddle-boxes were carried bottom up and using two separate pieces of tackle they first had to be turned over, then pushed outward and lowered down to the water. On the port side, the boat had been hoisted and almost righted when the tackle suddenly broke and the boat fell at one end and hung limply against the side of the ship. Most of the men, including Mr. Brodie, managed to jump clear as the boat crashed down but one or two soldiers overbalanced and fell over the side. On the quarter-deck John Rolt and a group of men had been able to free one of the gigs but as it was being lowered too many people tried to clamber on and it capsized. In the confusion that followed, Rolt and four others were hurled into the sea and the men on the tackle let go of the ropes, allowing the gig to fall. It hit the ship's side and slithered upside down into the water, smashing on to the men who had fallen, killing outright four of them. Rolt was lucky, he was struck a glancing blow but despite his injury, he managed to grab at some bits of wreckage and stay afloat.

It was more or less the same story with most of the other boats, and in all only three were successfully lowered to the water, one gig and two cutters, and it was into one of the cutters that the women and children were transferred.

The ship, still rolling badly, made the task of passing the women and infants into the cutter extremely difficult and matters were not helped by the reluctance of the women to be parted from their husbands who were left on board. It was necessary therefore for a certain degree of force and firmness to be executed by Ensign Lucas of the 73rd and Sergeant Kilkeary of the same regiment, in persuading the women to leave as it was essential for this agonizing job to be swiftly accomplished. Privates William Tuck of the Marines and John Smith of the Queen's had also been detailed to assist with this task and they were all struggling frantically in getting the women and children from under the poop and into the cutter. The slippery deck under their feet tilted first one way, then back the other, and it was as much as they could do to keep their balance while half pushing and half carrying the helplessly exhausted and terrified women and children to the side of the ship. Lieutenant-Colonel Seton himself stood by the gangway, afraid that some men might make a dash for the boat and endanger the safety of the women and children by crowding it. He stood, with a sword drawn in his hand, determined to prevent such a move, but this proved to be entirely unnecessary as not one soldier, nor seaman, made any attempt to jump into the cutter other than those ordered to do so to man the oars.

Rowland Richards, the young Master's Assistant, had been off duty and asleep in the fore cockpit when the ship's crash almost flung him from his hammock. He woke with a start and half jumping, half falling to the floor, made his way quickly to the top deck. The only garment he had on was his nightshirt. As he passed the gunroom, Mr. Hire, the ship's clerk, with just a blanket wrapped around him, stumbled forward from somewhere and collided with both Richards and Dr. Culhane who had come running from another direction. As Hire recognized the Doctor he gasped out in one breath, 'Good God, Doctor. All the people who were down in the cockpit fore of the ship are drowned. The water came rushing in through a hole in her bottom but I managed to get out of the hatchway.' Richards did not bother to stop and hear more, or to ask questions; he raced on up to the top deck only to hold his breath and recoil with disbelief at the spectacle that met his eyes.

A few yards from Lieutenant-Colonel Seton, who had now replaced his sword, stood Captain Salmond issuing further instructions to Colour-Sergeant John Drake, but on seeing Richards appear he beckoned him urgently over.

As he staggered across the deck, Richards, rather subconsciously, made a mental note of the fact that Colour-Sergeant Drake was fully dressed, even to his hat and immaculately polished boots. He also had his regimental sash across his shoulder. Must have been on duty, thought Richards, always very smart that man.

'Richards, quickly, over here, man,' ordered the Captain. Taking hold of Richards and pushing him towards the rail he added: 'The women and children are in the first cutter. Take charge and pull away immediately.'

Young Richards, still somewhat dazed by the bewildering rapidity of events, clambered down the rope ladder, almost overbalancing as he literally fell into the small boat. He suddenly heard shrill cries from above and looked up sharply to see Cornet Sheldon-Bond holding two small children in his arms. After the horses had been put over the side Sheldon-Bond decided to make one final check of the rooms not under water and had come across the two frightened infants, crying and holding on to one another, in one of the cabins. Taking hold of them he quickly rushed on deck in time to see Richards being ordered into the cutter. The children, whose mother was in the cutter in a state of near hysteria and shouting incoherently, were passed gently but speedily down into the boat, but Cornet Sheldon-Bond, who was offered a place in the cutter for his foresight and courage in rescuing the children, declined, stating he would rather stay with the men. Richards lost no further time in ordering the coxswain, George Till, to cut loose and pull away. All the women

A reproduction of an original drawing by Ralph Sheldon-Bond, 12th Lancers, who survived, of the *Birkenhead*'s last few minutes before her final plunge.

and children were huddled together at both ends of the cutter, the one woman whose children were returned to her, quiet now, and the soldiers and seamen who manned the oars rowed fast away. On Richards' orders the cutter stood off from the doomed *Birkenhead* at a distance of approximately 150–200 yards.

The other cutter with coxswain Able-Seaman John Lewis and three sailors, and the small four-oared gig with two men inside, were also got safely away and both boats were ordered by Captain Salmond to stand off where they would not be sucked down by the vortex caused by the *Birkenhead* sinking. The Captain then summoned Mr. Archbold the Gunner and ordered him to fire one of the guns continuously as this might be heard from the shore. But within minutes Archbold had returned, breathlessly gasping out that the magazine was under water but whilst in the Captain's cabin, fetching the keys to the magazine, he had found some blue lights and rockets which were now clasped in his arms. He was ordered to fire them off immediately, but as it transpired the gesture was to no avail as the distress signals were not sighted.

Archbold had climbed up on to the port paddle-box to fire the rockets, and when the last one had gone up he turned to where Mr. Brodie and his party of men were still struggling and straining to free the boat that had collapsed at one end. It was well over a ton in weight and he joined Brodie and others on the tackle, giving what help he could.

It was about fifteen minutes after the *Birkenhead* first struck and the situation was now critical. Water was rising rapidly up the hatchways, and no sooner had the cutters and gig moved away when, with an awesome and thunderous crunch the bow of the stricken ship broke clean away at the foremast. The vessel tilted crazily, with the stern high in the air and in those horrifying moments there were few men who had been working near where the ship tore apart, that escaped death. As the vessel buckled, men ran frantically back but many of them had no chance at all and were flung into the shark-infested waters. Their blood-curdling cries as the monsters of the sea took them were louder even than the dying screams of the *Birkenhead*.

At the same time, a swell rose against the jagged edge of what was left of the ship and as the water swept across, more men were lost, including Brodie and Archbold. Both men were able to cling to bits of wreckage in the water but poor Brodie was too badly injured and he died shortly afterwards.

A few more moments passed and then the funnel splintered and came crashing down on to the starboard side of the ship. It smashed the pinnace and the paddle-box, killing outright most of the soldiers and sailors working on the tackle there. Lieutenant-Colonel Seton shouted to the troops on the quarter-deck to break ranks and as they ran for safety, but only God knows where, dozens more were crushed to death by falling spars and portions of the masts.

The ship was now sinking by the head but the indefatigable Colonel Seton, still as calm and composed as ever, stood amongst the wreckage apparently oblivious to the turmoil about him as he ordered the officers to have the men go to the poop deck. The soldiers on the top deck moved quickly but the shrill cries of Girardot, Wright, Lucas, and the other officers carrying out these instructions went unheeded by the brave men on the chain pumps below who continued with their despairing duty in the hope the ship might be kept afloat. The remainder of the troops, those that had not been killed by falling wreckage or swept overboard, mustered on the poop. Some of the injured men were supported by comrades and others more seriously hurt were carried bodily. And although not one man was fully dressed, most were hatless and without boots, and some wore only a shirt or a blanket to cover them, those able to stand, about two hundred in all, fell into ranks almost as smartly and as perfectly as if they were on a parade ground. The officers, both naval and military, assembled with the men, and Colonel Seton, Wright, Lucas, Girardot, Sheldon-Bond, Doctor Bowen, and all the others stood clustered together, calmly awaiting their fate.

Suddenly, Captain Salmond, perhaps on an instinctive impulse of survival and preservation at the realization that time had finally expired, climbed two or three feet up the steps of the mizzen rigging and called out to the men, 'Save yourselves. All those who can swim, jump overboard and make for the boats. That is your only hope of salvation.'

On hearing this, Lieutenant-Colonel Seton dashed forward and faced the men. He paused long enough to quickly scan their drawn and pale faces, seeing in their eyes the pathetic and appealing look of tired, frightened men. Men who wanted to live. But he knew that any rush for the boats would mean the certain death of the women and children. He had no choice, no alternative, but to ask the men to go to their deaths. To make the supreme sacrifice so that others might live.

Raising his hands above his head, his voice torn with deep emotion, Seton begged the men to remain where they were. 'You will swamp the cutter containing the women and children. I implore you not to do this thing and I ask you all to stand fast.' Both Wright and Girardot moved forward together and echoed their commander's words, shouting to the men to 'Remain where you are'.

The request to stand fast in their ranks was heard by every man on the poop and this, to their eternal honour, they did to the very last man.

Simultaneously with the request from Lieutenant-Colonel Seton to 'stand fast', the hull of the ship cracked in two and with a dull moan the *Birkenhead* broke its back on the rock. The men on the chain pumps had no chance at all and as water flooded through the decks, they too perished. Lieutenant Booth of the 73rd who had relieved Griardot only a few moments earlier, died with the men. The stern of the ship, on which was the poop deck, now reared even higher in the air, as if to position itself for the final plunge, catching many of the men off balance by the quickness of her movement. Soldiers standing at the edge of the deck cried out as they stumbled against one another and those close to the rails clutched the bars tightly for support and held on desperately. But some who were too weak to help themselves toppled off, falling like fish tipped from a bowl. They went to their deaths in the inhospitable waters below while their comrades, helpless to save them, watched in horror.

The rolling and twisting of the ship struggling for life suddenly stopped, her movement now carrying an air of deathly grace as she fell back into the water, and with ever increasing momentum, disappeared for ever below the waves.

As the water swished across the deck of the poop the officers murmured goodbye to one another and shook hands, and someone shouted out 'God bless you all'. The troops, who had now regained their bearings, stood rigidly to attention like lines of living statues, each knowing in his own gallant heart the ghastly fate that awaited them. But amongst this motionless mass of truly brave men no one murmured and no one moved. With fists clenched tightly, bodies erect and stalwart, heads held high, two hundred or more British soldiers prepared to sacrifice themselves to the cruel sea rather than jeopardize the lives of the women and children.

If ever, throughout the whole of history, there was an act of heroism of such magnitude for which there are no adequate words, then this surely must rank as contender for that distinguished honour. Suffice it to say, men such as these men of the *Birkenhead* will never perish. Although their bodies may be taken by the sea, their memories are, as indeed they should be, immortal.

Throughout the entire disaster the one outstanding quality shown by all the men was discipline. And from this notable quality stemmed the courage that was to make these men unique. It must not be forgotten either that these were not battle-hardened troops facing an enemy on the field, but young, raw, untried recruits from ten different regiments, facing the hazards of the sea, and only forty-six days ago, strangers to one another. Many of them had not even seen the headquarters of their regiment so they had no chance of imbibing regimental pride and spirit, and most of the different batches had but one officer belonging to them. Yet every man stood silent, awaiting the word of command.

Captain Wright of the 91st, who was to survive, wrote afterwards:

> Every man did as he was directed and there was not a cry or a murmur among them until the vessel made her final plunge. I could not name any individual Officer who did more than another. All received their orders and had them carried out as if the men were embarking instead of going to the bottom of the sea, there was only one difference, that I never saw any embarkation conducted with so little noise or confusion.

Twenty minutes after first striking the rock, the *Birkenhead* had gone. Only the main-top mast remained above the water where she sunk. Many of the men who went down with her rose again, to begin yet another desperate fight for survival, and as they broke to the surface, choking and gasping for every breath, the sea about them was thick with oil, floating furniture, planks of wood, struts, spars, and other fragments of wreckage. And here and there, drifting to and fro with the currents, were the mutilated corpses of men who had lost their struggle for life. Some of the survivors, those that found the strength, tried to swim for land, risking the hungry sharks, and the thick and deadly seaweed that was known to border the shore. Others, too exhausted and too weak to attempt anything else, lay across the driftwood and other bits of debris that washed past them, and about forty or so, including Mr. Hire, clung feebly to the main-top mast, where most of them were to remain until taken off by a rescue ship the succeeding afternoon.

It was a dreadful sight. The water was literally alive with men. Some, in their last dying throes were pulling others down in their efforts to keep above the water, and others striking out manfully away from the wreck were suddenly, with loud shrieks of agony, dragged under by sharks. Private Page of the 2nd Regiment (Queen's) and twenty-seven other soldiers, all painfully trying to keep their heads above the surface, were grimly hanging on to a mess table that had been bobbing up and down in the water. Of this group of men only Page was to survive as his comrades gradually released their hold through sheer exhaustion and were either drowned or taken alive and screaming by the sharks. Another soldier, Private Boyden, also of the Queen's, managed to clamber on to the top of a bale of compressed hay and was eventually carried by the currents to the shore in that position. A cabin boy who was lying across part of a door and paddling it furiously like a canoe shouted over the water to Boyden 'Come on, Jack Straw', and this nickname stuck to Boyden, who eventually rose to the rank of colour-sergeant, for the rest of his service.

Mr. Brodie, the Master of the *Birkenhead*, who was washed off the ship, was last seen struggling in the water for a few moments before disappearing below the surface. Both the Second Masters were also drowned, as was Mr. Hare one of the Master's Assistants. Robert Salmond died too, in those first few minutes after his ship sank. He was seen being swept into the sea and then struck by the falling mizzen mast and pulled under. Cornet Sheldon-Bond at the last minute had located a Mackintosh life preserver and putting this hastily on before taking to the water, had successfully swum for the beach. Several hours later he was to discover that his own horse awaited him on the shore, being one of the five that survived.

Colour-Sergeant Drake, uninjured and one of the lucky ones destined to survive the torturous hours, struggled to the surface, his lungs almost at bursting point, and as his head broke through the water he coughed and choked, spitting out the foul taste of salt water and trying at the same time to swallow huge gulps of life-giving air. He was a strong man and as his head cleared and his eyes focused, he auto-

matically started the motions of swimming, making for a large plank of wood about
20 yards away which would serve as a raft. He had barely pulled himself on to the
wood when he became conscious of weak cries for help coming from behind him
and close by, and turning over on to his stomach he recognized a shape in the water
as young Rolt. His hair was clotted with blood, and his face creased in pain with
every movement of his arms. Drake lay across the wood and extending both arms,
reached out, and managed to grasp Rolt's shirt, pulling him slowly forward, first
to the edge of the wood and then with a sudden upward jerk he dragged him sharply
on to the plank. He let go of Rolt and lay back, momentarily exhausted and unaware
that they were being moved by the tide away from the wreck and nearer to some
rocks which were protruding from the water. With an unexpected movement the
wood suddenly surged against the closest rock and as Drake pushed himself into
a sitting position, the plank broke and both he and Rolt slid into the sea. Rolt was
too badly injured to save himself further, and without even a cry he folded limply
and allowed the sea to take him. Drake choked back a feeling of helplessness but he
had done all it was possible to do. He swam back to the wreck and joined Mr. Hire
and the others who were clinging to the rigging.

Poor Ensign Metford also died in the hell of that night. After several hours in
the water his injured body could take no more, and as his tortured mind finally
absorbed the realization it was the end, his last thoughts were of his beautiful young
wife thankfully safe in Simon's Bay.

Although steam still arose in ghastly shapes from the surface above where the
sunken ship lay, it was bitterly cold away from the immediate area, and the appalling
ordeal of the men in the sea during the remaining long dark hours of the night was
horrible to the extreme, leaving nightmarish memories that were to be remembered
vividly by the survivors for the rest of their lives. Pathetic and unanswered cries
for help, numerous and loud at first, could be heard for several hours but they
gradually diminished and finally stopped, as one by one the suffering men took their
last choking breath before dying.

Eventually all was quiet except for the occasional sob or the muffled words of a
prayer. And here and there, amongst the debris that floated about in the dark waters
now stained crimson with blood, lay the gruesome evidence of the unfinished work
of the killer sharks. Large pieces of flesh, barely recognizable as the arms and legs
they once were.

The two cutters and the gig which had witnessed the spectacular death of the
Birkenhead waited a further thirty minutes or so, and then began to move away
towards the shore. Dr. Culhane, who had struck out in the water for the gig, reached
it safely and was hauled in, and a few minutes later so was Mr. Renwick the
Engineer, who was spotted struggling close by.

The cutter containing Richards and the women and children was farthest from the wreck. The second cutter with Lewis and the three sailors, and the gig, had remained close to the *Birkenhead* and after the ship parted and sank soldiers appeared out of the water all around them. They were struggling frantically to grab the sides of the two boats, calling out to the Holy Mother to save them, and while Lewis sweated with the heavy gear and tackle in the cutter, throwing it overboard for lightness, the three sailors were pulling men out of the water and heaving them into the boat. Surgeon Bowen was one of the lucky thirty-two men that got in before Lewis, realizing they could hold no more without being swamped, ordered the oarsmen to pull away after the first cutter. The gig, having picked up another eight people, including Culhane and Renwick, was also full and they too moved off. It was heartbreaking but the men had no choice.

In the first cutter, just as Richards gave the order to make for the nearby shore he heard a shrill cry from the water and seconds later a young boy suddenly grasped the boat's gunwale. His weak pleading words to be saved were not necessary. The look on his face was enough. Richards had dreaded a moment like this and he felt even sicker. His boat was full and he had prayed to be spared the agony of having to refuse to take on any more. And now, here was just a boy, crying for his life, who would not last minutes if left in the sea. The women in the boat begged the sailors to pull him in and one or two men had half moved anyway. Richards hesitated no longer. He beckoned to two sailors and Second-Class Boy William Matthews was brought to safety. His life had been spared for the second time within the space of an hour and for the third time in his short career at sea. The first time had been a few months earlier on another ship. On H.M.S. *Illustrious*, when Matthews and another boy were playing about and decided to race each other aloft. Sixty feet up the rigging young Matthews slipped and fell. He hurtled into the sea and owed his life to an officer who dived overboard and brought him back. Unconscious, bruised, and battered. But alive.

Then, on the *Birkenhead*, during the last few minutes, one of the officers told Matthews to go below for an overcoat and on the way back he found to his horror the hatches had been battened down. He was trapped. Salmond had ordered the iron hatches closed in a desperate attempt to contain air in the hull, and there was no way of opening them from the inside. Fortunately, however, one of the seamen, Thomas Drackford, who had been screwing down the hatches heard the frantic banging and shouting and released the bolts. As he raised the cover the frightened boy scrambled through.

And now, less than an hour later, as Matthews squeezed into the cutter he felt an arm go around his shoulders, and looking up through tear-filled eyes, he saw for the second time the smiling, friendly face of Thomas Drackford the man who had almost certainly saved his life earlier.

The three boats were at more than full capacity, the second cutter under Lewis had a total of thirty-six on board, and the small gig had ten. There was nothing further they could do. It would have been madness to have considered picking up more survivors as this would have endangered the safety of the boats and the people in them who at least had some chance of reaching the shore.

They were a pitiful sight in the boats. Huddled together, wet and shivering. Many, including poor Renwick, were feeling the motions of the boat on the swell and were being terribly sick. The children were crying from hunger and the cold, and one or two of the women had their faces buried in their hands, softly praying.

The cutter with the women in was slightly damaged and had sprung a leak. Some of the men who had been wearing hats had taken them off and were using them to bail out the water. Others were using their hands cupped together and although they were not getting rid of much water, at least they were feeling some warmth from their movements.

It was still dark and very cold. As they neared the shore the survivors could hear the lapping of the waves on the beach above the regular swishing sound of their oars. Unfortunately, the seaweed was very thick, and with the combination of the darkness, the swell, and the tired condition of the men, it was impossible to safely manoeuvre the boats on to the beach. The oars became entangled with the weed, and as they could not simply abandon the boats and swim, Mr. Richards, as the senior officer and in charge of the two cutters and the gig, ordered the boats to pull back for an attempted landing farther along the coast.

As the cutter containing the men moved sharply away, Ensign Russell suddenly shouted, and pointed to where a man could be seen struggling in the water, close to the cutter. The man was obviously in a bad way and could not have lasted much longer without help. Without any hesitation Russell stood up in the boat and ordered that the man be hauled in, stating that he would take his place in the water. Half a dozen pairs of strong arms reached down and grasping the man by the waist and shoulders pulled him into the boat. At the same time Russell entered the water but tragically, within the space of not more than five minutes, as he swam strongly behind the cutter, he was seized by a shark and with a horrible scream was instantly pulled under and never seen again.

It was roughly 3.30 in the early morning when Russell died, and several hours later, as the three boats were still making their slow progress to a safe landing spot, the stars in the sky slowly began to dim, and the bright rays of dawn emerging from beyond the horizon fell on to the bodies of the men from the wreck who had managed to reach the shore.

Some had died as their finger-tips touched the sand, but with others life continued to flow through their still shapes, and as the warmth of the morning sun spread rapidly across the beach the limbs and muscles of the sprawled bodies twitched and moved as slowly the men began to stir and wake. Black and unkempt from long

A reproduction of the oil painting by Hemy, showing the scene where Ensign Russell gives up his place in the boat to a man struggling for his life in the water. The original painting, which measures 5 ft. × 4 ft., hangs in the Regimental Museum of the Highland Light Infantry, Glasgow. It is the property of Mrs. Eleanor Russell and her son, Captain J. Russell, to whom acknowledgement is made for their kind permission to reproduce the painting in these pages.

hours in the oil and filth of the water, some cut and bleeding and almost all completely naked, they rose unsteadily to their feet, aching and throbbing with pain
and helping to support one another in an almost comical fashion. Captain Wright
was one of the men to have successfully reached the land and as he gazed around
him, his mind slowly taking in the hideous reality of the events during the night,
he recognized many of the men on the beach, among them two fellow officers,
Giradot and Sheldon-Bond. On a later check, Wright was to discover there were
about sixty men in all, including eighteen seamen. The first thing to do was summon
help and to find food and clothes for themselves, so, rousing the groups of men,
Wright and the officers prepared everyone as best they could for the harrowing
torment of a long and agonizing trek over miles of bleak and barren countryside,
to the nearest habitation at Standford Cove which they eventually reached several
hours later.

Wright and his party were not in fact taken off by the rescue ship until three days
later but in the meantime food and clothes had been received, mainly from a Captain Smales, a retired military officer who occupied a farm a short distance from the
cove. The unpleasant task of burying the dead was carried out and thorough
searches organized by Wright's group for any more men who might have reached
the shore.

A full account of events until the rescue ship arrived is contained in graphic
detail in Captain Wright's official report to the military authorities which may be
found in Chapter 3.

Meanwhile, as it became lighter the three boats still making painfully slow progress, spotted a sail on the horizon. Almost frightened to look too hard in case it
should be a cruel trick played by the shadows of the early light of day, the survivors
rubbed their bloodshot eyes and stared again at the shape in the distance. It was
clearer now and they could make out the lines of the hull and the silhouette of the
masts and sails. There was no doubt, it was a ship. Hope rose in the empty hearts of
the poor people in the boats, and fresh strength came to their tired and numb limbs.
Their tongues and lips were sore and cracked but they managed to shout hoarsely
and wave their arms. A woman took off her shawl which was quickly tied to an oar
by one of the soldiers who stood up in the boat frantically waving his make-shift
signal back and forth.

But the ship, which later turned out to be the British schooner *Lioness*, was too
far away and the crew did not see the boats, nor at this stage were they even aware
of the disaster.

The schooner suddenly changed course and was no longer sailing towards the
three boats. The survivors were helpless to do anything. They could only watch
in horror and despair as the sail, which a few moments ago had meant food, warmth,
and clothes, and which had brought life back into their bodies, now moved farther

and farther away. Their shouting and waving stopped and they sank back against one another, silently resigned to their fate.

All of a sudden, Dr. Culhane stood up in the gig and called out for everyone's attention. He shouted across to Lewis in the nearest cutter that their best hope would be to transfer the eight strongest men to the gig, this being the smallest and fastest, and for the gig to make all speed for the schooner. This suggestion was accepted as sound, and with some difficulty the change over of men was carried out. Dr. Culhane remained in the gig but Mr. Renwick was one of those transferred to the cutter containing the men. When this operation had been accomplished, the gig pulled quickly away and energetically started off in pursuit of the schooner. The two cutters moved slowly in the same direction after the gig.

However, the attempt to catch the schooner was unsuccessful and the gig, now a considerable distance from the two cutters, decided to abandon the chase and make directly for the shore at a point which turned out to be about fifteen miles farther along the coast from the wreck and nowhere near the spot where Wright and his group of survivors lay on the beach.

The *Lioness*, under Mr. Ramsden the ship's Master, made yet another change of direction and was again approaching the boats. Hardly daring to believe it the survivors in the two cutters saw the sail looming closer and closer. There were no more changes of course by the schooner and this time they spotted the boats, reaching the one containing the men first. The survivors were taken on board and about an hour later, at 11 a.m., the cutter with the women and children was lashed to the side and these people gently transferred to the schooner. The *Lioness* then made all speed to the wreck. They reached it in the mid-afternoon and found a large number of the men still clinging to parts of the main-top mast that remained above the surface. Their condition after long hours in the water, first during the cold of the night, and then exposure to the hot sun, was appalling. Many could hardly move their muscles, or even their lips to speak, and the delicate task of the seamen moving these survivors to the schooner was an arduous and sickening labour taking almost the rest of the day.

The gig, with Dr. Culhane aboard, had landed at a point called Port D'Urban at approximately 3 p.m. that afternoon, and leaving the other men in the care of a Mr. Phillipson, the owner of a store, Dr. Culhane secured a horse and rode over one hundred miles across country to Cape Town to summon help. Nearly twenty-four hours later, at about 2 p.m. the following day, 27 February, the Doctor faltered into Cape Town.

The staggering news of the disaster brought by Dr. Culhane, was conveyed immediately to Commodore Wyvill on board H.M.S. *Castor*, who in turn sent word to Sir Harry Smith, adding that he had, without delay, dispatched H.M.S. *Rhadamanthus* to the scene of the wreck. Ordered aboard the *Rhadamanthus* was Com-

THE LAUNCH FROM H.M.S. *CASTOR*

At the end of March 1852, it was decided by the naval authorities to chart with accuracy the location of the rock on which the *Birkenhead* struck. Accordingly, a detachment of ten men, under Lieutenant O'Reilly, together with Mr. Mann the Assistant Astronomer at Cape Observatory, embarked in a launch from H.M.S. *Castor* and set off on what was to be the first attempt to survey the rock.

They had been at sea for two days when a sudden gale blew up during the second night, and in pulling away to avoid the worst of the storm they discovered at daybreak that they were well out to sea with no sight of land. The gale was still continuing and they endured a further day exposed to the full fury of the seas before they eventually made land three days after first starting out.

The above illustration of the launch caught in the height of the storm was made by a member of the party and published at the time in the *Illustrated London News*, to whom the author is indebted for their permission to reproduce it here.

mander Bunce (from the *Castor*) together with twenty-five additional men to form boat crews.

The *Rhadamanthus* left at once and late that evening located the *Lioness* making for Simon's Bay with a total of 116 survivors on board, those from the cutters and the main-top mast. There was little or no wind and the progress of the schooner was very slow, so it was decided that as she was still a considerable distance from Simon's Bay the steamer *Rhadamanthus* should tow her in, proceeding afterwards towards Danger Point in search of further survivors. The *Rhadamanthus* subsequently scoured this area extensively, in both directions of the sunken *Birkenhead*. There was no sign of life in the water but every so often a corpse, spotted lying across bits of wreckage that were drifting with the currents, would be taken on board by sailors already sickened by what they had heard and seen.

Captain Wright's group were found two days later in the evening of Saturday, 28 February, at Standford Cove, and on the following morning they were transferred to the *Rhadamanthus*. This group now also included Ensign Lucas who had reached the shore, badly injured, in the company of five others, and on the day prior to the rescue had met and joined up with the main party. One or two other survivors were picked up from various spots along the coast where they had reached the shore and there remained, exhausted and waiting for death or rescue, whichever came the sooner.

When Commander Bunce was satisfied there were no more survivors and that the area had been combed thoroughly, he returned to anchorage at Cape Town on the morning of 1 March. The other survivors from the three small boats had in the meantime been moved to Cape Town, the men put aboard H.M.S. *Castor* and the women and children comfortably housed in a barracks.

Commodore Wyvill reported to the Governor that the area had been searched, both on sea and along the shore. He attached a list of survivors which numbered 183, adding,

> All the sufferers of this unfortunate wreck are on board H.M.S. *Castor* and H.M.S. *Rhadamanthus*, and the soldiers are very thinly clothed. I have to request your instructions as to the disposal of the troops, and beg directions may be given for the necessary clothing to be furnished.

This request for clothing was met without delay and uniforms for the soldiers and clothing for the seamen were provided immediately. News of the survivors was published, also without delay, to relieve the acute public anxiety and consternation which had swept through Cape Town over the suddenness and magnitude of the disaster.

The toll of the *Birkenhead* was heavy. Captain Salmond had gone down with his ship, as had 10 of his officers and 72 of his crew. The courageous Lieutenant-

The 26-gun naval corvette H.M.S. *Amazon*, on which the *Birkenhead* survivors were brought back to England. By courtesy of the *Illustrated London News*.

Colonel Seton had also perished, along with 7 brother officers, 353 soldiers, and the two military surgeons, Robertson and Laing.

The five surviving military officers were Captain Wright, Lieutenant Girardot, Ensign Lucas, Cornet Sheldon-Bond, and the Staff Surgeon Bowen, and in all only 193 persons saved could be accounted for, including the women and children. Altogether 445 lives had been lost out of a total of 638. A disaster of no mean proportions, even by today's standards after two world wars. The names of the survivors, shown under their respective regiments, are listed in Chapter 5 together with a Roll of Honour of those who perished.

At the Cape, during the course of the following few days the surviving soldiers and seamen were closely questioned and statements taken. Official reports were also received from the military officers and from Commander Bunce of the *Rhadamanthus* and Mr. Ramsden of the *Lioness*, and these, together with a covering dispatch from Commodore Wyvill, were forwarded to the Admiralty in London, reaching the hands of their Lordships on 7 April 1852. Full copies of these documents, written in the survivors' own words have been included in Chapter 3. The dispatches were conveyed to England by Mr. Freshfield, the clerk from the *Birkenhead* who had disembarked from the ship at Simon's Bay through ill-health. He travelled home independently by the mail ship *Propontis* arriving on 6 April, and was thus the first to reach England with news of the disaster.

The Times and other newspapers carried the story in great length the following day and a deeply shocked but immensely proud nation learnt of the conduct and behaviour of the men of the *Birkenhead*. Their heroism that day in February was acknowledged by some of the greatest men of the day, including His Grace the Duke of Wellington who made several references to the event. And sixty years later, the *Observer* newspaper, reporting on the loss of the *Titantic* in 1912, commented that the strains of 'Nearer my God to Thee', the hymn played by the ship's orchestra on board the mighty *Titanic* as she went down, were worthy to be remembered along with the *drums of the Birkenhead*.

On 7 March the fifty-nine surviving ship's officers and crew were embarked on board the 26-gun naval corvette H.M.S. *Amazon* (all sail) which, en route from the China station to England, had docked at the Cape a few days earlier to take on provisions. She arrived at Spithead at the end of April after an eventful journey during which she was struck by a sudden squall while becalmed that made her heel over nearly 23 degrees. Of the thirteen sails which were out, ten were split by the force of the blast, and for the *Birkenhead* survivors this was yet another providential escape experienced.

On their arrival in England the survivors were conveyed to Portsmouth to undergo, in accordance with Royal Navy policy, a trial by court martial. The court martial held on board H.M.S. *Victory* is described in Chapter 4.

3. In their own words

The Official Reports and Statements
of some of the Survivors

The official reports are reproduced here in the order in which they were presented by Commodore Wyvill to the Admiralty. And here, in the survivor's own language, these details of the terrible loss of the *Birkenhead* contain all those elements of tragic and deeply pathetic interest which give to the stories of shipwrecks their painful fascination and their hold over the reader of an almost magnetic absorption.

The official military version of the disaster is that given by Captain Wright of the 91st, the senior surviving officer, and is contained in his initial report to Lieutenant-Colonel Ingelby, the Commandant of Cape Town, dated 1 March 1852.

Simon's Bay
March 1st 1852

Sir—It is with feelings of the deepest regret that I have to announce to you the loss of Her Majesty's steamer Birkenhead which took place on a rock about two and a half to three miles off Danger Point, at 2 a.m. 26th February.

The sea was smooth at the time, and the vessel was steaming at the rate of eight knots and a half an hour. She struck the rock, and it penetrated through the bottom just aft of the foremast. The rush of water was so great that there is no doubt that most of the men in the lower troop-deck were drowned in their hammocks. The rest of the men and all the officers appeared on deck, when Major Seton called all the officers about him and impressed on them the necessity of preserving order and silence among the men. He directed me to take and have executed whatever order the Commander might give me. Sixty men were immediately put on to the chain-pumps on the lower after-deck, and told off in three reliefs; sixty men were put on to the tackles of the paddle-box boats, and the remainder of the men were brought on to the poop, so as to ease the fore part of the ship. She was at this time rolling heavily. The Commander ordered the horses to be pitched out of the port gangway, and the cutter to be got ready for the women and children, who had all been collected under the poop awning. As soon as the horses were got over the side, the women and children were passed into the cutter, and under charge of Mr. Richards, master's assistant, the boat then stood off about 150 yards. Just after they were out of the ship the entire bow broke off at the foremast, the bowsprit going up in the air towards the foretopmast, and the funnel went over the side carrying away the starboard paddle-box and boat. The port paddle-box boat capsized when being lowered. The large boat in the centre of the ship could not be got at.

It was about twelve or fifteen minutes after she struck that the bow broke off. The men then all went up on the poop, and in about five more minutes the vessel broke in two, crosswise, just abaft the engine-room, and the stern part immediately filled and went down. A few men jumped off just before she did so, but the greater number remained to the last, and so did every officer belonging to the troops. All the men I put on the tackles, I fear, were crushed when the funnel fell; and the men and officers below at the pumps could not, I think have reached the deck before the vessel broke up and went down.

The survivors clung to some of the rigging of the mainmast, part of which was out of the water, and others got hold of floating pieces of wood. I think there must have been about 200 on the drift-wood. I was on a large piece along with five others, and we picked up nine or ten more. The swell carried the wood in the direction of Danger Point. As soon as it got to the weeds and breakers, finding that it would not support all that were on it, I jumped off and swam on shore; and when the others, and also those that were on the other pieces of wood, reached the shore, we proceeded into the country, to try to find a habitation of any sort where we could obtain shelter. Many of the men were naked, and almost all without shoes. Owing to the country being covered with thick thorny bushes, our progress was slow; but after walking till about 3 p.m. having reached land about 12, we came to where a waggon was outspanned, and the driver of it directed us to a small bay where there is a hut of a fisherman. The bay is called Sandford's Cove. We arrived there about sunset; and, as the men had nothing to eat, I went on to a farmhouse about eight or nine miles from the cove, and sent back provisions for that day. The next morning I sent another days provisions, and the men were removed up to a farm of Captain Smales', about twelve or fourteen miles up the country. Lieutenant Giradot, of the 43rd. and Cornet Bond of the 12th Lancers accompanied this party, which amounted to 68 men, including 18 sailors.

I then went down to the coast, and during Friday, Saturday and Sunday, I examined the rocks for more than 20 miles, in the hope of finding some of the men who might have drifted in. I fortunately fell in with the crew of a whaleboat that is employed in sealing on Dyer's Island; I got them to take the boat outside the sea-weed, while I went along the shore. The seaweed on the coast is very thick, and of immense length so that it would have caught most of the driftwood. Happily, the boat picked up two men and I also found two. Although they were all much exhausted, two of them having been in the water 38 hours they were all right the next day except for a few bruises. It was 86 hours on Sunday afternoon when I left the coast since the wreck had taken place, and as I had carefully examined every part of the rocks, and also sent the whaleboat over to Dyer's Island, I can safely assert that when I left there was not a living soul on the coast of those that had been on board the ill-fated Birkenhead.

On Saturday I met Mr. Mackay, the Civil Commissioner of Caledon, and also Field-Cornet Villiers. The former told me that he had ordered the men who had been at Captain Smales' to be clothed by him, he having a store at his farm. Forty soldiers received clothing there. Mr. Mackay, the field-cornet and myself, accompanied by a party of men brought down by Mr. Villiers, went along the coast as far as the point that runs out to Dyer's Island, and all the bodies that were met with were interred. There were not many, however, and I regret to say it could be easily accounted for. Five of the horses got to the shore and were caught and brought to me. One belonged to myself, one to Mr. Bond, of the 12th Lancers, and the other three to Major Seton of the 74th, Dr. Laing and Lieutenant Booth of the 73rd. I handed the horses over to Mr. Mackay, and he is to send them on to me here, so that they may be sold, and that I may account for the proceeds.

On the 28th of February Her Majesty's ship Rhadamanthus was seen off Sandford's Cove; so I went down there and found that Captain Bunce, the commander of the Castor frigate, had landed and gone up to Captain Smales', to order the men down to the Cove, so as to embark in the steamer to be conveyed to Simon's Bay. On Sunday, when I was down on the coast the field-cornet told me that at a part where he and his men had been a few bodies were washed up and buried; also a few boxes which were broken in pieces and the contents strewn about the rocks. I then ceased to hope that any more were living, and came down to the cove to join the other men. We arrived there about 6 p.m. The order and regularity that prevailed on board, from the time the ship struck till she totally disappeared, far exceeded anything that I thought could be effected by the best discipline; and it is the more to be wondered at, seeing that most of the soldiers had been but a short time in the service. Everyone did as he was directed; and there was not a murmur or a cry among them until the vessel made her final plunge. I could not name any individual officer who did more than another. All received their orders, and had them carried out, as if the men were embarking, instead of going to the bottom. There was only this difference, that I never saw an embarkation conducted with so little noise or confusion.

I enclose a list of those embarked, distinguishing those saved I think it is correct, except one man of the 91st. whose name I cannot find out. The only means I had of ascertaining the names of the men of the different drafts, was by getting them from the comrades who were saved. You will see by the list enclosed that the loss amounts to nine officers and 349 men, besides those of the crew; the total number embarking being 15 officers and 476 men (one officer and 18 men were disembarked in Simon's Bay).

I am happy to say that all the women and children were put safely on board a schooner that was about seven miles off when the steamer was wrecked. This vessel returned to the wreck at about 3 p.m. and took off 40 or 50 men that were clinging to the rigging, and then proceeded to Simon's Bay. One of the ship's boats, with the assistant surgeon of the vessel and eight men, went off and landed about 15 miles from the wreck. Had the boat remained about the wreck, or returned after landing the assistant-surgeon on Danger Point—about which there was no difficulty—I am quite confident that nearly every man of the 200 who were on the drift-wood might have been saved, for they might have been picked up here and there, where they had got in among the weeds, and landed as soon as eight or nine were in the boat. Where most of the driftwood stuck in the weeds the distance to the shore was not more than 400 yards, and as, by taking a somewhat serpentine course, I managed to swim in without getting fould of the rocks, or being tumbled over by a breaker, there is no doubt the boat might have done so also.

One fact I cannot omit mentioning. When the vessel was just about going down, the Commander called out, 'All those that can swim jump overboard and make for the boats', Lieutenant Giradot and myself were standing on the stern part of the poop. We begged the men not to do as the Commander said, as the boats with the women must be swamped. Not more than three men made the attempt.

On Sunday evening, at 6 p.m. all the men who were at Captain Smales' and the four I had with myself on the coast, were embarked in boats and taken on board the Rhadamanthus, and we arrived in Simon's Bay at 3 a.m. on Monday, the 1st March; eighteen of the men are bruised and burnt by the sun, and the Commodore has ordered them into the Naval Hospital. The rest are all right, and seventy require to be clothed. I need scarcely say that everything belonging to the men was lost.

I have, &c

EDWARD W. C. WRIGHT

(Captain 91st Regiment)

Lieutenant-Colonel Ingleby R.A.
Commandant of Capetown.

P.S.—I must not omit to mention the extreme kindness and attention shown by Captain Smales, to the men at his house; and by Captain Ramsden of the Lioness schooner, and his wife to those taken on board his vessel—E. W. C. W.

Captain Wright has referred to Lieutenant-Colonel Seton as 'Major' and it is by this rank that he is incorrectly referred to in other reports and in newspaper articles. In actual fact his promotion to Lieutenant-Colonel, in place of Lieutenant-Colonel John Fordyce the Commanding Officer of the 74th, killed in action, was published in the *Gazette* on 16 January 1852, to take effect from the previous November, and it can only be assumed that either Seton did not wish to take up his new rank until his arrival on the frontier, or, more likely that the promotion had not been notified at the regimental depot in Ireland before Seton sailed on the *Birkenhead* on 7 January.

In the third paragraph from the end, Wright refers to the gig containing the Assistant Surgeon (Dr. Culhane), and states that a great number of men who died could in fact have been saved had the gig landed immediately and then run a 'shuttle service' between the wreck and the shore. This suggestion is made in far stronger terms in the Captain's second report and was later taken up by the newspaper critics who, perhaps unjustly, laid blame on to the Doctor for his actions in leaving the wreck and making his way to Cape Town. Later in the chapter is the Doctor's answer to these inferences and statements.

The list of men enclosed with Captain Wright's report is not unfortunately accurate, but nevertheless, it was published in full in *The Times* of 7 April and proved extremely useful in the cross-checking carried out. The name of the man of the 91st whom Captain Wright did not know was in all probability Corporal O'Neill who embarked at Simon's Bay.

Given next is the dispatch by Commodore Wyvill to the Secretary of the Admiralty. It is dated 3 March 1852 and was compiled aboard H.M.S. *Castor*. Apart from giving details of the disaster it also contains conclusions drawn by the Commodore from the reports and evidence provided by the survivors. As with Captain Wright's report, there is a further discrepancy over the number of people aboard the *Birkenhead*, but, as stated in Chapter 1, the reader is asked to accept these figures shown on page 112 as being the accurate numbers.

An interesting fact to emerge on reading the Commodore's dispatch is the absence of any detrimental remarks, or comments of any nature, concerning the actions of Dr. Culhane. The fact that the boats left the scene of the wreck is referred to in paragraph no. 8, but there is no specific mention of the Assistant Surgeon. Instead, Commodore Wyvill has come down rather heavily on young Richards, the executive officer in charge of the boats. Whereas Captain Wright appears to have excused the two cutters of making any attempts to land and return to pick up more survivors, he criticizes only Dr. Culhane and the gig, the Commodore's remarks are directed to all three boats. However, his criticisms of Richards are softened by his further remarks that the excited and obviously highly emotional state of the people in the boats under the most appalling circumstanecs would not contribute to the best decisions being made. It is probably fair to say though, that whether or not the right, or best, decision was made by Richards or Culhane, what was done was done well and to the best of everyone's ability. The boats took on as many as they could safely carry and had they been able to land the survivors there is not much doubt that they would have returned to the assistance of the men still around the wreck.

The Commodore also criticizes Captain Salmond for the course of the ship so close to land and for the lack of either the Captain or the ship's Master on deck, and on duty, at the critical time. This latter point, however, could be considered unfair on just the purely simple basis that even captains and ships Masters must sleep at times. And all possible precautions had been taken by the Captain before retiring, leaving an adequate watch on duty.

The criticisms by Captain Wright and Commodore Wyvill, and those of Commander Bunce who made similar remarks concerning the boats, were to themselves no doubt justified, but in all probability they were full of indignation at what they considered to be a needless waste of human life suffered in a disaster which occurred in a calm sea and within three miles of land. It is always easy to look back at what someone else has done, and to find fault, but it is another thing entirely to be that person and live through the event.

The Commodore's dispatch is as follows, together with the statement and reports submitted to the Admiralty.

'Castor', Simon's Bay
March 3rd.

1 Sir—It is with much pain I have to report, for the information of my Lord Commissioners of the Admiralty, the disastrous wreck of Her Majesty's steam troopship Birkenhead on the morning of the 26th of February at two o'clock, on the reef of rocks off Danger Point about 50 miles from this anchorage, by which catastrophe I lament to state that the lives of 438 officers (Naval and Military), seamen, soldiers and boys, have been lost out of 630 who were on board the ship at the time. The circumstances, as far as I can recollect, are as follows:

2 The Birkenhead reached Simon's Bay from Cork on the 23rd. ult. in 47 days. She was immediately prepared for sea, receiving coals to 350 tons, some provisions, and the officers horses, disembarked the women and children (except those taking a passage to Algoa Bay), and was reported ready on the 25th. That afternoon Mr. Salmond received the Government dispatches for his Excellency Sir Harry Smith, my orders to proceed to Algoa Bay and Buffalo Mouth to land the drafts of the different regiments, and steamed on his passage at six o'clock in the evening, which was fine and calm, with smooth water.

3 At half-past two o'clock in the afternoon of the 27th. February Mr. Culhane, assistant-surgeon of the Birkenhead, arrived at Simon's Town by land to report to me the loss of his ship near to Point Danger that two boats with, as he stated, the only survivors were cruising at a distance from the land. I immediately dispatched Commander Bunce, of Her Majesty's ship Castor, with 25 men (to form boats' crews), in the Rhadamanthus, the only steamer in port, to the scene of the wreck. That evening he fell in with the schooner Lioness, of Algoa Bay, Mr. Ramsden master. This vessel had on board the persons who were in the boats and 40 others, whom they had succeeded in taking off the mantopsail yard of the ship, which was the only part of the vessel visible above water; altogether 116 in number, as per lists. It being calm, and the schooner some distance from this anchorage, the Rhadamanthus, towed her in, and proceeded afterwards to Point Danger in search of any people who might yet be clinging to the spars and pieces of wreck floating about; also for any who might have landed. An examination of the coast having been made for upwards of 20 miles by land and sea, and no other persons being found except those who had landed during the night and day of the wreck on Point Danger, the Rhadamanthus received them on board and returned to this port on the morning of the 1st. inst. The persons so saved were 68 in number, of whom six were officers, (four Military and two Naval). They reached the land by swimming and on pieces of wreck, &c. These, with nine others who escaped in the gig, and those who were rescued by the schooner, make the total saved 193.

4 It appears that Her Majesty's ship Birkenhead was duly pricked off on the chart at eight o'clock on the night of the 25th within False Bay by the master, Mr. Brodie, and officer of the watch, Mr. Speer, second master; that the course was shaped S.S.E. ½ E, and Cape Hanglip given a berth of about four miles. The man

at the wheel, John Haynes, A.B. from ten o'clock to twelve o'clock of the first watch, states that he steered that course with directions not to go to the eastward of it. A leadsman was on the paddle-box, and look-out men were placed. The night was fine, starlight, and calm, but a long swell setting in on shore. The land was seen all the night from three to four points on the port bow. At about ten minutes before two o'clock, in the middle watch, the leadsman, Abel Stone, ordinary seaman, got soundings in twelve or thirteen fathoms, of which he gave notice to the officer of the watch, Mr. Davies, second master. The ship was going about eight knots. Before he could get another case of the lead the ship struck and he found seven fathoms alongside; there were two fathoms water under the bows, and eleven by the stern.

5 It appears that Mr. Salmond, who was roused by the shock, inquired the time, a few minutes past two o'clock, and the course steered. It was reported to be S.S.E. ½ E, which he stated was quite correct. He immediately ordered the engines to be stopped, the small bower anchor to be let go, the quarter boats to be lowered and lie off alongside the ship, the paddle box boats to be got out, and a turn astern to be given to the engines. He ordered the military officers, who were all in attendance (Major Seton of the 74th Regiment, and Captain Wright of the 91st) to send troops to the chain-pumps. The orders were implicitly obeyed and perfect discipline maintained. As soon as Mr. Salmond heard that there was water in the ship, he directed the women and children to be put into a cutter in charge of Mr. Richards, master's assistant, which was done. In ten minutes after the first concussion, and while the engines were turning astern, the ship struck again under the engine-room, bulging the side in several feet and tearing open the bottom. The water rushed in, drowned the fires, and stopped the engines; the engineer, Mr. Renwick, and stokers making their escape to the upper deck. Instantly the ship broke in two abaft the mainmast and sank, leaving the maintopmast and topsail-yard only visible above water. Up to this awful moment the resolution and coolness of all hands were remarkable. Mr. Salmond gave his orders with much presence of mind to the last. The three boats which had stayed by the ship now left her to seek a landing or to save themselves, and at daylight they were out of sight of the wreck. The two cutters were picked up by the schooner Lioness, and the gig landed with eight men and Mr. Culhane at Port D'Urban.

6 Having called upon the surviving officers for their statements of the circumstances attending the loss of this ill-fated ship, I now have the honour to lay them before their Lordships for their information, together with lists of the people saved, but I regret I cannot furnish the names of the unfortunate individuals who have been drowned on this most melancholy occasion, as the muster books and rolls have been lost.

7 There is no doubt that the course of the ship was shaped to hug the land too closely, and as it does not appear that Mr. Salmond or the Master had attended on deck from ten o'clock in the first watch until the accident occurred, it would infer much inattention and extreme neglect of duty on their parts; and when soundings were first struck, had the helm been put to port, this ill-fated ship might have escaped the danger. It is much to be lamented that not an officer has been saved who can give any satisfactory information on these points.

8 It is also deeply to be deplored that a young officer, Mr. Richards master's assistant, should have been the only executive officer in command of the boats; and

but for the circumstances of their leaving the scene of the wreck before daylight, the landing place discovered on Point Danger by those who reached the shore on rafts would have shown itself and the helpless individuals who were clinging to the pieces of the wreck and spars might have been picked off and carried to the shore by the boats, and thus many more lives would have been saved. Also, when the schooner visited the wreck, had the cutters examined the coast in the locality, it is probable that they might have found a few others. I can only attribute this fatal error to want of judgement, and to the excited state of the people in the boats under such appalling circumstances.

9 Captain Wright of the 91st Regiment, who landed on a piece of the wreck, lost no time in procuring and sending assistance to his fellow sufferers. He walked several miles along the coast, obtained the use of a whaleboat, and returned again to give all relief in his power, taking charge of all who landed. The Civil Commissioner, Mr. Mackay, and a Captain Smales, residing near Sandford's Cove, were most hospitable and active in clothing and feeding the poor fellows as they reached that place. To Mr. Ramsden, the master, I have expressed my thanks for his humane kindness and exertions in proceeding in his schooner to the wreck and saving the people who were clinging to the topsail-yard. Commander Bunce, with the boats, though too late to save life, by his activity prevented a long and painful journey to the sufferers, and succeeded in embarking and bringing them to this port in the Rhadamanthus.

10 From the deep water and dangerous position in which the wreck has sunk, I do not entertain any hopes of recovery of anything of value; but I have sent Commander Bunce by land to the vicinity to recover and dispose of the property as he may think best, an account of which I will send their Lordships by the next mail.

11 The soldiers will shortly join their respective Regiments, and I propose sending the remaining officers and crew of the late Birkenhead to England by the first opportunity (Her Majesty's ship Amazon, which arrived here last night and will sail about the 12th inst.) to be dealt with as their Lordships may see fit.

12 I am glad to state that the subscriptions were immediately raised to relieve the distress of the unfortunate widows and children of the soldiers, who are comfortably housed in the barracks of this place.

I have the honour to be, Sir, your most obedient servant,

C. WYVILL, Commodore

I have deemed it advisable to entrust this dispatch to Mr. Freshfield, the late clerk of Her Majesty's steamship Birkenhead, who from his knowledge of the circumstances, though not present at the wreck, having been left behind at my residence sick, will be able to give their Lordships every information, and particularly as to the names of the drowned officers, &c. It will also enable the accounts of this unfortunate ship to be closed.

C. WYVILL, Commodore.

J. Parker, Esqre, Secretary to the Admiralty, &c., London

Statement of Dr. Culhane of
Her Majesty's Steamship *Birkenhead*

That Her Majesty's steamship Birkenhead struck the ground at about 2 a.m. on the morning of the 26th February, somewhere near Point Danger, and in 20 minutes after filled and went down. The quarter boats were lowered, and about 65 persons got into them; the gig was also down. Whilst getting the paddle-box boats out, the heave of the ship in sinking washed them away. Many were drowned below before they could effect their escape to the upper deck. Dr. Culhane and eight men landed in the gig, near Port D'Urban, where Mr. Phillipson has a store about 30 miles from the wreck. Nothing had been heard of the other two boats, except that they pulled out to sea to get picked up by a sailing vessel.

Report of the Master of the Schooner *Lioness*

Schooner 'Lioness'
Simon's Bay
February 27th

Sir,—I beg to report to you that when the Lioness was off Walker's Bay I observed a boat inshore pulling towards me on the morning of the 26th. inst. at about ten o'clock which I picked up, and found her to contain 37 survivors from the wreck of the Birkenhead. On hearing that there were two other boats I proceeded in search of them, and three-quarters of an hour afterwards I succeeded in picking up the other cutter with the women and children; but after cruising about for the third boat I made for the wreck, which I reached about two o'clock in the afternoon of the same day, and sent the cutters away to pick up the men hanging to the spars, by which we rescued 35 soldiers and sailors in a nearly naked state. The wreck had disappeared all but a piece of the maintopmast and topsail-yard, to which the men had been clinging. Nothing else could be saved. I observed that some had succeeded in landing on the Point, but only to the number of about ten. Finding that I could do no more at the wreck, I made for this anchorage, and was towed by Her Majesty's vessel Rhadamanthus when about nine miles from the anchorage. I was glad to have it in my power to relieve the sufferers of this unfortunate ship, who were on board with me about 36 hours. The women and children were provided with suitable clothing by my wife, and all that I and my ship's company could spare we supplied to the men.

As I am desirous of prosecuting my voyage to the west coasts of Africa without delay, I beg you will be pleased to order the provisions to be replaced and the defects of the ship made good, my boat and gunwhale being injured by getting in the cutters. The unfortunate people have been put on board the Castor at nine o'clock.

I have the honour to be, Sir, &c.,
THOMAS RAMSDEN
Master and owner of the Lioness.

Commodore Wyvill, Commander-in-Chief, &c.

Statement of Dr. Bowen, Staff Surgeon, saved by the first Cutter

Simon's Bay
March 1st. 1852

Sir,—In obedience to your command I have the honour to state that I was on the Birkenhead shortly after she struck about 2 a.m. on the 26th February. I remained in the vessel till she parted in two just before the paddle-boxes, as it seemed to me, and then seeing no hope of the ship floating, and Mr. Salmond saying that those who could swim had better try and save their lives, I lowered myself from the poop and swam. The ship went down in three or four minutes after I left her, so far as I can judge. I was picked up by the first cutter.

During the time I was on the deck the conduct of the officers and men, both Naval and Military, displayed the greatest coolness and the perfection of discipline. Mr. Salmond's orders were give, answered and carried out with as much quietness as if it had been only an ordinary occasion. I spoke to Mr. Salmond only a short time before the ship parted, and he was as cool and self-possessed as possible.

After I got into the cutter we took in as many men as she could with safety carry, and the crew behaved with the greatest courage and propriety with the exception of one marine, whose conduct was disrespectful to Mr. Renwick, and who appeared to grumble rather than assist.

The first and second cutters pulled in company for Cape Hanglip, under the orders of Mr. Richards, as when we neared the shore we found the surf breaking heavily. At daylight we all pulled seaward for a sail which was in sight, but after a long pull, as there seemed no chance of reaching her, we again pulled for Hanglip. A north-westerly breeze now sprang up and freshened, with a sea that was rather too much for our deeply-laden boat, and after hailing the gig that was ahead of us, and waving hats for some time without being able to attract the attention of her crew, we put the boat before the wind and pulled for a schooner that appeared to be standing in. This proved to be the schooner Lioness, and she took up about half past 11 a.m.

The master of this schooner then stood in shore for the second cutter with Mr. Richards, the women and children, and some soldiers. We picked them up. They were, like ourselves, pulling for the schooner. When we first made them out they appeared to be under sail, which proved to be a woman's shawl spread on a boat-hook. We could see nothing of the gig, but as she had a picked crew from the first cutter for the purpose of chasing the schooner in the morning, we were not in much apprehension on her account.

The schooner then visited the wreck and took many men from it. This was done by Mr. Renwick and Mr. Richards and the cutters' crews. These two gentlemen displayed the greatest courage, determination, and intelligence in getting the men away from the wreck, as well as during the whole affair. Their conduct was that of brave men.

Mr. Richards' duty in the boat with the women and children was arduous in the extreme and well performed.

Mr. Hire, who was on the wreck about thirteen hours, displayed the greatest courage and coolness.

Mr. Renwick was nearly exhausted and much bruised when we in the first cutter took him out of the gig, for the purpose of lightening her to chase the schooner, but after sunrise he soon rallied and behaved nobly.

Nothing could exceed the kindness and attention of Mr. Ramsden and his wife on board the Lioness; nothing was too good for us, and he made every effort to save as many souls as possible. He deserves the highest praise.

I have the honour to be, sir &c.
ROBERT BOWEN
Second Staff-Surgeon.

There is a stirring legend attached to Dr. Bowen's escape from the *Birkenhead* which, although bearing no truth whatsoever, has been accepted in a number of places including the Rifle Brigade where it has now become a tradition. A few years after the *Birkenhead* disaster, Dr. Bowen became Regimental Surgeon to the 1st Battalion Rifle Brigade, and the horse he rode, and was deeply attached to, was a magnificent white charger. Legend has it that the mare was on the *Birkenhead* and at the last minute when all hope appeared to have gone, the horse, which had remained at Dr. Bowen's side throughout, leapt into the sea with the Doctor on her back and carried him safely to the shore, thus saving his life.

A touching story, but regrettably not true. Nevertheless, Dr. Bowen could certainly be included among the notable figures on board the *Birkenhead*. He was a Fellow of the Royal College of Surgeons and held in high esteem by colleagues in his profession. He served in the British Army for thirty-six years, retiring in 1877 with the rank of Surgeon-General, and during his military career saw service in many parts of the world, including Gibraltar, Jamaica, South Africa, and Canada. He was also in the Crimean campaign and was involved in the battles of Alma and Inkerman, and the siege of Sebastopol.

Two years before his death in 1895, a photograph of Dr. Bowen was taken for the British Museum of Portraits, a copy of which was kept in the Art Library of the Victoria and Albert Museum, South Kensington. On the reverse of the portrait is a signed record of service on which it states the fact that Dr. Bowen was on the *Birkenhead*.

Statement of Mr. Richards, Master's Assistant, the Officer in Command of the Boats

Her Majesty's Steam Vessel 'Rhadamanthus'
Simon's Bay
March 1st 1852.

At the time the vessel struck I was in my hammock in the fore cockpit. I immediately ran on deck in my shirt, and on looking down the fore hatchway I saw the cockpit was half-full of water. It rising very fast, I then went aft and heard the Captain give orders to rig the chain-pumps. I went below in the after cockpit, and with the purser's steward and carpenter shipped the pump-handles. I then went on deck and assisted in clearing away the first cutter and starboard paddle-box boat falls. The vessel was then rolling heavily, and settling down by the head very fast. The Captain then ordered the soldiers on the poop, which was done in a quiet manner. He then called me and ordered me to get the women and children into the second cutter and save them if possible. The boat was lowered with a quantity of water in her, and nearly swamped alongside. The women and children were then passed into her, and some of the soldiers also jumped in off the gangway, in all thirty-five persons. I then got clear of the vessel, which immediately parted in two just before the paddle-boxes. I then heard the Captain calling for a boat to save Mr. Brodie, the master. I pulled to the wreck, but could not see him. I was obliged to get clear of the wreck again almost immediately, as the boat was nearly swamped and a great number of men swimming towards her. I then saw the first cutter and second gig astern of the wreck. I hailed and asked if they were full, and told them to take in as many as they could carry with safety. They then pulled towards me. I then heard Mr. Renwick call to me to pick him up. I told him we were nearly sinking and full of people, and to go on a little further to the gig, which picked him up shortly afterwards. We stayed by the wreck about an hour. After she parted in two, and having as many in the boats as we could carry, I stood in towards the shore to see if I could land those that were in the boats. We got in as far as the breakers, and I found the surf was running too high to land without staying the boats and endangering the lives of those that were already saved, especially those of the women and children. I then hailed the boats to keep further out, as I was nearly in the breakers, and should be swamped; we, however, succeeded in getting out of them, and then proceeded along the shore to the north-west six or seven miles, but could not see any place we could land at. At daylight we observed a schooner in the offing five or six miles off. I consulted with the other officers, and we considered it the best way to try and come up with the schooner. After chasing her between two and three hours a breeze sprang up from the westward and she stood off the land. The first cutter and gig were then very nearly out of sight ahead of me, as we could not keep up with them, only being able to pull six oars. I found it was useless me proceeding any further in chase, so I stood in towards the land. We were then in sight of the wreck, but could not distinguish any men on it. We made very little way towards the land, and the breeze freshening we were obliged to keep the boat before it to prevent her sinking. We were within two or three miles of the land when we again saw the schooner sailing towards us. We pulled the boat round, and with a woman's shawl for a sail succeeded in making a little way towards her. She hove to and picked us up at about two o'clock p.m., when I found the first cutter on board with Mr. Renwick, Dr. Bowen and 34 men. We could not see the gig and therefore made all sail towards the wreck, which we hove to off at half-past three. Mr. Renwick and myself then proceeded in the cutters and succeeded in saving 45 men off the topmast and topsail-yard. We could not see anything between the wreck and the shore, and thinking all were saved had reached the shore we proceeded in the schooner to Simon's Bay, having on board 116 people.

R. B. RICHARDS,
Master's Assistant.

Statement of Mr. Hire, the Clerk

Her Majesty's Steam Vessel 'Rhadamanthus'
Simon's Bay, March 1st

I slept in the fore cockpit, and between two and three in the morning of the 26th February 1852, I was awoke by the ship striking against something. I got on deck and went aft to the Commander, who told me to get the books ready to go in the boat, as he did not think there was any immediate danger. I did so, and went again on the poop. Had hardly got there when she went in halves amidships. I stopped by the Commander and Mr. Speer, second master, at the wheel until the poop went down, taking us with it. I came up again close to the mainyard, and went thence to the topsail-yard as she settled down where I remained. I did not see any officer or the boats. There were, I think, about fifty men on the yard with me, some of whom dropped off during the rest of the night, and at daylight some went on shore on parts of the wreck. I saw a vessel about five or six miles to windward, which afterwards proved to be the schooner Lioness. I tried to get one of the gigs, which appeared above water, but could not. At about half-past 3 p.m. the next day the schooner came down close to us, and the two cutters, with Mr. Richards, master's assistant, and Mr. Renwick, engineer, came and took us off to the schooner where we received the greatest kindness both from the master and his wife, who did everything in their power to assist and make us comfortable.

G. W. S. HIRE,
Clerk Her Majesty's Steam Vessel 'Birkenhead'.

Statement of Mr. Renwick, Chief Assistant Engineer

Her Majesty's Steam Vessel, 'Rhadamanthus'
Simon's Bay, March 1st.

I was awoke by the vessel going ashore and water rushing from the main deck into the fore cockpit. I ran into the engine-room in my shirt only, and found there Mr. Whyham, Mr. Kitchingham, and Mr. Barber. The engines were stopped and water pouring from the main deck through the door over the starboard cylinder. I shut the door, and about a minute afterwards orders were given to go astern. The engines, after making from sixteen to twenty revolutions, stopped, the water rising so high as to extinguish the fires.

While opening the starboard injection cock I observed a large portion of the starboard bilge buckled upwards, plates and ribs both started and water rushing in.

Mr. Whyham having reported to the Commander that the water had risen above the level of the air-pump lids, ordered all hands out of the engine room. I then went aft and remained on the poop until she broke in two. On rising in the water I swam towards the shore for about fifteen minutes, but observing what appeared to be two boats about a hundred yards to my left, I proceeded in that direction. On nearing the first one I hailed, and was answered by Mr. Richards, who told me to go ahead to the other boat, as his was full. At this time I was seized by a boy, who took me down, after struggling I rose and was picked up insensible by the second gig. On recovering I found Dr. Culhane and six or seven others in the boat. The three boats being full, closed and pulled in towards the shore to pick out a landing place, the surf breaking very heavily, as far as we could see. At break of day we saw a sail standing towards us, distance about five miles, we being then about four or five miles from the wreck and three or four from the shore. We consulted together and decided to pull towards her, as we were unsuccessful in finding a place to land without smashing the boat. We pulled two hours or so after her, and made very little progress in nearing her. Dr. Culhane then proposed to close with the first cutter, select eight good men, and to continue the chase, the second cutter being at this time about a mile astern. We did so, and no officer being in the first cutter I took charge of her and continued to follow the gig. A breeze sprang up, when the vessel quickly left us. Both gig and first cutter pulled in towards land; obliged to pull before the sea to prevent the boat swamping, there being in her 36 men. About 11 a.m. observed the vessel standing towards us on the port tack to leeward. At twelve were picked up by her, which turned out to be the schooner Lioness of Cape Town, Captain Ramsden. I pointed out to him the position, as I supposed of the other boats. He immediately made sail in that direction, and at 2 p.m. succeeded in picking up the second cutter, with men, women and children, in charge of Mr. Richards. A man at the mast-head being unable to see the gig, we made all sail towards the wreck, and arrived off the reef about 3.30 p.m.

Mr. Richards and myself, in the two cutters, proceeded to the wreck and succeeded in rescuing Mr. Hire, clerk and 36 men who were clinging to the maintopmast and topsail-yard. Having closely examined the whole coast without perceiving any other persons afloat made sail for Simon's Bay, having on board in all 116 persons.

CHARLES K. RENWICK
First Class Assistant Engineer

Statement of Mr. Archbold, Gunner

(Enclosure of No. 8, in No. 12 of 1852, from Commodore Wyvill)

On the morning of the 26th February I was aroused from my bed by a severe shock. I instantly ran on deck, and found the ship had struck on a rock and was rapidly sinking. I was ordered by the Captain to fire the rockets and both the blue lights, which I did; after so doing I went on the port sponson to clear away the port paddle-box boat.

We had canted the boat, when the fore part of the ship went down; at the same time I and Mr. Brodie (Master) were washed overboard. When rising to the surface of the water I held on to part of the wreck. Leaving the pieces of wreck, I swam towards a truss of hay, where I found Mr. Brodie. Finding it impossible to hold on with the hay any longer, I made for part of the wreck, where I found Captain Wright of the 91st. Regiment, and nine or ten men; they assisted me on to the raft floating towards shore. We picked up Mr. Barber, assistant-engineer, and a boatswain's mate (Lacey James). We arrived on shore about 1 or 2 o'clock. Previous to landing on shore I observed a sail in the offing, distant about eight miles. After landing I saw the schooner making for the wreck. We then proceeded on to Sandsford Bay, at which place Captain Wright left us, and procured some refreshment. Next morning proceeded to Captain Smale's, where we were clothed and fed until sent on board Her Majesty's steamer Rhadamanthus.

Memorandum: In respect of the boats, I saw none but the port paddle-box boat, bottom up, with some seven or eight hands on her, drifting towards the shore. I heard several voices calling loudly, and in that strain of voice that I fancied some boat or boats very near at hand; and, if there had been any boats present to have taken the men from the floating pieces of wreck, they might with good management have been safely landed in the same cove where Captain Wright and myself were landed, and could have made several trips to and fro to the shore, and saved a large number of men, as they were some time kept upon the surface of the water by the floating pieces of wreck. My opinion is that the boat that had the women and children in, saved time and lives by getting the assistance of the schooner, there being a great number on or about the wreck.

JOHN ARCHBOLD, Gunner
late Birkenhead.

Second Statement of Mr. Culhane, Assistant Surgeon

Naval Hospital, Simon's Bay
March 1st.

Sir—I have the honour to inform you that I was the last person to leave the wreck of Her Majesty's steam vessel Birkenhead when she got on the rocks off Danger Point. The poop was on a level with the sea when I swam from her, and at that time I could not see any of the boats. I succeeded after swimming about a mile or more, in reaching the second gig, and when I got into her we mustered ten. I remained there for some time. Could not see the wreck, it being dark, and did not see any men near. The two cutters were near, and they left and we followed, thinking to make the shore; but at daylight Mr. Richards saw a sail, and we all determined to pull for it, but after chasing the schooner for at least twenty miles in the gig, as I had eight men who volunteered from the cutter to pull for the schooner, she got ahead of us, and we did not come up until she was out of sight, and then thought it the most expedient way to reach you in order to let you know of the melancholy loss of the men and officers who were on board, except those who were on the mast. When I left the wreck we pulled for ten hours before we reached the shore and were six miles ahead of the cutter when we gave up all hopes of reaching the schooner. The people in the cutter say that they made signals to us, but the eight men and myself can assure you that we did not see any signal to us. I reached Port D'Urban about three o'clock p.m. The day after the wreck I rode on horseback from there to Cape Town, and arrived at Simon's Bay in about twenty hours from the time I started; and after pulling a space of about 50 miles and riding about 110 miles across the country, I am sorry to hear that it has been said that I left the boats. We saw the schooner tack, and come in the direction of where we last saw the cutt_rs, and she hove to as if to take them on board, and afterwards steered towards the wreck. We should have been very glad to be there at the time, as we dreaded that we could not get a landing place. I assure you that I tried every effort to reach you in order that you may be able to send a steamer to the wreck, and that was the object of the other eight of the boat's crew.

I have the honour to be, Sir, your most obedient servant,

W. CULHANE
Assistant-Surgeon.

C. Wyvill, Esqre., Commodore Commanding-in-Chief, Simon's Bay.

Report of Commander Bunce, sent to the Scene of the Wreck to afford Relief

Her Majesty's Ship 'Castor'
Simon's Bay
February 29th, 1852

Sir—I beg to acquaint you that I proceeded, in obedience to your orders, in Her Majesty's steam vessel Rhadamanthus to Danger Point arriving there on the morning of the 28th, and after examining the wreck with her maintopmast alone above water I proceeded in the boats to Sandford's Cove, where I found four of the men who had reached the shore from the wreck, from whom I received information that many more were at a farm called 'Klyne River', about 15 miles distant. I rode out to the farm and found 60 more, all of whom had been clothed, fed and housed most hospitably by Captain Smales, the proprietor, with whom I made arrangements for sending them down to Sandford's Cove in the morning to embark them in the Rhadamanthus—the sick to come in waggons.

The next morning I proceeded with Captain Wright, of the 91st Regiment (the senior surviving Military officer) and Mr. Mackay, the Civil Commissioner of the Caledon district, to the neighbourhood of the wreck, and travelling the beach for some distance found it strewn with small spars, pieces of deck &c., and the paddle-box boats, both of which were rendered unserviceable when the vessel broke in two pieces. Numbers of dead bodies had been found and buried, and great numbers must have perished by getting entangled in the large kelp weed which fringes the coast about Danger Point.

From the information I have been able to collect, it would appear that the Birkenhead rounded Cape Hanglip at about 9.30 p.m. on the 25th ultimo, at the distance of four or five miles; that a S.S.E. ½ E course, by compass, was steered; and at 2 a.m. on the 26th she struck on a pinnacle rock on the reef off Danger Point, a short two miles from the shore. The rock went right through her into the engine-room, and the engines being immediately reversed, rent her bottom, and in 20 or 30 minutes from the time she first struck she broke amidships, the bow part going down into deep water one way and the stern the other. The two cutters and one gig had been lowered and manned, and ordered to be off. All of the women and children were put into one cutter under the charge of Mr. Richards, master's assistant, the senior surviving Naval Officer. Some 30 or 40 of the men clung to the maintopmast and rigging; some swam to the boats, and getting heavily laden, the boats pulled out clear of the wreck. Many were below when the vessel broke and went down in her, and the rest on bundles of hay, spars, stools, doors, tables and the paddle-box boats bottom up were driven about between the shore and the wreck. The 68 officers and men whom I brought down in the Rhadamanthus are the only survivois out of those who were on those rafts, paddle-box boats &c. Many must have been drowned from exhaustion, and many have been knocked to pieces on the ledges of rocks over which the sea was breaking. By the exertions of Captain Wright and the Civil Commissioner of the Caledon district (Mr. Mackay) a whaleboat was procured the day after the wreck to search about, and five men landed by her from bits of wood drifting about, one soldier after being 38 hours in the water.

In communicating to you this disastrous occurrence, I cannot but express my opinion that if the boats had kept by the wreck until good daylight, landed the extra hands in one of the small creeks about, and then given their attention and assistance to the poor fellows floating and struggling in the water, a great many more might have been saved, for the weather was fine, the sea quite smooth, and not a breath of wind.

Mr. Culhane, the assistant surgeon of the Birkenhead, was in the gig and went in pursuit of a small schooner which was seen at daylight, but as he could neither reach her nor succeed in drawing her attention he bore up for Port D'Urban, about 12 or 15 miles from Danger Point, whence he communicated to you the loss of the Birkenhead.

The two cutters succeeded in getting to the English schooner Lioness, which vessel came in to the wreck and took off all those who were hanging to the mast and yard, making in all on board her saved from the wreck 117, which, with the nine landed in the gig and the 68 in the Rhadamanthus, makes a total of 194 of all denominations saved out of the 630 she left Simon's Bay with on board. I enclose you a list of the officers, soldiers, seamen, women and children who have been saved.

> I have the honour to be, Sir,
> Your most obedient, humble servant,
> B. H. BUNCE, Commander

To Commodore Christopher Wyvill, Commanding in Chief &c.

Second Statement of Captain Wright, 91st Regiment

Simon's Bay   March 1st.

About six p.m. of the 25th February Her Majesty's ship Birkenhead sailed from Simon's Bay on her passage to Algoa Bay to land the drafts of the 12th, 91st, and 74th, and then to proceed to Buffalo to land the remainder of the drafts, viz., 12th Lancers, 2nd, 43rd, 73rd, 45th, 6th and 60th Rifles. About half past ten I was on deck, and the officer of the watch, Mr. Speer, observed to me that he has passed the light, at the same time pointing out to me a light on the port side of the vessel. I made the remark at the time 'Surely that is not Cape Agulha's light, for if so the cape must have moved nearer the Cape (meaning Cape Point) than it was when I was here five years ago' From the appearance of the light I was satisfied that it was from a lighthouse, and not from a fire on the hills, many of which were burning, and therefore I concluded that another lighthouse had been built since I was here in 1847. I then went to bed.

About two o'clock on Thursday I was awoke by a severe shock, and on getting up found that the vessel had struck. I came up on deck and found the Commander, Mr. Salmond, and Mr. Davies second master on the poop. I was standing alongside them. The commander asked Mr. Davies how the light was bearing when he last saw it. Mr. Davies replied by naming some point of the compass. When the Commander turned away Mr. Davies remarked to me that it was odd where that light was, and he gave me distinctly to understand that he alluded to a lighthouse light, and not a fire on the hills. I have now every reason to suppose, that the light which was seen was a fire lighted of dry wood on Cape Mudge to act as a signal fire to the fishing boats which go out from that point. I saw the light for a long time myself, and certainly considered it a lighthouse light, as I have before stated.

After the vessel struck the Commander remained on the poop and gave his orders to Major Seton and myself. The utmost order was observed by all on board, and until the vessel totally disappeared there was not a cry or murmur from soldiers or sailors. It struck me as being one of the most perfect instances of what discipline can effect, and almost led me to believe that not a man on board knew the vessel was likely to go down. About ten minutes after the vessel struck the Commander sent me to Mr. Brodie, who was on the bridge, to know what assistance he required to get the paddle-box boats out. He told me to get 30 men put on to each tackle as to get the boats off. I did so, and then went to the Commander on the poop to see if he had any more orders; he told me to get 20 men more to the chain-pumps. I directed Lieut. Giradot, 43rd, to do this and it was done. Almost immediately the vessel's bows snapped off, the bow part going up in the air towards the foremast; the funnel fell over to starboard at the same time, almost carrying away the paddle-box and boat. The other paddle-box boat was being caned over just at this time, and Mr. Brodie disappeared from the bridge, having been knocked over somehow or other.

Just before the vessel broke at the bows the Commander had ordered the horses to be pushed overboard and directed Mr. Richards to get into the cutter to receive the women and children. All this was done with the utmost regularity, and the boats stood off about one hundred yards from the ship. The Commander also ordered out the large boat in the centre of the ship, but it could not be moved as the ship was breaking up at the bows.

Just before the vessel broke a second time, which was in about twenty minutes after first striking, the Commander called out for all officers and men who could swim to jump overboard, and make for the boats. Lieut. Giradot was standing alongside of me by the poop tails at the time. We called out to the men not to go overboard to the boats as we feared their being swamped, they being full of women and children (at least one of them we knew was). Very few men went and the rest remained on the poop until that part sank, and then down we all went together.

Every officer was on board the vessel when she sank except Mr. Richards, who was on board the cutter, and Dr. Culhane, of the ship who got into one of the gigs and then made the best of his way to Butt River, some fifteen or twenty miles from the wreck, rowed there by eight of his crew. I cannot express how much the loss of this boat was felt, and had it returned after landing Dr. Culhane I have no hesitation in saying that nearly every man of the two hundred (about) who were on the driftwood between the wreck and the shore must have been saved, as they could have been picked off the spars and wood on which they were when they were outside the seaweed, which prevented them from coming in to shore. The boat could have made forty or fifty trips to shore between daylight and dark and landed the persons in the boat in a cove just eastward of Danger Point.

As soon as I got on shore the party I was with (on the driftwood) and myself proceeded to Sandford's Cove; where there is a fishing station, about six or seven miles from Danger Point. As there was nothing to be had to eat there, left the men and went to a farmhouse about eight miles thence and sent provisions for the men. I also did the same next day, and then had the men removed to Captain Smales' farm about fifteen miles further up the country, sending Lieut. Giradot and Cornet Bond with them. I then went down to the coast and put up in a hut, and was occupied during Friday, Saturday and Sunday in examining every part of the rocks for at least twenty miles. I fell in with the crew of a whaleboat who were employed sealing at Dyer's Island. I got them to take the outside of the seaweed about a quarter of a mile from shore. while the purser's steward of the Birkenhead and myself examined the rocks. The boat got two men and we also had two who had been thirty-eight hours in the water; they were sadly exhausted, but a nights rest in the hut made them all right, except a few bruises. On the second and third day that I was on the coast I was joined by Field-Cornet Villiers and Mr. Mackay, Civil Commissioner of Caledon, and they had with them a number of men to assist in burying the dead and collecting what things were washed up on shore.

Very few bodies were found. On Sunday at 6 p.m. having perfectly satisfied myself that no living soul could be along the shore, and the men who were at Captain Smales' having been ordered down to the Cove to embark on board the Rhadamanthus, I left along with with, and arrived in charge of 46 soldiers and two officers at Simon's Bay at three this morning. Ensign Lucas, of the 73rd being unable to travel I had to leave him at Captain Smales' farm.

I cannot conclude this memorandum without alluding to Mr. Archbold, the master gunner, who was on the same raft with me for some time. While there he was as usual active to a degree, and encouraged the other 15 men who were also on it; but this was no more than his daily custom when on board the ship, for there he was perpetually at work, and to some purpose too. The ship's steward James

Jeffreys, although much exhausted after having been in the water so long a time, accompanied me in my search round the rocks on the coast and did his best to give me all the assistance in his power. I am happy to say that hardly a man of those saved of the party with me are anything the worse except for a few bruises.

W. W. C. WRIGHT, 91st

Statement of Mr. Barber, Assistant Engineer

Her Majesty's Steam vessel 'Rhadamanthus'
Simon's Bay, 1st March 1852

About two a.m. on the morning of the 26th February 1852 I was awoke by the ship striking, and ran into the engine-room, where I found Mr. Kitchingham, who was on watch, standing by the starting gear. He informed me he had just stopped the engines. We remained there until Mr. Whyham ordered the safety valves of the three boilers to be opened, which I did; shortly after, the order was given to turn astern, which was done; the fires were afterwards extinguished by the water rising rapidly in the engine-room. We then went on deck. Soon after, the ship parted; I went to the dingy's fall, and lowered myself into the water, but the weight of the soldiers who clung on me forced me to let go, and take to some of the main rigging, where I remained until the ship went down, taking me with her. I came up again, and held on to some of the wreck, until picked up by Captain Wright and some more men on a part of the fore sponson, on which we succeeded in reaching the shore at about one p.m.

(signed)   BENJAMIN BARBER
Assistant Engineer

Statements of the Look-out Man at the Wheel in the First Watch, the Sergeant of Marines who carried the Orders of the Commander, and of the Stokers in the Engine-room

John Haines, able seaman of Her Majesty's steam-ship 'Birkenhead' states,—That on the night of the 25th February 1852, he had the first watch, and took the wheel at 10 o'clock. It was a starlight night, smooth water, with a long rolling swell. Mr. Speer, second master, was officer of the watch, keeping the poop, and latterly on the paddle-box, looking out for a light (Alhulha's). The course he was steering was S.S.E. ½E. That the officer of the watch frequently looked at the compass, and gave orders not to steer to the eastward of the course, but a quarter of a point to windward of it. He was relieved by Francis Holditch, A.B. There was a leadsman in the chains all the watch, but no soundings given; the course was the same for two hours previously; a particular look-out was kept. On being relieved he turned in. The first intelligence of striking which he got, was by the hands being turned up to save ship. He thought she struck twice. On the first cutter being called away (to which boat he belonged) he turned out, and went into her, and remained by the ship, as ordered by the captain. Mr. Richards master's assistant, was officer of the boat, but afterwards went into the second cutter, to take charge of the women and children, by the captain's directions. The cutter was afterwards picked up by the schooner 'Lioness'. The ship struck the rocks about two o'clock.

his
(signed)   Johan + Haines
mark

Witness
(signed) C. A. Pritchard, Secretary

Thomas Daley, ordinary seaman, states—That he was look-out man on the starboard bow when the ship struck; he had been on since one o'clock, the water smooth and a starlight night. He saw the land about three points on the port bow. The ship struck about ten minutes to two o'clock, and there was no appearance of breakers.

On the cutter being called away, to which boat he belonged, he went into her, and remained by the ship. Mr. Davis, second master, was officer of the watch. The cutter was afterwards picked up by the schooner 'Lioness'.

his
(signed)   Thos. + Daley
mark

Able Stone; ordinary seaman states—That he was leadsman in the chains at one o'clock but got no soundings. At about 20 minutes to two o'clock he got soundings in 12 fathoms; but before he got another cast, the ship struck, and he got seven fathoms alongside. Mr. Davis was officer of the watch; the night was fine with smooth water. The land was seen on the port bow about four points. On the boat's crews being called away, he went to the gig, to which boat he belonged, and laid by the ship, as ordered.

his
(signed)   Able + Stone
mark

Serjeant Drake, R.N. states—That he was on the forecastle when the ship struck, about a quarter before two o'clock. He saw the land about four points on the port bow, the water perfectly smooth. On striking he went to the quarter-deck, and was directed by the Captain to carry his orders to Mr. Brodie, master. The engines had been stopped, and ordered to take a back turn. He carried orders to Mr. Brodie to let go the small bower anchor, to get out the port paddle-box boat, to get the women and children into the boats. He states that the paddle-box boats could not be got over by a pin jamming. That about 20 minutes after striking, the ship broke into two, the bow and stem cocking up. That the ship began to sink. He found himself in the water, and the captain Mr. Salmond, close to him swimming for a plank. That something struck Mr. Salmond, and he went down. After being about four or five minutes in the water, he observed the mainmast and main topsail yard out of the water. He swam to it, and got on it with 30 or 40 others. The hull of the ship was under water. He states that the military officers, and Major Seton of the 74th were in attendance on the captain, and had sent the soldiers to the pumps, as ordered; that all hands were steady, and obeyed orders with alacrity until the last moment; that the ship struck twice; the first shock stove in the bows, and drowned many men forward. that the second shock broke the ship in two. The men on the yard behaved with great coolness and firmness, several swam to the shore on pieces

of spar, and about 30 in number reached the land. Mr. Davis second master, was officer of the watch; he was picked up after being twelve hours clinging to the spars.
(signed)   John Drake, Colour Serjeant, R.M.

John Ashbolt, stoker, states—That it was his watch in the engine room when the ship struck. That Mr. Kiehenman was engineer of the watch. The first order given was to stop the engine, and shortly after to give a back turn, which was done, and the engine made about eight or ten revolutions, and the ship struck again; the water bgean to rush into the engine-room, and put the fires out. When the engines stopped he went on deck, the ship broke in two, and he found himself picked up by one of the cutters.

William Chase, stoker, states the same. The engineers were all in the engine-room.
(signed)   William Chase
John Ashbolt

All the preceding statements are the official reports studied at the court martial and taken into account by the officers of the Court. In addition to these documents there is a statement by Cornet Sheldon-Bond of the 12th Lancers, and a narrative by an unnamed non-commissioned officer, both of which were published in full in *The Times* of 7 April 1852.

Cornet Sheldon-Bond commences with the striking of the *Birkenhead* on the rock and confirms the initial action on board as stated in the official reports. He mentions the orders issued to himself to put the horses over the side and goes on to describe the breaking up of the ship and how, after her final plunge, he found himself in the water.

I rose to the surface almost immediately. I had one of Mackintosh's life preservers on, which may be filled in the water, which I did. The sea at the time was covered with struggling forms, while the cries, piercing shrieks and shouting for the boats were awful. I swam astern in hopes of being picked up by one of them. I hailed one sixty yards off, but could not reach it as they pulled away, I suppose for fear of too many attempting to get in. I then turned round and made for the shore, about two miles distant, which I finally succeeded in reaching at a little after 5 a.m. by swimming only. Two men who were swimming close to me I saw disappear with a shriek, most probably bitten by sharks.

He eventually reached the shore and found to his surprise his own horse standing there, as if waiting for its master. He then describes how a few hours later he meets Lieutenant Girardot who managed to reach land on a raft with nine other men.

I fortunately hit on a landing-place, but owing to the great quantity of seaweed I had to struggle through, and being quite exhausted, I almost failed in reaching it. I then walked up a sort of beaten track from the beach in hopes of finding some habitation. In doing so I perceived my horse at a short distance standing in the water on the beach. I got him out and then returned to the place at which I landed when I saw a raft with about nine men on it endeavouring to land, but they did not succeed in doing so until they saw me on the rocks standing opposite to the proper spot; they then steered straight for me and finally landed at 7 a.m. Lieutenant Giradot of the 43rd Light Infantry, was one of them.

They made their way inland to Captain Smales's residence where they were provided with food and clothes and where they spent the night. The following morning, Bond, in the company of Mr. Mackay, the district magistrate, and others, made their way to the beach meeting small numbers of men who had landed, including Captain Wright.

On our way thither we met numbers of men who had landed.Some came ashore in the paddle-box boats, which had floated up; the one was full of water and the other keel uppermost. One of the ships quartermasters told me that there were seven others in the boat with him, which was full of water. They, however, all died from cold, having been many hours in the boat and quite naked. He had his clothes on. We also met Captain Wright 91st, who had landed on the sponson; we had been along the shore and had picked up several men. Some rafts had reached the shore with the bodies lashed on them quite dead; other bodies washed up, some of them dreadfully mangled by sharks.

In conclusion Cornet Sheldon-Bond refers to the rescue of the men by H.M.S. *Rhadamanthus* and confirms that the time when the ship (*Birkenhead*) struck, to the period at which the poop sank, was no more than twenty minutes.

Then there is the narrative of the non-commissioned officer which is reproduced here in full. This is a very interesting and informative document and mentions several incidents, such as Captain Salmond's last few moments before drowning, which the other official reports have omitted to do. The writer was also an eyewitness to Colour-Sergeant Drake's efforts to save Cornet Rolt.

The Birkenhead left Simon's Bay at about 6 o'clock in the evening, and everything went on comfortably until about quarter before 2 in the morning, at which time the vessel struck upon a rock, which made a hole in the port side under water, but before the paddlewheel. She began to fill immediately; hands were turned up to get the boats out; lowered two cutters down and one gig, then turned to get the paddle-box boats out, but the pin of the davits was rusted in and would not come out. At this time the vessel was swinging and grinding and grating against the rocks very much. Some set to work at the chain pumps in the after cockpit. The next thing was to throw the horses overboard, and get all the women and children in the second cutter, which Mr. Richards took charge of, with orders to land them at the nearest place. They could not land on account of the breakers, so her head was put out to sea. Just at this time, the Birkenhead parting in two just before the engine, the fore part of the deck sunk with several people on it. Captain Salmond then gave orders to do the best they could to save their lives. The other cutter and the gig were then lying off, manned. Several men then jumped overboard and swam to the boats—the captain standing on the poop, giving orders. Up to this time perfect order and discipline were observed—all the men quiet and steady and obedient to orders. At this time the captain was standing on the poop with several others; the after part of the ship then lurched forward, and all were thrown into the water. Some swam to the boats, and some to the wreck. At this time the maintopsail and the maintopsail-yard were out of the water, and all who could made for the topsail-yard. Part of the forecastle deck was then floating at about 20 yards distance. Captain Salmond swam for the wreck that was floating; and as he was swimming something that was washed off the poop struck him on the head, and he never rose again. All were clinging to the raft till it broke up, and then some swam back to the wreck, and some to the maintopsail-yard. About 45 people were on the yard, where they remained about 12 hours, till the Lioness schooner came and took them off, about 2 o'clock on the Thursday afternoon. About 100 of the soldiers were drowned below. The vessel filled so fast that they had no time to get up. From the time we first struck, which was about 2 o'clock on the morning of Thursday, until the vessel was all to pieces, was about half an hour.

Captain Salmond might have saved himself easily, but he remained giving orders until the after part of the vessel surged and threw him overboard; he might still have been saved if it had not been for his accident. Young Mr. Rolt of the Lancers asked the sergeant of Marines to try and save him; he did try, and got him on the raft, but as it surged against the rocks, it parted and he sunk. About 117 men, women and children came into Simon's Bay on board the schooner, and about 30 or 40 landed on another raft. That number could be counted on the beach. Of the 45 that remained on the yard, were Mr. Hire, the clerk, John Drake, Sergeant of Marines; John Cooper, private Marine; John King, a stoker, and 42 soldiers, and all, with one exception behaved most admirably. They were rather in a hurry to get into the schooner's boat when she came to take them off which nearly caused an accident, but all were saved. The behaviour of the crew was admirable all obedient to orders. There is no chance of Captain Salmond being alive. Mr. Brodie, the master, was in the act of clearing the paddle-box boat, when the ship parted in two, and he was killed at once. Nothing could exceed the kindness of Captain Ramsden, of the Lioness schooner, who took us on board; he clothed and fed us as well as he could and we shall always remember his kindness. It is supposed when we left Simon's Bay that there were about 486 officers and men of different regiments, besides women and children, and ship's company of the Birkenhead, amounting to about 115. It is feared that, on the whole, not less than 500 lives have been lost.

A further document worth including amongst those official reports and other statements is a letter from Lieutenant Girardot of the 43rd to his father, written just a few days after the disaster. Lieutenant Girardot, the son of a minister of the Church, was born at Newark, Nottinghamshire, in 1829. He entered the Army in 1847, retiring thirty-three years later with the rank of Lieutenant-Colonel. He married late in life, at the age of 65 and was for many years, until his death in 1902, a justice of the peace for the county of Nottinghamshire. Within a year of his death the officers of the old 43rd arranged for a memorial to be placed in the colonnade of Chelsea Hospital as a mark of respect for the high esteem in which he was held.

The letter from Lieutenant Girardot to his father reads:

Lieutenant Giradot, 43rd Light Infantry—
Simon's Bay, March 1—My Dear Father—
I wrote one letter to say I was safe, but for fear that should not reach you, I will send this to say I am quite well. I remained on the wreck until she went down; the

suction took me down some way, and a man got hold of my leg, but I managed to kick him off and come up, and struck off for some pieces of wood that there were on the water, and started for land, which was about two miles off. I was in the water about five hours, as the shore was so rocky, and the surf ran so high that a great many were lost trying to land. Nearly all those who took to the water without their clothes on were taken by sharks; hundreds of them were all around us and I saw men taken by them quite close to me, but as I was dressed (having on a flannel shirt and trousers) they preferred the others. I was not in the least hurt and am happy to say kept my head clear. There was no time to get the paddle-box boats down, and a great many more might have been saved but the boats that were got down deserted us, and went off. From the time she struck to when she went down was twenty minutes. When I landed I found an officer of the 12th Lancers, who had swam off with a life preserver, and fourteen men, who had got on with bits of wood like myself. We walked up the country eleven miles for a farm belonging to Captain Smales, formerly of the 7th Dragoon Guards, who was very kind to us, and all the men that were got on shore came up to him—

Ever your affectionate son,
FRANK GIRARDOT

Whilst noting Girardot's statement '. . . the boats that were got down deserted us . . .' and the earlier-mentioned remarks of Commodore Wyvill concerning the boats, it must be remembered that the boats were full to capacity and attempts to take on more people would have swamped them. Furthermore, the boats did try to land and would then have returned to the scene of the wreck, but as Richards has so clearly stated in his report, this was found to be impossible. When daylight came he could perhaps have made a further attempt to land instead of chasing the schooner, as possibly several hours were wasted by doing so, but obviously at the outset Richards felt that to make for the schooner was the safest course and the lesser of several evils. And his task first and foremost, was to save the women and children in his care.

Finally, to return briefly to the matter concerning Dr. Culhane. Premature to the naval court martial, a number of adverse articles appeared in various newspapers and journals in connection with the actions of the Doctor, among them the following particularly bitter and sarcastic comments in the *Examiner* of 10 April 1852.

His object in trotting to Cape Town, he tells the Commodore, was that he might be able to send a steamer to the wreck, and such also was the object of the other eight of the boat's crew. That is, his shipmates were to struggle in the water, floating on driftwood, knocked on the head by spars, bitten by sharks, or sinking by sheer exhaustion, though some hundred and fifty of them might have been picked up and rescued by half-dozens at a time with the gig of which this doctor deprived them. And these men were in their death-struggle, while the zealous doctor was trotting a hundred miles across the country to inform the Commodore that there were Englishmen a drowning, and that it would be well for him to send a steamer out. England having thus paid the lives of more than a hundred of her bravest sons for the preservation of Mr. Culhane, will no doubt feel bound in honour to take care of a gentleman whose retention in her service cost so large a sum in death and widowhood and orphange.

Meanwhile, the Doctor, obviously concerned and upset at the implications of the remarks made by Captain Wright, had written to his uncle, Dr. Morgan Culhane, who lived at Worthing, and his letter had elaborated somewhat on his method of escaping from the striken *Birkenhead* as she went down, and of his reasons for leaving with the gig and then riding all the way to Cape Town. *The Times* of 9 April 1852 published a letter received from Dr. Morgan Culhane which contained relevant extracts from his nephew's communication.

To the Editor of *The Times*

Sir—I beg to call your attention to the following statement made by Captain Wright, of the 91st Regiment, which appeared in your paper today.

'One of the ship's boats with the assistant-surgeon of the vessel and eight men went off and landed about 15 miles from the wreck. Had the boat remained about the wreck, or returned after landing the assistant-surgeon on Point Danger, about which there was no difficulty I am quite confident that nearly every man of the 200 who were on the drift wood might have been saved.'

This statement I shall beg of you to again insert in your paper of to-morrow, with the following extracts from a letter which I have this afternoon received from my nephew, Mr. Culhane, assistant-surgeon of the late Birkenhead:

'I was one of the last who left the wreck. When the poop was on a level with the sea the captain said "Now all you that can swim leave the ship". I saw the captain in the mizzen rigging about that time. I then determined to have a tug for it, took off my clothes, except for my flannel jacket and my cap, and stood on the after-most part of the poop, and remained on board about 5 minutes. I swam about for some time before I reached a small boat (the second gig); I hailed the men in the boat and knowing my voice they took me in; it was then dark. We remained there for a short time to see if we could pick up any of the sufferers. The two cutters had then left we followed, came up to them and intended to try for a landing place as soon as light should appear. The first thing we saw was a schooner in the distance, to which we gave chase, but she gained way on us. We then pulled towards the cutter, and got a few men to volunteer who could pull well, to try to come up with the schooner, but she went on at a smacking place. We had no sails. We then turned back, and tried to make the shore. When we reached it, the men had been pulling for ten hours, and had pulled 50 or 60 miles since we had left the wreck. I thought the most expeditious way to render assistance would be to get here (Simon's Bay) as soon as possible, to send a steamer down, as the boat I was in was of little use on that coast. I rode as far as Cape Town (95 miles), leaving Port D'Urban at 4 o'clock p.m. the day of the wreck, and arriving at Cape Town at 9 o'clock the following morning.'

I am, Sir, your obedient servant,
MORGAN CULHANE.

7, Steyne, Worthing, April 7.

In any event, the question of Dr. Culhane's conduct at the scene of the wreck was finally disposed of, officially anyway, at the court martial during the third day of the trial when he was aquitted of any blame or dishonourable conduct.

Some of the prejudice against Dr. Culhane was still retained by many of the survivors however, even for as long as fifty years after the event in the case of Lieutenant Girardot who, in 1902 (then a colonel) a few months before his death, wrote a letter commenting on reports in the press on the fiftieth anniversary of the disaster, and in his letter he mentions the Doctor, again in an unsavoury light.

The cuttings [wrote Girardot] are, that I have seen except that by General Maurice in the Cornhill Magazine of February 1897, which is about as correct as any that could be given even by those who were present, when each Officer was attending to his own duties. The boats never passed between the ship and the land, but remained near the ship. No-one knew where the land was, as it was pitch dark. The only boat that did not stay by the ship was that Dr. Culhane was in, which went away; had it remained until it was light, it might have saved many lives, as there was no-one in it but the doctor and the crew. I was in charge of my party at the chain pumps below until about five minutes before the Birkenhead parted and went down, when I was on the poop with Colonel Wright and a number of men. The behaviour of the troops on board as mentioned in the Cornhill Magazine was thought much more of in Prussia than it was in England, where no order was given to read the record at the head of every Regiment, as in Prussia.

In actual fact the letter is not strictly accurate in the reference to the boats as all three eventually left the scene of the wreck, not just the gig containing Dr. Culhane. Fifty years had obviously made the memory a little hazy.

H.M.S. *Victory*, Portsmouth Harbour.

4. The naval court martial

Her Majesty's Warship *Victory*, lying at Portsmouth Harbour was chosen to be the court-room for the trial of the survivors of the *Birkenhead*, and on the morning of 5 May 1852, within the timbers of this famous ship where, listening quietly the ghostly footsteps of some of England's greatest seamen could be heard pacing the quarter-deck, the court martial of the fifty-nine officers and crew members began.

In effect, the trial took the form of two separate courts martial, and as the Court could only hear evidence concerning the behaviour of the survivors at the wreck, they were conducted more along the lines of courts of inquiry. There were no surviving officers who could answer charges for the actual loss of the ship.

The first court martial, lasting two full days, was held against five men, Mr. Richards the young Master's Assistant, and four seamen, Brown, Dunn, Ashbolt, and Stone, with the evidence being given by the other survivors. The verdict against these five men was made known at the end of the second day, and on the following morning, 7 May, the remaining fifty-four survivors, including Dr. Culhane, were put on trial and the evidence supplied by the five men whose court martial had been held the previous two days. Although fifty-four men were involved, their hearing lasted less than a day and was very much a matter of formality. The verdict of the Court was given during the afternoon.

The officers of the Court were the same for both courts martial, and consisted of:

President: Rear-Admiral Henry Prescott, Second-in-Command of Her Majesty's
Ships at Spithead and Portsmouth
Captains: Henry Chads of the *Excellent*
    Edward Scott of the *Neptune*
    Granville Loch of the *Winchester*
    Robert Harris of the *Prince Regent*
    George Martin of the *Victory*
    William Henderson of the *Blenheim*
    Robert Robinson of the *Arrogant*
    Frederick Warden of the *Retribution*
    Henry Matson of the *Highflyer*
    Lewis Jones
    Charles Wise
Sir G. L. Greetham, Deputy Judge Advocate of the Fleet

The court martial of Richards and the four seamen opened at 10 a.m. The
audience were admitted and the five men were brought in as prisoners. A few
legal formalities took place, such as the reading out aloud of the Admiralty Authority
for the court martial and the apologies which had been received from certain officers
of the Court who were absent through either duty or illness. The various oaths were
sworn by the officers sitting, as required by law, and finally the hearing itself
started. Nine of the survivors not on trial in the first hearing were called in turn, in
the following order, to offer evidence and be questioned by the Court.

Thomas Cuffin, Seaman
Thomas Daly, Seaman
John Drake, Colour-Sergeant, Marines
John Archbold, Gunner
Dr. Culhane, Surgeon
Edward Wilson, Boatswain's Mate
George Till, Able Seaman
John Lewis, Able Seaman
Charles Renwick, Assistant Engineer

The procedure was more or less the same with each witness. He was first required
to state on oath his whereabouts on the *Birkenhead* prior to the collision, then to
state the circumstances as known by him relative to the loss of the ship, and thirdly,
he was questioned in detail and to some length by the Court. The five prisoners
were also permitted to put questions to the witnesses if they so desired. As far as
this book is concerned, not all the questions asked have been included. Only the

particularly relevant questions of either the Court or the prisoners have been taken, word for word, from the original transcript of the trials and set out here.

Cuffin, the first witness, was called and sworn in. He confirmed his own position at the helm, the course of the ship, and the fact that Mr. Davis, the Second Master, had taken bearings just prior to the ship striking. He also confirmed Captain Salmond's order to the engine-room for a back turn and his further instructions for all the boats to be lowered. He described how he left the *Birkenhead* and the events effecting him which followed, until he made land.

> ... I belonged to the cutter, (not the one with the women and children) and I left the wheel at the time, and the quartermaster Fleming, who was drowned, took the helm from me. I went into the boat, and the Captain ordered the boat to be lowered down, and I left the ship in the boat, and two or three soldiers jumped from the gunwale of the ship into the boat while she was lowering down. The boat took away from the ship the crew, and some who were by at the time, and we pulled off from the ship to pick up any person who was found swimming in the water. We did not pick up any.
>
> I left the cutter after daylight, and volunteered for the second gig, and went in her to pull after the schooner which was in sight. We pulled for about four hours, and finding she was gaining on us, and the breeze freshening, we found it useless to pull longer. The land being nearly out of sight, we thought it best to make for the land as soon as possible. Being a small boat, and the breeze beginning to freshen, we thought it dangerous to remain out. We then lost sight of both cutters, and pulled for the land as quick as we could, and reached the land about half-past four in the afternoon.

The Court then asked Cuffin the following questions, and as will be observed here and with the other witnesses, the questions do not always follow in sequence. They tend to jump from event to event, presumably because an officer would suddenly put a question which did not necessarily follow on from his preceding colleague.

Was there any officer in the second gig with you? YES, DR. CULHANE.

Did you act under the direction of Dr. Culhane in regard to your proceeding on shore, or was it the joint opinion of the persons in the gig? DR. CULHANE DIRECTED IT.

Where was the wheel placed in the Birkenhead*?* ON THE POOP.

Was she under sail or steam? STEAM ONLY.

Was the wind off, or on the land? THERE WAS NO WIND, EXCEPT WHAT THE SHIP MADE FORCING THROUGH THE WATER.

Was it clear or dark night? STARLIGHT.

Did you see the land? YES.

How far did you suppose yourself off? BETWEEN TWO AND THREE MILES.

How long was it after the ship struck that Mr. Salmond was on deck? NOT MORE THAN A MINUTE.

Was he dressed or not? NOT DRESSED.

When she struck, what was the effect upon the ship? IT CAUSED THE SHIP TO ROLL,
AND SHE MADE A ROLLING NOISE BELOW.

What state was the ship in when the cutter was lowered? A SINKING STATE; THE
FORE-PART OF THE SHIP WAS NEARLY UNDER WATER.

Was the foremast standing? YES.

Who was coxswain of the cutter? JOHN LEWIS, A.B.

What was the size of the cutter? A TEN-OARED BOAT.

How many people had you in her altogether? THIRTY ODD.

Did the boats stay by the wreck till daylight? NO, NEARLY DAYLIGHT.

When the boat left the wreck, where did she pull for? FOLLOWED MR. RICHARDS
ALONG THE COAST, TO TRY TO FIND A LANDING-PLACE.

Did you attempt to make any landing? NO; ON ACCOUNT OF THE SURF RUNNING
ON THE SHORE, IT WAS DANGEROUS FOR THE BOATS TO LAND.

Did you remain at the back of the surf till it was open daylight? YES, AND THEN
WE SAW THE SCHOONER, AND WE THOUGHT IT WAS SAFER TO PULL FOR HER THAN
TO MAKE FOR THE LAND.

How far were you from the wreck when you were at the back of the surf? ABOUT
FIVE MILES.

Could not the cutter have held more men, considering it was calm and smooth water?
NOT WITH SAFETY.

How many men were in the gig? I CANNOT SAY BEFORE DAYLIGHT, BUT AFTERWARDS
THERE WERE EIGHT OF US, BESIDES THE DOCTOR.

Was Dr. Culhane in the cutter? NO, IN THE GIG THE WHOLE OF THE TIME.

Why did you volunteer from the cutter to the gig? BECAUSE I WAS STRONGER THAN
ANY WHO WERE IN THE GIG.

*Was Mr. Salmond on deck at any time while you were at the wheel before the ship
struck?* NO.

Had he to come out of his cabin which was under the poop? YES.

Did you see Mr. Brodie on deck at any time during your being at the wheel? NO.

Did you see him after the vessel struck? NO, BUT I HEARD HIS VOICE FORWARD
GIVING ORDERS.

Are you aware what look-out men were placed in any part of the ship? THOMAS
DALY ON ONE BOW, AND JOHN BUTCHER, WHO WAS DROWNED, ON THE OTHER.

Who composed the party of thirty in the cutter in which you left the ship? SOME
OF THE CREW; SOME WERE STOKERS; THERE WERE NO WOMEN OR CHILDREN;
THEY WERE IN THE FIRST CUTTER.

Did the Birkenhead *steer easily?* SHE STEERED VERY STEADILY, BUT THE WHEEL
WAS VERY HEAVY.

Was the compass sluggish or not? RATHER SLOW IN MOVING.

Was there a good light in the binnacle? YES.

Did the officer of the watch look at the compass while you were at the wheel? YES,
SEVERAL TIMES.

After the ship struck, and before the back turn was given, did she bump? YES.

Do you think if the back-turn had not been given she would have remained more steady? I CANNOT SAY.

From where did they heave the lead in the Birkenhead*?* THE AFTER PART OF THE PADDLE-BOX.

If Abel Stone had called his soundings, would you have heard him? I COULD HAVE HEARD IT HAD I BEEN LISTENING, BUT MY ATTENTION WAS KEPT TO THE WHEEL.

Do you believe that at the rate the ship was going, that accurate soundings could have been obtained at 12 or 13 fathoms? IT MUST HAVE BEEN A VERY QUICK HAND.

Could you yourself have obtained accurate sounding in 12 or 13 fathoms water, the ship going between 7 and 8 knots? NOT AT ALL TIMES.

Was the course you were steering by the binnacle or standard compass? BY THE BINNACLE.

Do you know whether the binnacle differed from the standard compass? I DO NOT KNOW.

Was it usual to compare the two by the officer of the watch or master when the course was altered? IT WAS BY THE OFFICER OF THE WATCH.

Was the ship swung at the Cape of Good Hope to ascertain the deviation of the compass? NO.

Could you see the outline of the shore distinctly before she struck? NO.

What light did Mr. Davis take the bearings of? I CANNOT SAY THE NAME OF THE LIGHT.

How long did you lose sight of it before the ship struck? A VERY FEW MINUTES.

Did Mr. Richards do everything he could do to save the people from the wreck? YES.

Have you any misconduct to allege against either of the prisoners? NO.

Thomas Daly, who had been in the cutter containing the women and children was called and sworn in. He made his initial statement to the Court and, in common with the other witnesses, it included confirmation of the events of the disaster as already known and did not disturb to any significant extent the main features of the story. He was then questioned by the Court.

What number of men, women and children were in the cutter? THIRTY-SIX IN THE WHOLE; I BELIEVE; ABOUT SEVEN WOMEN, FOUR SOLDIERS AND SEVERAL CHILD-REN; BUT I DO NOT REMEMBER THE NUMBER.

Could the boat have held more with safety? NO, I DO NOT THINK SHE COULD.

What lights did you observe? IT LOOKED LIKE TWO LIGHTS IN ONE PLACE.

Did you watch the light the whole time of your watch? YES, I WAS LOOKING AT THE LIGHT AND THE LAND ALL THE TIME.

Was the light pointed out to you by the man you relieved? YES.

What officers did you see on deck during your watch? MR. DAVIS WHO WAS THE OFFICER OF THE WATCH, BUT NO OTHER.

Mr. Richards being commanding officer of the boats, do you think he did everything in his power to save the people from the wreck? YES.

Have you any instances of misconduct on their part to state to the Court? NO.

When you went on the look-out, what distance did you think yourself from the land? THREE MILES.

Did you think you were nearing the land by the course you were steering? NO.

What distance did you suppose yourself when you struck? THREE MILES.

Did you attempt to take any people up from the water into the cutter when 12 yards off the ship? NOT AT THAT TIME.

Did you consider your boat too full to attempt it? YES.

Did you make any attempt to land through the surf by daylight? NO, WE COULD NOT SEE ANY LANDING-PLACE.

Who was coxswain of your boat? GEORGE TILL.

The questions were switched back to the *Birkenhead* before the collision.

Did you report the lights to the officer of the watch? NO.

Did the lights alter their bearings while you were on watch? YES, THE LIGHT WAS A LONG WAY OFF THE QUARTER WHEN THE SHIP STRUCK.

Where did you first see them? ON THE BEAM.

Did you consider the light you saw to be a lighthouse, or lights from houses on the shore? THE LIGHT SHONE VERY BRIGHT.

Mr. Richards then requested that he be allowed to put a question to the witness.

Do you think it possible we could have effected a landing through the surf? NO.

The next witness called was Colour-Sergeant John Drake of the Marines. His initial statement to the Court included the words, 'They could not get the port paddle-box clear, because of the pin jamming.'

He was questioned by the Court as follows:

Did you observe any lights previously to the ship striking? NO.

Do you know of any cause of complaint against Mr. Richards, or the seamen now on trial, in regard to the loss of the ship? NOT THE SLIGHTEST.

Was everything done, in your opinion, which could be done, to save the crew and the passengers on board the ship after her loss? YES.

Were you on the forecastle during the whole time from 12 to 2? NO; I HAD ONLY BEEN THERE TWO OR THREE MINUTES; I DID NOT GO FORWARD AFTERWARDS. I WAS ON OTHER PARTS OF THE DECK.

What officers did you see on the deck previously to her striking? MR. DAVIS AND NONE OTHER.

Did you see the land? YES.

Did it appear unusually close? NO, TWO OR THREE MILES.

Mr. Richards asked:

Could you see the surf breaking when you were on the wreck? YES.
Do you think it possible for a boat to have landed there with safety? NO, NOT ABREAST OF THE WRECK.
Did you see any breakers to seaward of the wreck? YES.
Which bow were they on? THEY WERE ON THE STARBOARD BOW.
How far do you think the vessel struck off the land? TWO AND A HALF OR THREE MILES.
Could you, when I took you off the wreck, see any spars floating between the wreck and the shore? NO.

John Archbold, Gunner of the *Birkenhead*, was called and sworn, and related his story to the Court before being questioned.

Do you know of any cause of complaint against Mr. Richards, or any of the seamen now on trial, in respect to the loss of the ship? NONE.
Was everything done to save the crew and passengers? YES.

In his initial statement, Archbold had referred to his method of reaching the land. He had been in the water for several hours when:

. . . At daylight I saw a large piece of wreck, and found Captain Wright and ten soldiers on it. We picked up Mr. Barber, an engineer, and a boatswain's mate, and we paddled ashore on the piece of wreck. It was about three miles from the wreck to the shore.

Questions were put to him concerning the spot on the coast on which they were able to land.

What means had you of managing the raft? SMALL PIECES OF WOOD WE PICKED UP.
Was the discovery of the place at which you landed accidental? NO, IT APPEARED LIKE A SMALL SANDY COVE WHEN WE WERE IN THE OFFING, AND WE MADE FOR IT.
Did it differ from the remaining parts of the coast in sight? YES.
At what hour did you discover it? BETWEEN SEVEN AND EIGHT IN THE MORNING.
Would it be easy of access to boats? YES.
Would the boats have been able to discover it before daylight? NO.
Would more lives have probably been saved had the boats have remained until daylight at the back of the reef? I HAVE EVERY REASON TO BELIEVE THERE WOULD.
Do you think that the boats going out to the schooner was an injudicious measure? I THINK IF THEY HAD REMAINED AT THE BACK OF THE REEF MORE LIVES WOULD HAVE BEEN SAVED; AFTER THE BOAT'S CREW WERE CALLED AWAY, THEY DID EVERYTHING THEY COULD TO PICK THE MEN UP, WHICH WAS MY MEANING IN STATING PREVIOUSLY THAT EVERYTHING WAS DONE TO SAVE THE CREW AND PASSENGERS ON BOARD THE SHIP.

D.B.—8

Was it possible to know or conjecture before daylight that there was such a cove as you described? NO.

Looking back to the circumstances, had you been in command of the boats, and had seen a vessel in the offing, would you have thought it the most advisable mode of proceeding to go out after her? YES.

Then with your present knowledge, and judging after the event, do you think it would have been more advantageous to have kept near the reef? YES.

Taking the surf generally on the beach, could those cutters have gone through the surf? NO.

Dr. Culhane was the next witness to be called and sworn. His initial statement to the Court was very lengthy and he described in great detail his escape from the *Birkenhead*, the events in his gig, and his final dash on horseback to Cape Town. He mentions Mr. Brodie the Ship's Master, who was on the bridge attempting to get out one of the boats, and he confirms the Captain's words at the end for all those who could swim to leave the ship.

The Doctor was closely questioned on the events in the gig.

How many people were in the gig when you were taken on board? ABOUT TEN.

Was any person taken into the boat after you? NO; BUT A SOLDIER GOT IN JUST BEFORE I DID.

Was there any instance of refusal to take any person in after you were there? NO.

What changes took place between the gig and cutter? MR. RENWICK AND THREE OR FOUR SOLDIERS WENT INTO THE CUTTER, AND FOUR OF THE BEST SAILORS, VOLUNTEERS, GOT INTO THE GIG. THERE WERE EIGHT IN THE GIG AFTER WE TOOK THEM IN.

What size was the gig? SECOND GIG. SHE HAD FOUR OARS.

How long were you after you changed crews? THREE HOURS.

Had you any spells at the oars? YES.

Was the water perfectly smooth? YES.

Did you attempt to take in any man after you got into her? I DID NOT SEE ANY MAN.

Did you pull up to the wreck to tender further assistance? NO.

How far were you from the wreck then? I SHOULD SUPPOSE HALF A MILE.

How did you get to the boat at half a mile distance? BY SWIMMING.

Did you not think it necessary to pull up to the wreck, being at a half a mile distance from her? AFTER CONSULTING WITH MR. RENWICK AND THE MEN, WE DID NOT THINK WE COULD DO ANY GOOD BY GOING THERE, AS MR. RENWICK SAID THE CUTTERS HAD LEFT, AND WE PULLED TO THE DIRECTION WHERE MR. RICHARDS WAS, AND WE THOUGHT IT BETTER TO GO TOWARDS THE SHORE TO LAND THOSE WHO WERE IN THE BOATS.

Were all three boats together at half a mile from the wreck? YES, I COULD DISTINGUISH THE BOATS.

Did Mr. Richards then take the command, and pull away? YES.

Am I to understand that the three boats were half a mile from the wreck, and that half an hour afterwards they pulled in for the land? I CANNOT SAY EXACTLY WHERE MR. RICHARDS'S BOAT WAS; HE WAS CLOSER IN TO THE LAND THAN WE WERE; IT WAS MORE THAN AN HOUR FROM THE TIME THE SHIP STRUCK BEFORE MR. RICHARDS TOOK COMMAND.

What steps did you take after you got into the boat? AFTER CONSULTING WITH MR. RENWICK AND THE OTHER MEN, WE WERE WAITING IF WE COULD PICK UP ANY POOR STRAGGLERS, AS I HAD BEEN PICKED UP BEFORE; AND AS THE MEN INFORMED ME THAT OTHERS HAD PICKED UP AND TAKEN INTO THE CUTTERS, WHICH COULD TAKE NO MORE.

When you went in chase of the schooner, had you any directions from Mr. Richards to pull in for the shore in the event of your not reaching her? NO.

Did you quit the other two boats without communicating with them? I SAW MR. RICHARDS TURN BACK; I HAD NO OPPORTUNITY OF COMMUNICATING WITH HIM, AS I SAW HIM PULLING SEVERAL MILES ALONG THE SHORE.

What was the last you saw of Mr. Salmond? I WAS ON THE BREAK OF THE POOP, AND HE WAS UP TWO OR THREE STEPS OF THE MIZZEN RIGGING, AS I BELIEVE.

When you were in the boat, did the men obey orders? MR. RENWICK HAD PARTLY THE CHARGE OF THE BOAT, AND I CONSULTED WITH HIM; THE MEN OBEYED THE ORDERS GIVEN.

How was it that you did not reach the schooner? A BREEZE SPRUNG UP, AND SHE WENT TO SEA, ALMOST OUT OF SIGHT.

Were the cutters with you? NO; MR. RICHARDS TURNED BACK WHEN HE OBSERVED THE OTHER BOATS GOING SO MUCH AHEAD OF HIM, HAVING THE WOMEN AND CHILDREN IN THE CUTTER; THE OTHER CUTTER WENT ALSO IN PURSUIT OF THE SCHOONER, BUT WE GAINED SO MUCH ON HER, THAT WHEN WE TURNED BACK WE FOUND SHE HAD TURNED BACK.

Was there perfect unanimity in the gig among the officers and men, as to the mode of proceeding? VERY MUCH SO.

It was now 6 p.m. and at this point the court adjourned until the next day, 6 May. The first witness called and sworn the following morning was Edward Wilson, the Boatswain's Mate, who had been on watch on the starboard side of the quarter-deck when the *Birkenhead* struck. In answer to questions from the court he stated that when he relieved the watch at midnight he observed a light on land but took no particular notice of it. He confirmed the speed of the ship and did not consider the vessel to be travelling dangerously close to land.

Further questions from the Court included:

Did you think that the ship was abandoned by the boats while they might have rendered any assistance? I CANNOT SAY; I DID NOT SEE THEM.

Have you any misconduct to allege against either of the prisoners? NONE WHAT-EVER.

In his initial statement to the Court, Wilson had stated he reached the shore in the company of Mr. Barber and Mr. Archbold on a large piece of wreckage which served as a raft, and he was now questioned closely about the difficulty experienced landing.

> *What sort of a beach did you land on?* ROCKY.
>
> *Had you much difficulty or danger in doing so?* WE HAD A GREAT DIFFICULTY IN GETTING THROUGH THE WEEDS, AND I FELL OVERBOARD ONCE OR TWICE PADDLING, AND TRYING TO GET THROUGH.
>
> *Would there have been any danger for boats?* THEY COULD NOT GET THROUGH THERE WELL, UNLESS IT WAS A REGULAR LIFE BOAT.
>
> *What would prevent it?* THE SUNKEN ROCKS AND THE KELP.
>
> *Was the place where you landed smoother than the general run of the beach?* NO.
>
> *Was there not a high surf on the beach?* YES, WHERE WE WENT THROUGH BETWEEN THE ROCKS.
>
> *Taking the general run of the beach, could the two cutters, loaded with people, have gone through the surf without endangering them?* NOT WHERE WE LANDED.

Questions were put to him concerning the soundings taken by the leadsman.

> *How long before the ship struck did you see the officer of the watch?* I SAW HIM ON THE POOP WHEN THE SHIP STRUCK.
>
> *Do you know whether Abel Stone is a good leadsman?* NO.
>
> *If he had called his soundings, do you think the officer of the watch would have heard him?* YES.
>
> *Do you think that, the ship going at the rate she was, it is at all likely he got accurate soundings in 12 or 13 fathoms water?* IT WOULD TAKE A GOOD MAN.

The next witness to be called was George Till who had been coxswain of the cutter containing Mr. Richards and the women and children. The questions from the Court included:

> *Were you regular coxswain, or did you act as coxswain on that occasion?* REGULAR COXSWAIN, AND DID ACT AS COXSWAIN ON THAT OCCASION.
>
> *Whom did you consider to have command of the boat?* MR. RICHARDS.
>
> *Did the boat take in as many people as you could with safety receive?* SHE COULD NOT TAKE ANY MORE.
>
> *Was admission refused to any person who approached the boat?* NO-ONE CAME ALONGSIDE; BUT WE COULD NOT TAKE ANY MORE.
>
> *Do you consider that, under Mr. Richards' direction, the management of the boat and proceedings were well-judged?* YES.

Mr. Richards asked:

> *Do you think, as a seaman, we could have landed through the surf we saw at daylight, without endangering the lives of the people in the boat?* NO, WE COULD NOT.

John Lewis, the following witness, made his initial statement to the court and described how Captain Salmond had ordered him into one of the cutters as coxswain, that they took in thirty-two men from the water after the *Birkenhead* had parted, and how they then tried to make the shore.

> . . . Captain Salmond said to me 'Go in the boat'. I went in the boat, and she was lowered down; we went under the starboard quarter when the steamer parted. There were so many in the water, that we had to shove on one side and went about forty yards from the vessel when the vessel parted. There were so many hanging on the gunwale, that I could not take them all in. We had thirty-six altogether in the boat, thirty-two of whom we took from the water, which was as many as the boat would safely carry. I have the boat's slings overboard, and all the heavy gear. We immediately afterwards tried to land, as did the other cutter and the second gig. We would not land on account of surf, and we thought we had better wait till daylight; we remained until daylight, but we found we could not land.

He went on to describe the events leading up to the time they were sighted and rescued by the schooner *Lioness*. He was then questioned at length by the Court.

> *Was there any officer in the boat?* YES; MR. RENWICK, THE ENGINEER, AND A SOLDIER OFFICER.
>
> *In whose charge did you consider the boat?* I WAS THE ONLY ONE IN CHARGE IN THAT BOAT, UNDER THE COMMAND OF MR. RICHARDS, WHO WAS IN THE OTHER CUTTER.
>
> *By what means did you prevent those people whom you speak of as hanging on her, coming into the boat?* WE COULD NOT TAKE THEM ALL IN AT FIRST, BUT WE DID AFTERWARDS, WHEN WE HAD LIGHTENED THE BOAT BY THROWING THE GEAR OVERBOARD.
>
> *Was admission into the boat refused at any time?* NO.
>
> *Where were the other boats when you took the people from the water?* CLOSE ALONGSIDE OF MY BOAT.
>
> *How many persons were there in the gig?* I CANNOT SAY.
>
> *From her appearance, do you think she had as many as she could carry without endangering the gig?* YES.
>
> *Do you think the same of the other cutter?* YES.
>
> *How was it you reached the schooner before the gig?* WE LOST SIGHT OF THE SECOND GIG AFTER WE GAVE UP THE CHASE OF THE SCHOONER.
>
> *Did not the gig beat you in pulling?* YES.
>
> *Was she not then nearer the schooner than you?* YES.
>
> *How was it you reached the schooner, and the gig did not?* BECAUSE I PUT ABOUT FOR THE SCHOONER, AND I LOST SIGHT OF THE GIG, WHICH, WHEN I LAST SAW HER, WAS PULLING FOR THE LAND, HAVING GIVEN UP THE CHASE OF THE SCHOONER.

How were you pulling at that time? ALL THREE BOATS WERE PULLING FOR THE
LAND.

Was the schooner beating up to windward? YES.

*Was it a matter of chance, or by any signal made, that the schooner joined the
cutters?* WE HAD A SIGNAL ON A BOAT-HOOK.

*Do you know from the people of the schooner whether it was in consequence of that
signal that they bore up for the cutters?* NO; I UNDERSTOOD FROM THEM THAT
THEY WERE NOT MAKING FOR US.

*When the day broke, and Mr. Richards gave orders for the three boats to pull away
from the wreck, and towards the schooner, did you think he was taking the best
means of saving the greatest number of lives?* YES.

Is that your opinion still? YES.

Mr. Richards asked:

Do you think it was possible for us to have gone through the surf at daylight? IT
WAS IMPOSSIBLE.

Did you see any part of the coast where the surf was not breaking? NONE.

Did you see any appearance of a landing-place? NONE.

Mr. Renwick, the Assistant Engineer, was the last witness from the survivors to be
called, and by his initial statement and answers to the questions put to him was
able to describe the effect of the *Birkenhead* running on to the rocks and exactly
what happened in the engine-room.

Were you an assistant engineer on board the Birkenhead *on the 26th February
last, when she struck?* I WAS.

Where were you at that time? ASLEEP IN MY COT.

Do you know what occurred in the engine-room in consequence of her striking? THE
ENGINES WERE STOPPED WHEN I ARRIVED IN THE ENGINE-ROOM. THE CHIEF
ENGINEER, MR. WHYHAM, AND TWO OTHERS, MR. KITCHINGHAM AND MR.
BARBER, WERE THERE. ORDER WAS GIVEN TO REVERSE THE ENGINE, WHICH WAS
DONE, AND CONTINUED TO WORK THE STAND UNTIL THE FIRES WERE EXTIN-
GUISHED FOR THE SPACE OF ABOUT TWO OR THREE MINUTES. THE FIRES WERE
EXTINGUISHED BY THE WATER RISING SO RAPIDLY IN THE ENGINE-ROOM. WE
TOOK THE INJECTION FROM THE BILGE; BUT IT DID NOT LESSEN IN ANY DEGREE
THE FLOWING IN OF THE WATER. MR. WHYHAM THEN REPORTED THE FIRES
BEING OUT TO THE CAPTAIN, WHO SENT FOR ME, AND ASKED ME IF NOTHING
MORE COULD BE DONE. I ANSWERED, THAT THE WATER WAS MAKING THREE OR
FOUR FEET A MINUTE, AND THAT ALL HANDS WERE OBLIGED TO FLY THE ENGINE-
ROOM. I PROCEEDED ON THE POOP, AND WITNESSED THE EFFORTS TO GET THE
PADDLE-BOX BOATS OUT. ABOUT A MINUTE AFTER I WENT INTO THE ENGINE-
ROOM, THE SAFETY-VALVES WERE EASED A LITTLE.

What effect do you believe the back-turn had on the ship? I AM OF OPINION IT
HASTENED THE CRISIS OF THE WRECK.

In what way? BY RENDING THE BILGE OF THE VESSEL, AND ADMITTING AN
IMMENSE FLOW OF WATER.

Did you observe a greater flow of water into the ship after the turn than before? YES.

Did you hear any sound indicating a rending of the plates? YES, I OBSERVED IT.

What do you believe would have been the case, had the back-turn not been made? I BELIEVE THAT THE FRAME-WORK OF THE VESSEL WOULD HAVE REMAINED IN TACK SOME TIME, SUFFICIENTLY SO TO HAVE GOT THE PADDLE-BOX BOATS OUT CLEAR.

Was the flow of water considerable before the back-turn was given? NOT IN THE ENGINE-ROOM, BUT IT WAS IN THE FOREPART OF THE VESSEL.

Did she strike a second time? YES; VERY SEVERELY AFTER THE BACK-TURN.

Do you believe that to have made a second hole? NO; I BELIEVE IT TO HAVE EX-TENDED THE PREVIOUS RENT.

Was the ship divided by bulkheads below into compartments? IT WAS; THREE MAIN COMPARTMENTS; THE FORE AND AFTER ONES WAS SUBDIVIDED.

Were they watertight? YES.

State what injury you believe to have been done to them, or any of them? I BELIEVE THAT THE WHOLE FOUR DIVISIONS WERE MADE COMMON.

Do you mean burst in by the force of the water coming in forward? NO; BY THE BILGE BEING BUCKLED UP THE WHOLE EXTENT OF THE FOREMOST DIVISION, OR NEARLY SO.

Where do you consider the hole was made in the vessel? THE FOREPART OF THE BILGE OF THE VESSEL.

Ought not then the main and after compartments have resisted the water, and kept the vessel afloat? YES, IF THEY HAD REMAINED INTACT.

Can you account why they did not do so? THE MAIN DIVISION WAS FILLED WITHIN FIVE OR SEVEN MINUTES OF THE SHIP'S STRIKING, CAUSED BY THE EXTENSION OF THE FRACTURE FORWARD.

How do you account for the ship breaking to pieces? I BELIEVE THAT THE ACTION OF THE SWELL WITH THE MOTION GIVEN BY THE ENGINE TO HAVE SHIFTED THE VESSEL, SO AS TO REST ON THE ROCK, AND BREAK HER BACK.

Do you know of any instance of misconduct on the part of either of the prisoners? NONE.

Mr. Richards asked:

Do you consider we could have landed without staving the boats? NO.

Did you see any appearance of a landing-place? NO.

Do you consider that the second cutter had as many people in her as she could carry with safety? I DO.

The final witness was Mr. William R. Madge, Master of the *Victory*, who gave evidence concerning the 'swinging' of the Birkenhead under his direction for the purpose of checking the accuracy of the compass. He was asked:

Has the late Birkenhead ever been swung under your direction in this harbour? YES.

At what date? I THINK ONE WAS ON THE 15TH FEBRUARY 1851, ON HER GETTING A NEW STANDARD COMPASS; SHE WAS SWUNG BEFORE THAT, I THINK ON THE 22ND OCTOBER 1850.

Was the commander of the vessel supplied with a copy of the result? YES.

Is it within your knowledge that she has been swung at any other place? I THINK AT GREENHITHE, BY CAPTAIN JOHNSON, BUT NOT ON ANY FOREIGN STATION.

Look at the chart now produced, and state whether, taking the point of departure as there laid down, you would have taken the course there indicated? IT DEPENDS WHETHER THE DEVIATION WAS EASTERLY OR WESTERLY; IT IF HAD BEEN EASTERLY, IT WOULD HAVE CLEARED THE POINT, BUT IF IT HAD BEEN WESTERLY, AS LAID DOWN IN THIS CHART, IT WOULD HAVE CLEARED TWO MILES OF THE INNER POINT; IF IT HAD BEEN VERY SMOOTH, I MIGHT HAVE TAKEN THAT COURSE, BUT IF THERE HAD BEEN ANY SWELL OR ANY CURRENT, I SHOULD NOT HAVE TAKEN THAT COURSE.

There was also a letter produced from Captain Salmond, addressed to the Secretary of the Admiralty, dated 7th April 1851, in which he expressed satisfaction with the correctness of the ship's compasses.

Her Majesty's Steam-vessel 'Birkenhead'
Woolwich, 7th April 1851

Sir,

In reply to your letter of the 1st instant, requiring a report from me regarding the compasses of Her Majesty's steam-vessel under my command;

I have the honour to inform you, that during my voyage from Portsmouth to Cork (touching at Plymouth), from Cork to Gibraltar, and thence back to Portsmouth, I have every reason to be satisfied with the correctness of the table of deviation applied to the courses steered by the standard compass; and further, from the opportunities I have had of testing the courses, corrected for deviation, by running along the land up and down channel, I have every confidence in steering the corrected courses.

So far as my experience to this date will permit me to judge, both the standard and steering compasses are sufficiently steady.

Any further information I will be most happy to give when opportunities offer.

I have, &c.
(Signed)   R. Salmond, Master Commanding

To the Secretary of the Admiralty
London

This concluded the evidence in respect of the first court martial and Mr. Richards and the other four prisoners were asked if they wished to make any statements in their defence but all five declined to do so. The Court was therefore cleared and the officers retired for two hours to consider the evidence that had been laid before them. After this time the Court was re-opened, the prisoners were brought in and the audience re-admitted, to hear the Court's verdict. The findings of the court martial were read by the Judge Advocate who, after reading the Authority for the court martial and other preliminary details, went on to state:

> . . . that they [the Court] had to observe, in the first place, that from the unfortunate circumstances of the master commanding, and the principal officers of the ship, having perished, they feel that it was in the highest degree difficult, and that it might be unjust to pass censure upon the deceased, whose motives for keeping so near the shore cannot be explained; but they must record their opinion, that this fatal loss was owing to the course having been calculated to keep the land in close proximity. If such be the case, they still trusted that they were not precluded from speaking with praise of the departed, for the coolness displayed in the moment of extreme peril, and for the laudable anxiety shown for the safety of the women and children to the exclusion of all selfish consideration. In respect of the prisoners tried under the authority of the abovementioned order, the Court was of opinion, that no blame was imputable to them, and did adjudge the said Mr. Rowland Bevan Richards, John Bowen, Thomas Dunn, John Ashbolt and Abel Stone, to be fully acquitted.

On the following morning, 7 May 1852, the court martial reassembled to conduct the trial against Mr. John Archbold, Dr. Culhane, and the remaining survivors, except, of course, Mr. Richards and the four men already acquitted. After the preliminary formalities the trial, which was to be a very brief affair, began. Richards, Brown, Dunn, Ashbolt, and Stone were called in turn as witnesses, and after being sworn each one was asked by the Court, 'Do you know of any instance of misconduct by any of the prisoners now on trial, in respect to the loss of the ship, or subsequent thereto?' to which all five answered with an emphatic 'No'.

There were no other questions from the Court, but Dr. Culhane required that he be allowed to put questions to the witnesses. The request was granted but his questions produced nothing new, they simply confirmed facts always known about the Doctor's movements and actions after the collision.

The final question from the Doctor concluded the proceedings. The prisoners were then removed and the Officers of the court martial retired for deliberation. A short while later, a verdict having been reached, the Court was again opened and the prisoners brought in to hear the Judge Advocate read out the findings.

> The Court agree that no blame was imputable to Mr. John Archbold, or the other surviving officers and crew of the said ship, tried under the authority of the above-mentioned order, for the loss of the said ship, or for their conduct consequently thereto: but on the contrary the Court saw reason to admire and applaud the steadiness shown by all in most trying circumstances, and the conduct of those who were first in the boats, and who, to the best of their judgement, made every exertion for the rescue of that portion of the crew and passengers who remained upon the wreck. In this expression of praise, they desired to include those who had been aquitted on the previous and present Courts Martial. And the Court did fully aquit the said Mr. John Archbold and

the other surviving officers and crew of the said ship 'Birkenhead', tried under the authority of the above-mentioned order.

Those then were the courts martial of the surviving officers and crew of Her Majesty's Troopship *Birkenhead*.

The verdicts which naturally were more than satisfactory for the survivors, gave complete exoneration to everyone, including young Richards and Dr. Culhane.

Nevertheless, there were a few discrepancies in the evidence and one or two points which may, or may not, have some significance. For instance, Dr. Culhane states in his second report that he left Port D'Urban at 3 p.m. and arrived in Simon's Bay in about twenty hours which puts his arrival at about 11 o'clock the following morning. We then find in his personal letter to his uncle in Worthing that he has said he left Port D'Urban at 4 p.m. and that he arrived at Cape Town at 9 o'clock the following morning. Commodore Wyvill, however, in his dispatch to the Admiralty states in paragraph 3 that 'At half-past two o'clock in the afternoon of the 27th February, Mr. Culhane, assistant surgeon of the *Birenkhead*, arrived at Simon's Town by land . . .'

Then there is the question of the number of persons in the cutters and the gig. The survivors have stated that without doubt these boats were at full capacity and could not have taken even one more survivor safely aboard. Yet, we have the incident of the change-over of a number of persons between the gig and one of the cutters when it appears that the same number of people did not move between the two boats. According to Dr. Culhane when answering questions put to him at the court martial, there were ten men in the gig prior to the transfer and then he later states there were only eight aboard when they chased the schooner. More men were moved into the cutter than out of it, so if, as the survivors have stated, it was impossible to have taken more survivors into any of the three boats, it would be interesting to learn where the two 'missing' men went.

There are discrepancies too, over the period of time that the three boats stayed by the wreck of the *Birkenhead*. This is important in so much as it would be expected they would leave straight away and attempt to land so that they could return for more survivors. They would not have been aware at that stage they would be unable to land. Richards has stated they remained by the wreck for about an hour whereas Cuffin says they stayed until nearly daylight which would have been several hours. Yet John Lewis, the coxswain of one of the cutters, told the Court that as soon as the cutter was lowered and had cleared the wreck '. . . we immediately afterwards tried for land'. Other survivors gave varying periods from half an hour, to two hours.

There could obviously be some quite simple explanation for these discrepancies so the reader should not speculate on this to any great extent nor try to find some sinister reason for the differences.

The question of the ship's compasses, however, does lend itself to an interesting thought. As stated at the court martial, the compasses had not been checked in the waters off the South African coast and it is a known fact that the iron ore contained in the Sugar Loaf Mountain near Cape Town could have a magnetic pull on the compass thus giving an incorrect reading. So it is just within the realms of possibility that the *Birkenhead*, at the time of the collision, was not in the exact position that the duty crew thought they were, and this theory would also account for the confusion over the lights seen by Captain Wright and some of the crew. In his second report Captain Wright states:

About half past ten I was on deck, and the officer of the watch, Mr. Speer, observed to me that he had passed the light, at the same time pointing out to me a light on the port side of the vessel. I made the remark at the time, 'Surely that is not Cape Agulha's light, for if so the cape must have moved nearer the Cape (meaning Cape Point) than it was when I was here five years ago'. From the appearance of the light I was satisfied that it was from a lighthouse, and not from a fire on the hills, many of which were burning, and therefore I concluded that another lighthouse had been built since I was here in 1847. I then went to bed. About two o'clock a.m. on Thursday, I was awoke by a severe shock, and on getting up found that the vessel had struck. I came up on deck and found the Commander, Mr. Salmond, and Mr. Davis, second master, on the poop. I was standing alongside them. The Commander asked Mr. Davis how the light was bearing when he last saw it. Mr. Davis replied by naming some point of the compass. When the Commander turned away, Mr. Davis remarked to me that it was odd where that light was, and he gave me distinctly to understand that he alluded to a lighthouse light, and not a fire on the hills. I have now every reason to suppose that the light which was seen was a fire lighted of dry wood on Cape Mudge to act as a signal fire to the fishing boats which go out from that point. I saw the light for a long time myself, and certainly considered it a lighthouse light, as I have before stated.

Lieutenant Girardot and Ensign Lucas were on watch duty that night and they too confirmed afterwards they saw the light which at the time was taken to be the Cape Agulhas lighthouse. Cape Agulhas, however, was a good 80 miles away.

These points were not pursued by the courts martial, neither were any comments, good or bad, made in respect of the construction of the ship which is rather strange in view of the controversy raging between supporters, both in and outside the Admiralty, of vessels made of wood and those constructed of iron.

But although the Admiralty made no official statement regarding the *Birkenhead*'s iron construction, there was much correspondence in the newspapers on the advantages and disadvantages of either wooden-built ships or iron vessels. A writer in *The Times* strongly in favour of iron ships put forward the following remarks:

All accounts from the survivors of the Birkenhead's melancholy loss agree in one respect that the cause of the accident was striking upon a sharp pointed rock

while going at a speed through the water of 8½ knots, and when we consider
that her weight or displacement, at her load draught as a troopship was upwards
of 2,000 tons, the effect of such a blow may be readily imagined. The Birkenhead was divided into eight watertight compartments by athwart-ship bulkheads, and the engine rooom was sub-divided by two longitudinal bulkheads into four additional compartments, forming the coal bunkers making in
all twelve watertight compartments. The first blow (from the description cf
Captain Wright and other survivors) evidently ripped open the compartment
between the engine room and the fore peak, and to such an extent that the water
instantaneously filled it, as stated by the engineer, Mr. Renwick; and the next
blow stove in the bilge of the vessel in the engine room, thus filling the two
largest compartments in the vessel in four or five minutes after she struck. Had
she been a wooden vessel, or not built in compartments, she must have gone
down like Her Majesty's frigate Avenger, in five minutes after she first struck.
As it was, the buoyancy of the after compartment alone was the means of giving
time to get the boats out and saving most of those who were rescued from death.
Evidently the long swell and at least 1,000 tons weight of machinery, coals &c.
admidships, acting against the buoyancy of the after division, caused her to
break off as described and sink in deep water. The case appears to be parallel
with the Orion's the side and bilge having in both instances been ripped open
in the forward and engine room compartments.

To give a random view of both sides of the argument a further letter is reproduced, also published in *The Times* and written by a captain in the Royal Navy who
wrote in answer to an earlier letter in the same newspaper which contained a question as to whether or not the *Birkenhead* was fitted with watertight compartments.
This earlier letter appeared on 14 April 1852 and was signed 'Navigator'.

To the Editor of The Times

Sir—Among the various remarks that have been made by professional gentlemen upon the melancholy loss of the Birkenhead steamship, I am surprised to
find that no allusion has been made to its water-tight compartments. Now, in
a vessel of the size of the Birkenhead there could not be less than three, but
more probably there were four or five water-tight compartments. If ever there
were a case in which the value of water-tight compartments could be tested it
surely must be that of the Birkenhead. The vessel has a hole driven through
her bottom, by which one or at most two compartments are filled with water.
The vessel then parts in the middle, leaving either end of the ship to its own
buoyancy. The weather was calm, the shore at no great distance, the crew and
troops in perfect order, so that had the vessel floated but a single hour, or any
part of it, for that time, probably 200 lives of our soldiers and sailors would
have been saved.

It seems[1] almost inevitable to conclude that the ship had no water-tight
compartments, or that they were fictitious. When the comparative merits of
iron and wooden steamers were considered, so much was said as to the value

1. See also, Barnaby's *Some Ship Disasters and Their Causes*, in which this eminent naval
architect covers the subdivision failure of the *Birkenhead*.

of water-tight compartments in the former that it is impossible to imagine that no attention was paid to this in the construction of the Birkenhead. If, on the other hand, the ship was so rent and torn by the straining of the parts before break up that all the water-tight compartments were rendered unserviceable, so impossible a fact in the construction of iron steamers ought not to be passed over in silence.

I am, Sir, your obedient servant,

April 10   NAVIGATOR

The captain's reply was as follows:

I can answer that she was and that, having been originally intended to carry heavy armament (as a ship of war) her talented and well-known builders, Messrs. Laird, spared no trouble and expense in constructing her as strongly as iron could make her. When she struck on the rock off Point Danger, it appears that as soon as the foremast compartment filled all that part of the vessel broke from the midship compartment; that on this filling it broke from the after one; and in 20 minutes, in a fine night and the sea so smooth as not to endanger her two overloarded cutters, did this large ship break into three pieces as if she had been built of card-paper, sending 438 human beings to a horrible and sudden death. It appears from the loss of this ship and that of the Pasha in the China Seas that the so-called water-tight compartments are useless; that the destructions of these iron ships was so rapid as not to afford time for getting out their boats or resorting to many of the usual means of saving life; and that iron is unable to bear the weight of the sea when one compartment is full of water, immediately tearing away, as in the case of the Birkenhead, and the ship sinking in three separate pieces.

However, the questions involved over this issue, iron ships or wooden ships, have long been resolved but what seems to have been overlooked both by the critics who wrote to the newspapers, and again by the court martial, was that the direct cause of so much loss of life was not only perhaps the character of the ship but also the complete inability to successfully launch all the ship's boats and the apparent lack of Mackintosh life-preservers, except for one which Cornet Sheldon-Bond appears to have worn. This latter point though was in fact picked up. A letter appeared in the columns of The Times on 19 April by a writer who also suggested 'Life-Boat Drill' and then went on to criticize Captain Salmond for being asleep at the moment of danger.

To the Editor of The Times
Sir—Will you allow an officer who has been twice wrecked to offer a few ideas, principally occasioned by the melancholy loss of Her Majesty's ship Birkenhead.
  1. That each man embarking on board a troop ship be served out with a life preserver, the said life belts to be returned into store at the end of the voyage, when they would be available for the invalids or regiments returning home. The cost being little, say 10/-d each and they would last for years.

2. That it be a rule on board all troop steamers that once a week at sea, or in harbour, be the weather calm or rough, the word 'Out boats' be given. Were this the case, and the order strictly carried out, we should no more hear of rusted pins preventing the paddle-box boats being launched, or unmanageable cranes doing the same.

But if the Admiralty would study economy a little less, and the lives of those on board a little more, they would give the command of troop steamers to post captains or commanders, with a proper complement of officers. We should then hear no more of the commanding officer being below when the lead was going, and the vessel close in shore.

I enclose my card, but as the Admiralty equally dislike suggestions and the suggestors, I beg you will not publish my name, but allow me to subscribe myself (although now on half pay) what I have been many years.

                                                                          A. RIFLEMAN
Traveller's Club, April 8.

However, disregarding for a few moments the hows and the whys of the circumstances leading up to the situation where the men were assembled on the poop deck of the sinking *Birkenhead*, the fact remains that they were there, and they faced the alternative of either making a dash for the boats and apparent safety, each with the thought 'There must surely be room for just one more', or, remaining where they were, allowing the boats, one of which contained women and children, to go free and safely while they themselves awaited almost certain death under the most diabolical of conditions.

What happened prior to the collision and immediately afterwards, were for these brave men but stepping-stones to the threshold of a situation that was to ensure for them their deserving place within the pages of history, and the earlier circumstances do not detract in any way whatsoever from the eventual final moment of pulsating discipline and courage that is beyond any form of praise.

5. The Roll of Honour

Despite thorough and meticulous searching through records and reports, it has been found impossible to state with absolute accuracy the number of persons aboard the *Birkenhead* on her last fateful voyage. Apart from the fact the disaster happened over one hundred years ago, which in itself presents certain problems, all the muster and roll books concerning the persons on board went down with the ship. Nevertheless, the military records of the troops embarked on the *Birkenhead* appear to be clear and accurate and an exact number of soldiers aboard can be calculated, as is the case with the women and children. The discrepancy arises over the crew. Apart from the survivors, and the officers of the ship, there are no complete records available to confirm the names of the men who formed the crew, nor consequently the number involved.

When the news of the *Birkenhead*'s fate reached England, the newspapers and other journals of the day all included in their reports a list of those aboard and the number of deaths, but these differed considerably from paper to paper. Communications then were not as they are today and, presumably partly due to the long delays in conveying news, a number of facts concerning the disaster, including the question of the precise number of people on board, were badly distorted by the time they appeared in print. For instance the *Illustrated London News* of 10 April 1852, describing the event as 'A catastrophe of the most disastrous character . . .' goes on to report '. . . on board, only 184 have been saved'. *The Scotsman of* 7 April, states that of a total number of 491 troops aboard, including officers, the military loss was 358. And *The Times*, on 8 April, states '. . . the total number of lives which have been lost on this sad occasion amounts to 438'. There are also many other reports giving various figures, both at the time and years later when referring to the incident.

However, from a careful study of the documents available and from cross checking all the lists published, the numbers shown and the names presented in this book are as near as possible correct.

The following table will show at a glance the numbers on board the *Birkenhead* at the crucial points en route, up to the time of striking the rock.

Note. The names shown in the list of survivors and the Roll of Honour have been spelt exactly as they appear in the official records and on the memorial at Chelsea and there are a number of inaccuracies. Lieutenant Girardot for example is shown as Lieutenant Gerardol. Also it will be observed that in one or two instances the same man is shown as belonging to more than one regiment.

	Depart Cork	Arrive Simon's Bay	Dis-embarked	Embarked at Simon's Bay	On board at Danger Point	Died	Survived
Children	31	34	23	2*f*	13	—	13
Women	25	21	15	1*g*	7	—	7
Naval Surgeon	1*a*	1	—	—	1	—	1
Ship's officers	17	17	1*b*	—	16	11	5
Crew	121*e*	121	—	—	121	68	53
Army surgeons	3	3	—	—	3	2	1
Army officers	12	12	1*c*	—	11	7	4
Other ranks	479	479	17*d*	3*h*	465	356	109
Civilian servant	—	—	—	1*i*	1	1	—
	689	688	57	7	638	445	193

a. Dr. William Culhane, ship's surgeon.
b. Mr. Freshfield, ship's clerk.
c. Lieutenant Fairclough, 12th Foot.
d. These 17 men, together with Lieutenant Fairclough and Mr. Freshfield, were disembarked through ill-health.
e. Included in the crew was a small detachment of Royal Marines under Colour-Sergeant John Drake, R.M.

f. The two Nesbit children, Richard and Henry.
g. Mrs. Nesbit.
h. Corporal O'Neil and 2 men.
i. Andrew White.

Note. The discrepancy between the totals for 'Depart Cork' and 'Arrive Simon's Bay' is due to the deaths of the women and the births of the children.

Then amidst oath, and prayer, and rush, and wreck,
Faint screams, faint questions waiting no reply,
Our Colonel gave the word, and on the deck
Formed us in line to die.

Sir Francis Doyle's verses

This painting by Thomas Hemy, more than any other, captures absolutely the calm, simple dignity and amazing grace of the scene on deck just moments before the stricken ship took her last plunge.

As the measurement of life ticked slowly by, these men had time to think, time to reflect, to wish and to hope, and time to be afraid. They suffered the awful anguish and perplexity of despair in knowing that, like the death-ship on which they stood, for them there would be no more joy and no more sadness, no more sleep and no more awakening. They knew too, there would be no to-morrow.

When the bell finally tolled and the relentless whispers of doom rose from the abyss of the dark, forbidding waters, these brave men of the *Birkenhead* enacted a drama that no imagination could ever have created.

Great and splendid was their final moment of supreme tragedy, yet greater still and more splendid was their glory.

In all the sea's long tale of acts of heroism and self-sacrifice, there are perhaps some to equal, but none to surpass, the chorus of human courage that lifted from the *Birkenhead* like a mighty hymn into the spaceous darkness as these men crossed the threshold of life and death into the arms of eternal peace.

The following list which has been reproduced from the 1905 *Chronicle* of the Oxfordshire Light Infantry, by kind permission of the 1st Battalion Royal Greenjackets, gives full personal details of the men of the 43rd Light Infantry who embarked at Cork. The names only, of these men will also be found among the list of survivors on page 116 and the Roll of Honour on page 120 respectively.

The Wreck of the Birkenhead

NAMES of the DRAFT of the 43rd LIGHT INFANTRY which embarked, under the command of Lieutenant John Francis Girardot, at Cork, on board Her Majesty's Steam Frigate Birkenhead, which was wrecked off Point Danger, Cape of Good Hope, on the night of 25th February 1852.

Place	Date	Age yrs.mths	Drowned or Saved, with Subsequent Disposal of those saved	Service when Drowned or on Discharge Years	Days	Regtl No.	Rank and Names	Married or Single as per Records	Birth Place
Plymouth	6. 8.37	14 9	Drowned	11	103	1195	Sergeant William Hicks	Single	Nuneaton, Warwick
Taunton	7.11.36	23 0	- - -	15	111	1121	Corporal Benjamin Cozens	"	Thurminster, Somerset
London	30.10.33	17 0	A transfer from 46th Regiment 1st July 1834. Drowned	16	256	1037	Joseph Harrison	"	Cambridge, Cambridge
Naas	4.11.39	19 0	Saved. Discharged 18th July 1861. Granted pension of 8d. a day for life.	21	226	1582	Private Peter Allen	Married	Millingar, Westmeath
Buttevant	20.10.51	18 4	Drowned	-	128	2706	John Anderson	Single	Limerick, Limerick
"	27.10.51	18 0	Saved. Died 21st. Aug. 1852	-	298	2707	Edmund Ambrose	"	Newmarket, Cork
Westminster	18.10.51	21 0	Saved. Discharged 31st.Oct.1861	10	12	2712	George Brackley	"	Aylesbury, Buckingham
Kilkenny	10.11.49	18 0	Drowned	2	106	2582	Daniel Brennan	"	Kilkenny, Kilkenny
Bury St. Edmunds	4. 9.39	17 6	Drowned	12	173	1557	William Bullen	"	Bury St. Edmunds, Suffolk
Oxford	29. 3.46	26 0	Saved. Died 25th March 1857	10	360	2336	Love Daniel Bunker	"	Oxford, Oxon
Dublin	16. 5.50	22 0	Drowned	1	295	2620	John Butler	"	Thurles, Tipperary
Dublin	20.10.32	19 4	Drowned	19	9	960	John Byrne, 2nd	"	Red Cross, Wicklow
London	20. 4.40	17 11	Drowned	11	310	1674	Thomas Cave 1st	"	Newport, Hants
Dublin	2. 1.33	18 0	Drowned	18	271	978	John Cosgrave	"	Dublin, Dublin
Wolver-hampton	29. 5.35	18 0	A transfer from 46th Regiment 1st. Sept, 1835. Drowned	16	270	1055	William Debank	"	Witney, Oxon
Westminster	15.12.51	22 0	Drowned	-	72	2736	Thomas Dews	"	Bristol, Somerset
Clonmel	2. 2.36	19 3	Drowned	15	328	1067	William Donnell	"	Caher, Tipperary
Westminster	3.10.51	17 11	Drowned	-	145	2703	George Gillham	"	Dartford, Kent
Sudbury	12.11.51	17 11	Saved. Discharged 16th April 1862. Granted compassionate Campaign pension of 9d. a day for life from 17th Dec.1903. Died 13th Jan, 1904.	10	152	2723	Francis Ginn	"	Sudbury, Suffolk

NAMES of the DRAFT of the 43rd LIGHT INFANTRY - Cont.

Particulars of Attestation			Drowned or Saved, with Subsequent Disposal of those Saved	Service when Drowned or on Discharge		Regtl No.	Rank and Names		Married or Single as per Records	Birth Place
Place	Date	Age (yrs.mths)		Years	Days					
Buttevant	15.11.51	17 6	Saved. Died 8th May 1858	5	357	2718	Private	Michael Harnett	Single	Askeaton, Limerick
Leeds	20.2.32	18 5	" Died 4th April 1854	22	34	930	"	George Harrison	"	Doncaster, York
Buttevant	4.11.51	17 0	" Died 23rd Oct 1858	6	351	2715	"	Michael Healy	"	Fermey, Cork
"	4.11.51	18 0	" Died 22nd March 1857	5	138	2724	"	John Hearn	"	Crumcolloher, Limerick
Sudbury	12.11.51	17 0	Drowned	-	105	2688	"	Edward Outing	"	Sudbury, Suffolk
Westminster	21.7.51	17 9	Saved. Discharged 8th.Mar.1864	12	139	1969	"	George Lyons	"	Sutton, Bedford
Omagh	1.12.42	19 0	Drowned	9	86	1029	"	Lackey McPacklin	"	Black Lion, Fermough
Bury St. Edmunds	8.8.33	18 0	"	18	201	1063	"	John McQuaid	"	Clogher, Tyrone
	8.12.35	19 0	"	16	79		"	Joseph Penning	"	Coventry, Cambridge
Royston	1.11.42	19 0	Saved. Died 19th.Dec.1858	16	47	1965	"	George Peters	"	Linton, Cambridge
Buttevant	30.10.51	18 0	Drowned	-	118	2710	"	Edmund Quinn	"	Killinman, Limerick
"	10.2.47	17 0	A transfer from 6th Regiment 1 April 1850, Drowned	4	15	2611	"	Timothy Sheehan	"	Doneraii, Cork
Westminster	8.10.51	17 8	Drowned	19	140	2705	"	Charles Ranshaw	"	London, Middlesex
Leeds	18.4.32	22 0	"	-	265	934	"	John Riddlesdin	"	Wakefield, York
Buttevant	12.11.51	18 0	"	-	101	2716	"	Daniel Riordan	"	Ruthca-e, York
Westminster	6.11.51	17 11	"	-	98	2720	"	George Sheppard	"	Melksham, Wilts
Buttevant	18.11.51	17 11	"	-		2721	"	Timothy Sullivan	"	Kanturk, Cork
Oxford	15.2.46	17 0	"	6	113	2296	"	Henry Tucker	"	Oxford, Oxon
Westminster	4.11.51	20 0	"	-	125	2719	"	Edward Vickery	"	Newbury, Hants
"	22.10.51	16 0	"	-		2713	"	Morris Walsh	"	London, Middlesex
Bury St. Edmunds	7.10.39	24 0	Saved. Discharged 8th Oct 1853. Granted a pension of 1s. a day for life	13	364	1576	"	Joseph West	"	Newmarket, Cambridge
Oxford	18.12.48	19 0	Saved. Discharged 8th.Oct 1853. Granted a pension of 6d. a day for 2 years conditional.	4	294	2557	"	John Wroduards	"	Oxford, Oxon

The above list is now published for the first time (1905), and is accurate in every particular. On comparing it with the list of survivors given in Levinge's Historical Records of the 43rd, and the list of the drowned on the Memorial Tablet at Chelsea Hospital it will be found that there are a few discrepancies, due doubtless to clerical errors in former lists.

The lists set out below show those persons who survived the *Birkenhead* disaster. The names marked thus † were, as far as can be ascertained, those saved by the ship's boats, and those indicated by an asterisk * are the men who formed Captain Wright's party and were taken off Danger Point by H.M.S. *Rhadamanthus*.

OFFICERS

*Wright, Captain, 91st Regiment   *Bond, Cornet, 12th Lancers
*Gerardol, Lieutenant, 43rd Foot   *Bowen, Staff Surgeon
*Lucas, Lieutenant, 73rd Regiment

SOLDIERS

2nd Regiment

Privates
†John Moore   †P. M'Crery   †John Peters   A. Anthurs
†P. Peters   W. Budd   †Robert Page   G. White
†Thomas Chadwick   John Banden   †Henry Vernon   John Smith
†Henry Double   T. Gleeson   †Benjamin Worill   S. Hales
†James Gildea   †M. Malay

6th Regiment

† — Terbe, Serjeant
Privates
†William Clark   *John Kitchen   †William Bushe   †William Welch
†James Goldin   *Thomas Hortly   †Thomas Con   *R. Hunt
†James Wade   E. Walshe   †John Herrich   P. Gleeson

12th Regiment

Privates
†Daniel Waters   C. Kerrigan   †Thomas Langan   Michael Hearty
†John Irvin   *George Bridges   †James Johnson   *George Wells
†Robert Dolan   *William Smith   †John Yule   *Thomas Higgins
†John Simon   *John McDonald   †P. Ward   G. Walker

43rd Regiment

Privates
†John Herin   *Michael Hornet   — Harrison   William Sharp
†James West   *James Woodward   *George Peters   M. Healey
*Thomas Ginn   D. Bunker   *George Brackley
*George Lyons   †Edward Ambrose   *Peter Allen

45th Regiment

†Adam Keating, Private

60th Rifles

Privates
†William Burlon   *Henry Foss   †William Sooter   *J. Stanfield
†Thomas Smith   *Henry Mather   *A. Lackie   M. Laffey
*D. Andrews   †Thomas Nutall   *J. Hanlon

73rd Regiment

† — Kilberry, Serjeant

Privates

†Thomas Cash	*D. Sullivan	†William Bushe	†William Wood
†William Halfpenny	*William Dobson	†James Fitzpatrick	*John O'Reilly
†Michael O'Brien	D. Maloney	†Patrick May	*Patrick Taylor
†John Sullivan	R. Green	†Patrick Lynch	J. Maloney

74th Regiment

†— Harold, Serjeant

Privates

†Charles Ferguson	*John Kriffe	†William Boyce	*Richard Hartley
†D. Kirkford	*James M'Gregor	†James Henderson	*D. Munro
*Thomas M'Mullin	A. Nathanniel	*George Taylor	*John M'Kee
			J. Sharp

91st Regiment

Privates

†John Stanley	*Allen M'Kay	†D. Carey	*Mark Hudson
†Patrick Mullins	*John Lancey	†Patrick Cunnyngham	*John Haggart
†John Congham	*J. Robinson	*John Holden	†John Lamb
*Patrick Flinn	†John Wamsley	*John Cordie	†Fred Winterbottom

12th Lancers

Privates

| *John Dodd | M. Schofield |

Ladies and women

| †Mrs. Darkins | †Mrs. Mellins | †Mrs. Gwichar | †Mrs. Hudson |
| †Mrs. Nesbit | †Mrs. Montgomery | †Mrs. Spruce | |

Thirteen children

Officers, 5
Soldiers (126 shown on list but 17 left at Simon's Bay), 109
Women, 7
Children, 13
TOTAL, 134

Ship's officers and crew

William Culhane, Assistant Surgeon
C. R. Renwick, Assistant Engineer,
   First Class
*Benjamin Barber, Assistant Engineer,
   Second Class

†R. B. Richards, Master's Assistant
†G. W. S. Hire, Clerk
*John Archbold, Gunner, Third Class

Ship's company

†John Bowen, A.B.
†Thomas Dunn, A.B.
†George Till, A.B.
†John Smith, A.B.
†Charles Noble, A.B.
†Thomas Daley, A.B.
†Thomas Langmand, A.B.
*Henry Maxell, Quartermaster
*Edward Wilson, Boatswain's Mate
*James Lacey, Captain Main Top
*James Messum, Sailmaker's Mate
†William Neal, Carpenter's Mate
*Thomas Handrain, Leading Stoker
*J. Jeffrey, Pay and Purser's Steward
*Edward Gardner, Stoker
*John Hoskins, Stoker
*Edward Croker, A.B.
*Samuel Harris, A.B.
  R. Tiggle, A.B.
†Henry Cheesman, Stoker
†Able Stone, Ordinary

†John M'Cabe, Stoker
†William Chuse, Stoker
†John Ashbolt, Stoker
†George Randall, Stoker
†John King, Stoker
†Thomas Drew, Stoker
†George Kelly, Stoker
†Martin Ruth, A.B.
†Robert Finn, A.B.
†George Windon, A.B.
†Thomas Harris, A.B.
†John Lewis, A.B.
†John Wood, Stoker
†John Phalan, A.B.
†John Dyke, A.B.
†John M'Carthy, A.B.
†Thomas Forbes, A.B.
†Henry Bewhill, Seaman
†William Woodward Seaman
†Thomas Driackford, Seaman
†Thomas Coffin, Seaman

Boys

†W. Gale, Boy, First Class
†Charles Matthews, Boy, Second Class
  J. R. Howard, Boy

*George Wyndham, Boy, First Class
*Benjamin Turner, Boy, First Class

Marines

†John Drake, Colour-Serjeant
†William Northoven, Private
†Thomas Daniels, Private

†John Cooper, Private
*William Tuck, Private
*Thomas Keans, Private

Officers, 6
Seamen, 42
Boys, 5
Marines, 6
TOTAL, 59

Total saved from wreck

Naval persons, 59
Military, 134
TOTAL, 193

THE ROLL OF HONOUR
of those men of the *Birkenhead* who perished

Stars and moon and sun may wax and wane, subside and rise,
Age on earth, as flake on flake of showering snows be shed:
Not till earth be sunless, not till death strike blind the skies,
May the deathless love that waits on deathless deeds be dead.

SWINBURN'S 'Grace Darling'

THE NAVAL OFFICERS

Mr. R Salmond, Master Commanding
Mr. W. Brodie, Master
Mr. R. D. Speer, Second Master
Mr. J. O'Davis, Second Master
Mr. W. Whyham, Chief Engineer
Mr. C. W. Hare, Master's Assistant

Mr. J. M'Clymont, Assistant Engineer
Mr. Deely, Assistant Engineer
Mr. Kitchingham, Assistant Engineer
Mr. T. Harris, Boatswain
Mr. J. Roberts, Carpenter

And the 68 members of the ship's crew who, through lack of proper records must regretfully remain unidentified.

THE MILITARY

Draft 2nd or Queen's Regiment

Ensign Boylan
Corporal M'Manus
Privates

H. Cull	T. McKenzie	W. H. Wheeler	Charles Cornell
James Rowley	Joseph Burke	A. Mills	John Greenleaf
Wm. Forbes	J. Green	Geo. Marsh	James Nason
John Howard	George Knight	Wm. Clay	G. Shaughnessy
John Martin	Charles Mooney	Patrick Lavery	Richard Coleman
Michael O'Connell	James Oxley	George Price	B. Webster
John Quinn	Timothy Simmons	George Weller	James Coe
Nathaniel Thomas	Samuel Vesse	Zwyker (bandmaster)	
J. Walker	Thomas Woolfall	Wm. Day	

Draft 6th Royal Regiment

Ensign Metford
Privates

Abraham Bark	George Worth	Michael Beckett	J. West
Joseph Bryan	James Millham	Patrick Bryan	Henry Jacobs
Joseph Bromley	Patrick M'Cann	Dennis Caulfield	Joseph Harris
Hugh Dickson	John Croker	R. Finn	James Handley
John Grady	Wm. Brown	Joseph Hudson	Wm. Bryan
M. Kelly	Patrick Carrigan	Wm. Kitching	Wm. Fletcher
John Mayn	Henry Keane	Hugh Meara	Henry Lombrest
Patrick Maloney	Cornelius Maloney	Thomas Maloney	Michael Morgan
John Colrenshaw	Patrick Ryan	Charles Prince	Thomas Spicer
John Rider	Thomas Smith	John Rennington	John Tierney
Mark Summerton	Thomas White	Michael Starr	John Lewis
Edward Torpy	Alfred Clifford	George Tully	

Draft 12th Royal Lancers

Cornet Rolt
Sergeant John Straw
Privates
G. Hutchings   Coalborn   I. Englison

Draft 12th Regiment

Privates
Thomas Archer	T. Kelcher	C. Lambden	W. Palmer
T. Bellingham	M. Lawler	W. Matravis	C. Reynolds
J. Bryne	J. McDonnel	D. O'Connor	W. Smith
M. Clince	A. Meally	J. Roche	W. Tigne
J. Cragg	R. Morrison	T. Wales	Barrett
J. Armstrong	J. Owen	J. Field	M. Cellars
W. Boswell	T. Purcell	T. Flanley	J. Durkin
M. Carrington	R. Sheppard	A. Grimshaw	O. Freeman
B. Cummins	J. Thompson	Samuel Johnston	J. Wootton
W. Denmack	W. Wilson	J. Kelly	J. McDermott
J. England	George Bradley	E. Lee	T. Morgan
P. Flanagan	J. Costello	T. McMorrow	J. Pettifer
W. Fynn	T. Fitzgerald	J. Mullany	W. Springs
S. Hayward	F. Hart	R. Munns	

Draft 43rd Light Infantry

Sergeant Wm. Hicks
Corporal Joseph Harrison
Corporal Benjamin Cousins
Privates
John Anderson	John Riddlesden	Thomas Cave	D. Riorden
Daniel Brennan	T. Sullivan	Wm. Bullen	Vickerey
John Byrne	Edward Quin	George Gilham	Maurice Welch
John Cosgrove	Charles Ranshaw	Thomas Dews	G. Sheppard
William de Bank	John M'Quade	Joseph Penning	Michael M. Parklin
Wm. Donnel	Timothy Sheehan	J. Houghton	H. Tucker
Kelly	John Butler		

Draft 45th Regiment

Privates
G. Cocker   M. Dockery   Wm. Connel

Draft 60th Rifles

Corporal Francis Curtis

Privates

James Brown	John Rees	James Brookland	Thomas Peacock
James Callaghan	H. Scutts	Wm. Chapman	Wm. Russell
Eli Elliott	Patrick Stokes	Thomas Frost	James Story
Arthur Hamilton	Wm. Wilkins	Michael Kelcher	James Thompson
Wm. Kelly	James Wilson	Charles Lucas	Wm. Wilkinson
James Maher	John Wallis	James Moore	Wm. Woolward
John McAcy	Joseph Ladd	Daniel McQuade	Simon Jacobs
Patrick O'Brien			

Draft 73rd Regiment

Lieutenant G. W. Robinson

Lieutenant A. H. Booth

Privates

H. Birmingham	Robert Houchin	James Bernard	Michael Hurley
James Biggam	Wm. Kearns	Wm. Brennan	Timothy Kelly
Daniel Buckley	George Lawrence	John Byrne	Thomas Larkin
Wm. Barton	Michael Maber	E. Bryan	John Haher
Michael Caffrey	John Murphy	Mathew Collins	Thomas Murray
Patrick Cooney	Patrick O'Brien	John Clements	Wm. O'Connell
Charles Dawson	Michael Tonen	Hugh Deegan	George Randall
J. Dudley	George Darsey	Patrick Doyle	Wm. Flynn
Hugh Feeley	Philip Scott	Matthew Fitzpatrick	P. Sheehan
Michael Flanagan	Daniel Shea	Michael French	James Sullivan
Malachi	Robert Shephard	Gavin	George Smith
Michael Gavin	James Wilson	L. Giles	H. Holmes
John Grant	James McMurray	Wm. H. Hall	W. Buckley
John Hannen	C. Wells	Patrick Hanley	

Draft 74th Highlanders

Lieutenant-Colonel Seton

Ensign Russell

Corporal M. Mathison

Corporal Wm. Laird

Privates

George Anderson	George Miller	Archibald Baxter	Alexander Miller
John Bennie	James Mackinnon	Robert Blackie	Wm. McAnley
Walter Bruce	John McElarney	John Cantaneech	Edward MacLeod
John Cowan	John Sharp	David Cousin	Thomas Robertson
Wm. Donald	Duncan Shaw	David Donaldson	Ebenezer Rutherford
James Gibson	Wm. Smith	Charles Gowan	Robert Smith
D. R. Goman	Wm. Steward	J. H. Graham	Robert Steward
Thomas Harrison	Adam Thompson	Alexander Hendry	John Thompson
David Hunter	Robert Walker	James Kirkwood	Francis Turner
John Lowrie	Peter Hamilton	James Morton	George Watson
Alexander Murdock	Thomas Pride	Alexander Mathison	John Nelson
Thomas Maxwell			

Ensign Alexander Russell, 74th Highlanders. Taken from a miniature oil painting in the possession of Mrs. Eleanor Russell, by whose courtesy it has been reproduced.

Draft 91st Regiment

Sergeant Wm. Butler
Corporal Alexander Webber
Corporal Smith
Privates

Joseph Birt	James Tarney	George Kemp	Henry Hayward
James Buckingham	Joseph Grant	James Evans	Patrick Hussey
James Cavanagh	John Moore	Wm. Mathieson	David Pratt
James Drury	George Justice	Wm. Clark	Wm. Sedgwood
Patrick Gaffey	James Brian	Christopher Wyer	James Delayney
Stephen Haggan	Wm. Wybrow	Alex. Winnington	Alex. McFadden
Thomas Jays	Daniel Daley	Wm. Woodman	John Sweeny
Francis Mackenley	Ford	James Moon	T. Walsh
A. Montgomery	John Harpey	Wm. Measures	W. S. Smith
Patrick Smith	Patrick Hagg	Patrick Kelly	John Smith

Andrew White (a servant)
Staff Surgeon Laing
Staff Assistant Surgeon Robertson

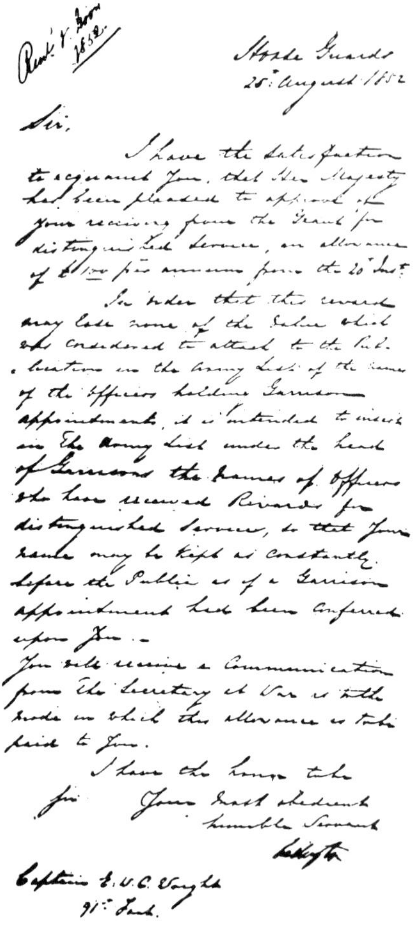

[handwritten copy of the letter appears on the left side of the page]

Horse Guards,

25th August I852.

Sir,

I have the satisfaction
to acquaint you, that Her Majesty
has been pleased to approve of
your receiving from the Guards for
distinguished service, an allowance
of £100 per annum from the 20th inst.

In order that this reward
may lose none of the value which
was considered to attach to the Pub-
lication in the Army List of the names
of the Officers holding Garrison
Appointments, it is intended to insert
in the Army List under the head
of Garrisons the names of Officers
who have received Rewards for
distinguished Service, so that your
name may be kept as constantly
before the Public as if a Garrison
appointment had been conferred
upon you.

You will receive a Communication
from the Secretary of War as to the
mode in which this allowance is to be
paid to you.

    I have the honour to be
Sir   Your most obedient
        humble Servant

        WELLINGTON

The letter from the Duke of Wellington to Captain Edward Wright, informing him of
the award of an allowance of £100 per annum for his part in the *Birkenhead* disaster.

6. Tributes to the brave

The men of the *Birkenhead* were heroes and their's indeed was the glory. England was a great nation and here in the strength and magnificence of the behaviour of these men lay the reasons for her greatness.

For over half a century the story of the *Birkenhead* disaster was on the lips of every man, woman, and child in the country and there could not have been one person unable to recite by heart the account of almost superhuman courage and discipline shown by the soldiers on board. And by allowing the women and children to be saved while they themselves, calmly and with dignity, went to their deaths, not only did they establish a tradition, they set a standard to which later acts of bravery were often compared.

At the time of the disaster the wave of praise and admiration came mainly from the press and the public. The Government and the Admiralty, for reasons best known to themselves, chose to make no official recognition of the event. There were no medals awarded and no form of promotion for the survivors. The only exception being Captain Wright who, with the direct approval of the Commander-in-Chief of the British Army, his Grace the Duke of Wellington, was awarded a Distinguished Service Pension of £100 per annum. But the press and the public made no secret of their feelings and for over two generations the story of the *Birkenhead* was not forgotten.

The news of the disaster broke loose in England on Tuesday, 6 April, when Mr. Freshfield, late clerk on board the *Birkenhead* and now the courier with Commodore Wyvill's dispatches, arrived at Plymouth in the early hours of the morning. The *Propontis* on which he had travelled docked at 3.30 and the ship was met by journalists from the London newspapers all eager for the foreign news. But not in their wildest dreams did they ever imagine the story that was to be told to them within minutes of talking to the passengers and crew.

They soon discovered Mr. Freshfield and although the contents of the dispatches were not disclosed to them, he was questioned at length and the reporters gained enough information for their stories. They now had to get this tremendous item of news back to their papers in London. After some quick discussion they decided to combine forces and charter a special train to Bristol where there was a direct electric telegraph link to London. By this means the news reached the capital in time for the preliminary details to be included in the late morning editions, and by midday the headlines were screaming out the fate of the *Birkenhead* and the great loss of life.

By early afternoon most of London had heard of the terrible destruction of the troopship. It was on everyone's lips. At the Houses of Parliament there was intense excitement and anticipation amongst the Members as questions demanding full details of the disaster were thrown from all quarters at the Duke of Northumberland, First Lord of the Admiralty, and Mr. Stafford, the Secretary for the Colonies. But these two highly distinguished, but embarrassed, gentlemen knew no more than their colleagues who were asking the questions, only what they themselves had read in the press.

The newspapers it seemed had been faster, and certainly more enterprising, than the official channels. Mr. Freshfield had not travelled with the journalists on the specially chartered train from Plymouth to Bristol nor had he taken advantage of the electric telegraph. He travelled later in the day on an ordinary train, and with the official reports and dispatches eventually arrived in London late that evening, many hours after the news he carried was out. The contents of the dispatches were made public on the following day, 7 April, when the story was carried in full by every newspaper in London, and within days by almost every newspaper in the country.

Most of the news reports centred around deep admiration for the conduct of the troops, but unfortunately a desire crept in for a scapegoat. Someone at whose feet the blame for such an appalling disaster could be laid. And who better than the captain of the ship. Commodore Wyvill's report had not spared him. His words, taken obviously as gospel, were damning and the newspaper comments rather unfairly were based on this.

The Times, in a leading article, proclaimed:

> There is no mystery about the calamity. We are not left, as in the case of the *Amazon*, to conjecture the origin of the disaster. Just what happened to the

Orion off the Scottish coast, and to the Great Liverpool off Finisterre, has happened now. Captain Salmond, the officer in command, anxious to shorten the run to Algoa Bay as much as was possible, and more than was prudent, hugged the shore too closely; 454 persons have lost their lives in consequence of his temerity. As soon as the vessel struck upon the rocks the rush of water was so great that the men on the lower troop-deck were drowned in their hammocks. Theirs was the happier fate: at least they were spared the terrible agony of the next 20 minutes. At least the manner of their death was less painful than that of others who were first crushed beneath the falling spars and funnel, and then swept away to be devoured by the sharks that were prowling round the wreck. From the moment the ship struck all appears to have been done that human courage and coolness could effect.

After stating that Captain Salmond appears to have done his duty when the vessel struck, the same newspaper added further:

It certainly cannot be imputed as a fault to the Admiralty or the Government that a Naval officer of good repute for skill and competency should, in an unhappy moment of temerity, have navigated his ship in so reckless a manner.

The 'Scotch Press' had this to say:

A man may be sent to prison, like the captain of the Orion, or to the bottom, like the captain of the Amazon, and the next week we will find other commanders of vessels 'hugging the shore' to shorten a voyage by a few hours, or proceeding to sea with a ship nearly in a state of ignition. Habituated to danger, accustomed to hairbreadth escapes, and removed a great portion of their lives from that healthful communion of thought and feeling which operates so powerfully on other men, the officers in charge of ships are, many of them, reckless to a degree which surprises and (too often by the catastrophes which ensue) appals us. Of this last description is the loss of the Government steamer Birkenhead.

Other newspapers followed in a similar vein with only one or two springing to the Captain's defence. And poor Captain Salmond's case was not helped a month later either, when the court martial declared:

... that they [the court] had to observe, in the first place, that from the unfortunate circumstances of the master commanding, and the principal officers of the ship, having perished, they feel that it was in the highest degree difficult, and that it might be unjust to pass censure upon the deceased, whose motives for keeping so near the shore cannot be explained; but they must record their opinion, that this fatal loss was owing to the course having been calculated to keep the land in close proximity.

However, Robert Salmond R.N. had gone down with his ship. He did not survive to hear and answer the implications and accusations cast against him at what was almost a trial and judgement by the press. But in any event, after the ship had struck there is no doubt that Captain Salmond's conduct had been exemplary. Remaining calm and composed he showed great presence of mind and spared no effort to save the women and children and as many men as possible. And there were a good number of prominent persons, including naval colleagues and other captains, who made it quite clear that in their considered opinion Captain Robert Salmond had done nothing for which he could be reproached, and at all times had acted in a proper and competent manner as befitting a ship's captain in the Royal Navy.

The laments and the glowing praise in the press for the behaviour of the troops on board the stricken *Birkenhead* went on. In Europe, America, and particularly at home in England.

Although, prior to 1852, the past had not been without its other disasters and great moments of tragedy, nothing had ever caused such a tremendous impact as the wreck of Her Majesty's Troopship *Birkenhead*. Never before had an event ever caught and held the attention, imagination, and prolonged heartfelt sympathy of the public so utterly and so deeply.

Perhaps it was because of the sheer gallantry and chivalry of the men on board. Their's was a romantic age. The age of quality and chivalry and the troops, quite simply, behaved as every man in England would like to think he himself would have behaved, and they did what every woman would wish her man to do. That was the mood of the country, and what could have been more romantic, or more gallant and chivalrous, than so many men nobly laying down their lives so that a handful of women and children could be saved. And after all, they did have a choice. The choice between a slim chance of life, or certain death. There was no hesitation in their decision.

Or perhaps it was just the final moment on the deck of the troopship that captured the emotions of the people. The unsurpassed splendour and dignity of those last few seconds before death, in the unparalleled scene of two-hundred-odd men facing the end so magnificently.

Who really knows? As Captain Wright in his report comments:

> Poor fellows! Had they died in battlefield and in their country's cause their fate would have excited less poignant regret; but there is something inexpressibly touching in the quiet, unflinching resolution of so many brave hearts struggling manfully to the last against an inevitable disaster.

The *Illustrated London News* on 10 April 1852, under the headline 'Fatal Wreck of Her Majesty's Steamer Birkenhead and Large Loss of Life', refers to 'a catastrophe of the most disastrous character . . .', and after giving details of the vessel and those aboard, goes on:

> . . . the coolness and steady obedience to orders which the troops manifested on that awful and trying occasion present an instance of the noblest results of discipline.

From the *Examiner* of the same date is the comment that:

> . . . the long annals of shipwreck furnish no picture more impressive than that which is conveyed to us of this large body of men labouring calmly in the face of death.

And the *Morning Herald*, after a rather doleful and somewhat resigned paragraph, thus:

> By this distressing accident, seven Military officers and 350 soldiers were lost, and with them perished eight Naval officers and 60 seamen. The cries of some of our most severe and bloody actions have been determined at a smaller amount of sacrifice than what we have now to record as the result of this awful and tremendous calamity. The heart sickens as we contemplate a scene so dreadful. It is bootless now to ask whether it might have been avoided. The commander of the unfortunate vessel is no more, and the bulk of his officers and crew have perished with him.

went on to voice the public sentiment:

> But it is due to the memory of the brave men who perished to hold up their conduct to that admiration which their heroism and devotion so richly merit. We venture to assert that the whole annals of Naval disaster afford no nobler instance of coolness, true courage, and steady discipline than was exhibited by the ill-fated Major Seton, and the officers and soldiers under his command. We defy the whole history of our race to produce a more striking instance of bravery and coolness.

All the London and provincial newspapers were the same. As were the periodical magazines and the Service journals. The praise and admiration could not have been higher. Not for the men, nor for their commanding officer, Lieutenant-Colonel Seton.

Many years later references could always be found to both the disaster as a whole, and to the individual courage and fortitude of Alexander Seton of Mounie.

In the *Biographical Dictionary of Eminent Scotsmen*, by Rev. Thomas Thomson, the feelings and respect towards the Colonel are expressed in the following quotation:

> In Britain, India, Australia and Ireland he had always maintained the character of a strict disciplinarian, so that no breach of duty could escape his notice or reprehension. But he was as strict with himself as with others, and whatever might be their labour or fatigue, he was ready to bear his part in it. This combination of two opposite qualities, so rare in Military officers, attracted the admiration of his soldiers, and their usual remark was, 'If he does not spare others, he does not spare himself'. It was a union of qualities only belonging to those who are born to be the veritable leaders of men, and through which they convert their men into heroes. By the controlling might of such an example, wielded by a superior intellect, a captain may become a conqueror or

a king; and all that such aptitudes require for the purpose is a proper field of action, which is not always to be found. These professional qualities of Colonel Seton, during this voyage were called into full exercise. The men under his command, instead of composing a single regiment and possessing the usual regimental esprit de corps, were drafted from ten regiments, and therefore had no such bond of union; they were also a motley assemblage of Irish, English, and Scotch, who had never been under fire, and most of their officers were young and inexperienced. How then, in the hour of such fearful peril, did they exhibit a courage, a firmness, a devotedness to which few veterans would have been found equal? It can only be attributed to the admirable discipline which their commander had established among them, and by which he acquired such marvellous power over them in the valley of the shadow of death.

And the *Comprehensive History of England*, after referring to the heroism and courage displayed, adds:

As long as the British Army nurses such a spirit as that which was shown upon the deck of the Birkenhead, and possesses such officers as Colonel Seton, our country, let the enemy be who they may, has nothing to fear.

No matter which medium of print, which story, article, feature, or comment, all sincere words, stirring words, and words to be remembered.

The disaster fired the imagination of poets like Sir Francis Hastings Doyle, Professor of Poetry at Oxford (1867–77) and he was moved to put pen to paper with the following beautiful and captivating result:

Right on our flank the sun was dropping down;
The deep sea heaved around in bright repose;
When, like the wild shriek from some captured town,
*   A cry of women rose*

The stout ship Birkenhead lay hard and fast,
Caught without hope upon a hidden rock;
Her timbers thrilled as nerves, when through them passed
*   The spirit of that shock.*

And ever like base cowards, who leave their ranks
In danger's hour, before the rush of steel,
Drifted away, disorderly, the planks
*   From underneath her keel.*

So calm the air—so calm and still the flood,
That low down in its blue translucent glass
We saw the great fierce fish, that thirst for blood,
*   Pass slowly, then repass*

They tarried, the waves tarried, for their prey!
The sea turned one clear smile! Like things asleep
Those dark shapes in the azure silence lay,
*   As quiet as the deep.*

Then amidst oath, and prayer, and rush, and wreck,
Faint screams, faint questions waiting no reply,
Our Colonel gave the word, and on the deck
*   Formed us in line to die*

To die—'twas hard, while the sleek ocean glowed
Beneath a sky as fair as summer flowers:
All to the boats! cried one—he was, thank God,
*   No officer of ours.*

Our English hearts beat true—we would not stir;
That base appeal we heard, but heeded not;
On land, on sea, we had our Colours, sir,
*   To keep without a spot.*

They shall not say in England that we fought
With shameful strength, unhonoured like to seek;
Into mean safety, mean deserters, brought
*   By trampling down the weak*

So we made women with their children go,
The oars ply back again, and yet again;
Whilst, inch by inch, the drowning ship sank low
*   Still under steadfast men.*

—What fellows, why recall? The brave who died,
Died without flinching in the bloody surf,
They sleep as well beneath that purple tide
*   As others under turf.*

They sleep well! and, roused from their wild grave,
Wearing their wounds like stars, shall rise again,
Joint-heirs with Christ, because they bled to save
*   His weak ones, not in vain*

If that day's work no clasp or medal mark;
If each proud heart no cross or bronze may press,
Nor cannon thunder loud from tower to park,
*   This feel we non the less:*

That those whom God's high grace there saved from ill,
Those also left His martyrs in the bay,
Though not be siege, though not in battle, still
*   Full well had earned their pay.*

There were other poems, none the less inspiring. And years later, when another
ship, the *Victoria*, plunged to the depths this too was seized upon by men of literature
as a theme for their prose and poetry. Rudyard Kipling wrote on that occasion and
one verse in particular aptly sums up the sort of courage needed for any comparison
to that which took place on the deck of Her Majesty's Troopship *Birkenhead*.

To take your chance in the thick of a rush, with firing all about,
Is nothing so bad when you've cover to 'and an' leave an' liking to shout;
But to stand and be still to the Birken'ead Drill is a damn tough bullet to chew;
An' they done it, the Jollies—'er Majesty's Jollies—soldier and sailor, too!

Today the term 'Birken'ead Drill' is a familiar expression in the Royal Navy. It's used to describe an incident of crisis when the persons involved, showing complete disregard for their own fears, remain calm and disciplined and display a courage and endurance above and beyond the call of duty.

Artists, too, found themselves compelled by the grandeur of the disaster to capture the scene on canvas, and paintings and prints soon appeared depicting the last few moments on deck. Possibly the most well known and famous of these were those executed by Thomas M. Hemy. Thousands of printed reproductions of his works sold to a public who wanted a constant reminder of one of the most noble acts of heroism ever recorded. Originals of three of these magnificent paintings are in the possession of descendant regiments of the drafts on board. They hang proudly in their respective regimental museums amongst other treasured items from the regiment's history.

Both artists and poets alike went to great lengths to convey the splendour of the moment and, regretfully, in doing so allowed some inaccuracies into their work which had the effect of distorting the truth when the story was taken up. Writers, also, were guilty of embellishing and exaggerating the scene somewhat. There was one version of the story for instance which had the soldiers standing firmly to attention on the deck of the ship, in full-dress uniform with shouldered rifles, singing, 'God Save the Queen', as the *Birkenhead* slid down into the water. This naturally conjures up a tremendous picture but unfortunately it is not true and such exaggeration is not necessary. However, no real harm was done. It certainly shows the mood was there, and after allowing for 'poetic', 'artistic', and 'literary' licence, the basic elements that have made the *Birkenhead* disaster a part of our national history are all there in the material published afterwards.

A considerable number of prominent persons pressed for official recognition of the event, one of whom was General Sir William Napier of Peninsular fame, who turned out to be the *Birkenhead* survivor's most ardent and enthusiastic supporter. Included in his efforts is the following letter which was published in *The Times* on Friday, 9 April 1852:

WRECK OF THE BIRKENHEAD

To the Editor of the Times
Sir,—Were the late ministry still in power we should doubtless have an official letter from Lord John Russell prating of 'discretion', and from Lord Grey a 'despatch' censuring Captain Wright for not sinking with his men; but, under

the present Ministers, it may be hoped that the matchless chivalry of Captain Wright and Lieutenant Girardot, and the responding generous devotion of their men, who went down without a murmur rather than risk the safety of the women and children in the boats, will meet with some public honour and reward,—honour for the dead as well as the survivors; for surely the occasion was great, was noble, was good,—the heroism never surpassed! And it was not calculated,—there was no time for that; it was the strong fount of military honour gushing up from the heart.

Yours respectfully,

W. NAPIER, Lieutenant-General.

Similar letters from a host of important people also appeared in other newspapers, all calling for some kind of honour and award. A few months earlier, on 20 February, there had been a change of government, and the General's scorn for the late Party and his assumed faith in the new government under Lord Derby is reflected in what he wrote. This letter was followed by correspondence to influential friends and to Members of Parliament known to him but although he gained support his moves were to no avail.

The day after General Napier's letter in *The Times*, but not necessarily because of it, a meeting of naval and military officers took place at Portsmouth. Its purpose was to open a Fund for the relief of the widows, orphans and relatives of the men who perished with the *Birkenhead*. A committee of high ranking and distinguished officers was formed and a subscription list opened. Heading the list of names that were to eventually appear were those of Her Majesty Queen Victoria and Prince Albert, followed by Admirals and Cabinet Ministers. One of the most spontaneous and generous acts came from the officers and men of the fleet. Every single captain and crew member gave one day's pay to the fund and by the end of the month almost £1,000 had been collected.

Reports of the events at Portsmouth were being carried by every newspaper in the country. *The Scotsman*, for instance, after referring to the scene at the harbour, went on to describe the gesture by the officers and sailors of the fleet.

PORTSMOUTH—It is impossible to describe the sensation that the loss of the Birkenhead has occasioned in this port, to which nearly all the crew belonged. The dockyard has been the scene of many heart-rending exhibitions of grief to-day, and numerous have been the applications for information by widows and orphans. The Birkenhead was an iron steam-vessel, of 1400 tons, built by Laird, of Birkenhead. She left this port last on the 2nd of January, on which day she victualled as her own troop service complement 129 persons, her apportioned complement being 131. As a navigator Mr. Salmond ranked among the most skilful of the Masters of the Royal Navy. Admiral Sir Thomas Briggs, the Commander-in-Chief at this port, has proposed, and his views are most warmly espoused by Rear-Admiral Superintendent Prescott, C.B., that they, together with the captains, officers, and ship' companies of her Majesty's

ships and vessels at Spithead and in Portsmouth Harbour, should, in demon-
stration of their deep regret at the loss of the Birkenhead, subscribe one day's
pay towards the pecuniary relief of the widows and orphans of the seamen
and marines who perished on that melancholy occasion.

Although donations came readily and willingly to the fund, there was a certain
indignation felt at the lack of government action to grant some kind of official
pension or payment to the dependants, and further letters, along these lines,
appeared in the press. One such letter, signed 'JUSTITIA', could be read in *The
Times* on 14 April.

To the Editor of the Times

Sir,—Private charity is a very good thing, but, like every other virtue, liable
to be abused; and I think the present attempt to raise money by subscription
for the widows and orphans of the unfortunate sufferers in the Birkenhead is
an instance of its abuse. Why should a few charitable persons be called upon
to do that which ought to be done by the whole nation, many of those so called
upon probably, being in circumstances little enabling them to contribute, but
from their position compelled to do so? I consider it very unjust and a hard
case upon the officers and crews of those ships now at Portsmouth and Spithead
to be called upon to subscribe each a day's pay towards the charity, some
of them with large families and very limited means, while millions will pay
nothing. Why should not the widows and orphans be properly relieved at the
public expense? Did not the sufferers perish in the public service, quite as much
as if they had fallen in battle? How can you expect men to enter into the
service of their country, when, if by any misfortune they perish, their widows
and orphans are to be left destitute or dependent on private charity? The
case is very different from emigrants or merchant sailors, who are not in the
service of the country, but are going out for their private ends and benefit; such
are fit cases for charitable subscriptions. But in this case, where a parcel of poor
fellows are sent out, not at their own will and pleasure, to fight for their
country and perish in their country's service, can there be a doubt that their
widows and orphans are entitled to public relief? The widows ought to have
pensions, and the children to be maintained and educated according to their
station, and then placed in a position to maintain themselves in every way
as well, as it is probable they would have been, had they not been deprived
of their husbands and fathers.

JUSTITIA

However, in spite of the immense outburst of public sympathy and emotion
caused by the circumstances of the disaster, and in spite of the efforts of men like
Sir William Napier, no official aid was sanctioned, until, on 26 April, instigated by
Henry Drummond, M.P., a friend of General Napier, the matter came up in the
House of Commons. Addressing his remarks to the Secretary for War, Major
William Beresford, Mr. Drummond reminded the Minister that it was within the
Queen's royal power to grant compensation to survivors, in instances such as the

Lieutenant-Colonel Girardot. A photograph taken shortly before his death in 1902.

wreck of the *Birkenhead*, of amounts up to £80, and also of rewarding deserving officers by promotion. He went on to ask that Her Majesty be recommended to authorize the payment of such compensation without delay.

Major Beresford, in his lengthy reply, expressed his admiration for the conduct of the troops and ship's crew on board the *Birkenhead* and explained the two aspects of the matter in question, that of compensation and promotion. He confirmed Mr. Drummond's statement concerning the payment to survivors and stated The War Office would be only too happy to receive applications from survivors for compensation for their losses and that within the limits permitted he would ensure a distribution of money to these persons. Dealing then with the subject of promotion he said this was entirely in the hands of the Commander-in-Chief (the Duke of Wellington), adding, '. . . he is as desirous of rewarding Military men as he is capable of appreciating their services'.

Nevertheless, although the Iron Duke did not by any means allow the *Birkenhead* heroism to completely pass by, and in fact referred several times in speeches to the conduct shown, paying a high tribute to the discipline and humanity displayed by the men at the wreck, he was known as a commander not normally given to rewarding soldiers by promotion for any sort of bravery unless it was on the field of battle facing an enemy.

So although the men of the *Birkenhead* were showered with the praise they so richly deserved, neither the survivors nor the dependants reaped any form of substantial reward. The survivors, apart from Captain Wright, both naval and military, received just a small pecuniary payment, and the dependants shared only the proceeds of the fund started at Portsmouth. There was no government pension or any other official payment made.

During the course of their later career a number of the survivors were in fact promoted. Captain Wright eventually became colonel, as did Lieutenant Girardot. And Staff Surgeon Bowen attained the rank of surgeon-general. Many of the men, too, received promotion at various times, to corporal and sergeant. But these awards were often years after the disaster and there is no evidence to suggest that any of the promotions were as a direct result of the men's conduct on that dreadful day in February 1852.

There is little doubt that Wellington was impressed by the behaviour of the troops on board the *Birkenhead*, hence his award of a Distinguished Service Pension to Captain Wright as the senior surviving officer. And it is possible therefore he may have decided to study the reports of the disaster more closely with a view of other awards, but unfortunately at this time his health was failing and he was shortly to die. Any recommendations he may have intended went with him to the grave and there is no later evidence that the subject was given any consideration by his successor.

Wellington, however, could not have failed to recognize the conduct of the troops on board the *Birkenhead*, if only for the unquestionable discipline which prevailed throughout the disaster. Discipline, as far as the Duke was concerned, was the start and the finish to everything. He lived by it and trained his troops to do so too. It was the force which held his army together when the tide of battle went against them and it was the foundation stone on which his great victories were built.

His Grace the Duke of Wellington.

When Wellington formed the famous squares at Waterloo he knew it was in those formations that his strength lay. And he knew, too, that they had to remain unbroken if victory was to be his. In the frenzied attacks by the French that followed they hurled themselves time and again against the squares but the British troops held firm. The formations remained intact and the French eventually broke and withdrew with heavy losses. Only discipline held those squares together and gave Wellington his victory, so it is extremely unlikely that such a rigid disciplinarian as the Iron Duke would not appreciate the example of discipline shown on the *Birkenhead*.

It is very sad that the matchless heroism and chivalrous self-sacrifice displayed on the deck of the *Birkenhead*, so warmly applauded by almost the entire world, was never officially recognized nor rewarded in material terms as it should have been.

Nevertheless, it was not forgotten and as the years passed General Napier and others pursued their course. Then, in 1859, seven years after the disaster and one year before the General's death, it was announced that Her Majesty Queen Victoria had ordered a memorial to be erected in the colonnade of Chelsea Hospital, London, in honour of the men who died with the *Birkenhead*. So, by the personal intervention of the Queen, official recognition, at least for the dead, came at last. The subject of the wreck of the *Birkenhead* was frequently brought up in conversation by Her Majesty, and apart from her name heading the subscription list to the fund, and her direction for a national memorial, there is ample evidence to indicate she was deeply touched and moved by the courage of the men of the *Birkenhead*.

The memorial, which may be viewed today, carries the following inscription:

THIS MONUMENT
is erected by command of
HER MAJESTY QUEEN VICTORIA,
to record the heroic constancy and unbroken
discipline shown by Lieutenant-Colonel Seton,
74th Highlanders, and the troops embarked under his
command on board the Birkenhead, when that vessel was
wrecked off the Cape of Good Hope on the 26th Feby. 1852,
and to preserve the memory of the Officers,
Non-Commissioned Officers and Men who perished on that occasion

Their names were as follows.

LIEUT.-COL. A. SETON, 74th HIGHLANDERS, COMMANDING THE TROOPS
Cornet Rolt, Sergt. Straw, and 3 Privates, 12th Lancers
Ensign Boylan, Corpl. McManus, 34 Privates, Queen's Regt.
Ensign Metford and 47 Privates, 6th Royals
55 Privates, 12th Regiment
Sergt. Hicks, Corpls. Harrison and Cousins, and 26 Privates, 43rd Light Infantry.
3 Privates, 45th Regiment
Corporal Curtis and 29 Privates, 60th Rifles
Lieutenants Robinson and Booth and 54 Privates, 73rd Regiment
Ensign Russell, Corpls. Mathison and William Laird, and 46 Privates, 74th Highlanders
Sergt. Butler, Corpls. Webber and Smith and 41 Privates, 91st Regt.
Staff-Surgeon Laing, Staff Assistant-Surgeon Robertson
In all three hundred and fifty-seven officers and men. The names of the privates will be found inscribed on the brass plates adjoining.

After the disaster the soldiers were posted to their respective regiments where they served with the colours for the remainder of their military career. The seamen too, once the formalities of the court martial were over, found themselves dispersed to various ships to continue their service. The survivors were thus completely split up and the cruel incident of the *Birkenhead*, which had drawn them so closely together, was over, and that was the end of it as far as they were concerned. They quickly lost contact with each other, going different ways to lead their own individual lives. Only a handful actually kept in touch for any length of time. And although for more than fifty years afterwards articles and reports on the disaster constantly appeared in the press, and in a variety of magazines, very seldom was there any mention of a survivor's current location.

Eventually, one by one, as age overtook them, they retired from their active lives to settle down with their families in all parts of the country, there to live out the rest of their days in peaceful and uneventful retirement.

In 1902, on the fiftieth anniversary of the disaster, efforts were begun to trace as many living survivors as possible and appeals in the newspapers were instrumental in bringing forward response from people who claimed to know the whereabouts of someone from the *Birkenhead*. The search started in earnest and it was by no means an easy task. The men of the *Birkenhead* were modest heroes, extremely reluctant to announce themselves of their own account. Nevertheless, the movement set in motion to find these men, which had the support of such prominent persons as Field Marshal Lord Roberts, Commander-in-Chief of the Forces, and His Highness the Prince of Wales, was successful in finally tracking down eleven

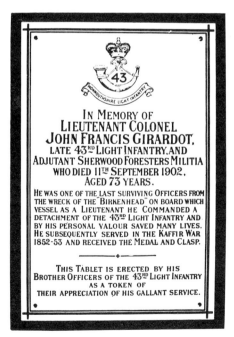

The memorial to Lieutenant-Colonel Girardot.

survivors. To mark the occasion a document of parchment was prepared, inscribed as follows:

> The Birkenhead 1852–1902 Roll Call of survivors living on the 50th Anniversary of the Birkenhead Troopship disaster. February 26th. 1902.

This was signed in turn by the eleven men and then presented to His Majesty the King who accepted with pleasure the honoured and historic document.

The survivors who were traced and whose signatures appeared on the 'Roll Call' were:

> Lieutenant-Colonel Frank Girardot, late Lieutenant, 43rd Light Infantry. Living at Northlands Road, Southampton.
> Captain Sheldon-Bond, late Cornet, 12th Lancers. Living in Ireland.
> Colour Sergeant John O'Neil, late Corporal, 91st Regiment. Living in Boston, Lincolnshire.
> Colour Sergeant Bernard Kilkeary, late 73rd Regiment. Living in Dungannon, Co. Tyrone.
> Colour Sergeant John Drake, late Royal Marines. Living at West End, Hayes, Middlesex.
> Private John Smith, late Queen's. Living at St. Ives, Hunts.
> Captain Lucas, late Ensign, 73rd Foot. Living at Penkridge, Staffs.
> Private William Tuck, late Royal Marines. Living at Gosport.
> Mr. J. Thomas Archbold, the naval gunner. Living at Buckland, Portsmouth.
> Mr. Thomas Cuffin, 'the man at the helm'. Living at Bristol.
> Mr. Benjamin Turner, late Second-Class Boy. Living at Fratton near Portsmouth.

Apart from these men, as a later result of the publicity given to the fiftieth anniversary a further seven survivors came to light, unfortunately after the 'Roll Call' had been presented to the King. The additional survivors were Corporal William Smith, late of the 12th Foot, of Middleton Cheney near Banbury; Sergeant Francis Ginn, late of the 43rd Light Infantry, living at Sudbury, Suffolk; Mrs. Parkinson of Beckingham near Gainsborough who, as 4-year-old Marian Darkin was one of the children on the *Birkenhead*, and four men located in South Africa. William Butler of the 12th Lancers, Sergeant McClusky, Mr. Charles Daley, and Colonel Nesbitt who with his brother and mother joined the *Birkenhead* at Simon's Bay.

These then were the eighteen living survivors of the wreck of the *Birkenhead* fifty years after the disaster.

By this time, 1902, other memorials had been placed in churches in various parts of the country by regiments that had been represented on the *Birkenhead*. One such memorial was placed in St. Giles's Cathedral, Edinburgh, in honour of Lieutenant-Colonel Seton and the men of the 74th Highlanders. Another memorial was unveiled on 19 June 1905 at Beckingham Church, near Gainsborough, in honour of Mrs. Marian Parkinson (née Darkin) who had died the previous year. The memorial,

IN MEMORY OF THOSE WHO PERISHED
IN
H.M.S. BIRKENHEAD
26TH. FEBRUARY. 1852

THE SHIP CARRYING REINFORCEMENTS
FOR THE EIGHTH KAFFIR WAR, STRUCK
A SUNKEN REEF APPROXIMATELY
2 SEA MILES SOUTH-WEST BY SOUTH
FROM THIS POINT.

NINE OFFICERS, THREE HUNDRED &
FORTY-NINE OF OTHER RANKS AND
EIGHTY-SEVEN OF THE SHIPS
COMPANY LOST THEIR LIVES
EVERY WOMAN & CHILD WAS SAVED

The *Birkenhead* memorial at Danger Point, South Africa.

surmounted by a brass representation of the sinking of the *Birkenhead*, bore the inscription:

SACRED TO THE MEMORY
of
MRS. MARIAN PARKINSON
a survivor of the troopship
BIRKENHEAD
wrecked off the Cape
26th Feby. 1852
under circumstances which
evoked the admiration of
all countries
She was a daughter of
Drum-Major John R. Darkin
of The Queen's Regt.
and died on 17th November, 1904
Erected by the Officers and all Ranks
1st Bn. The Queen's Regt.

Known endearingly as 'A Daughter of the Regiment', Marian Darkin had, throughout her entire life, always enjoyed a close and affectionate relationship with her father's old regiment, the Queen's, who were represented at both her funeral and the unveiling ceremony.

South Africa, too, sanctioned the erection of a memorial to the *Birkenhead*. This was built at the foot of the lighthouse on Danger Point, the scene of the disaster, and an illustration on page 143 shows the laying of wreaths in 1952 at the Centenary Service held there. And less than three miles away, beneath the silent waters of the South Atlantic, lies perhaps the greatest memorial of all, that of the *Birkenhead* herself, and marking the spot so accurately is the apex of the rock she struck which, at low tide, projects through the water like an accusing finger pointing upwards towards the God who deserted the men on that terrible day.

A further tribute came in 1914 when the Royal Navy gave the name *Birkenhead* to one of its cruisers. Although there is no direct evidence she was named specifically after the original troopship, it has always been naval policy to continue with the use of famous and honoured names.

The *Birkenhead* of the First World War was an improved Chatham Class Cruiser of 5,235 tons, initially ordered by Greece as the *Antinauarkos Condouriotis* and subsequently purchased by the Royal Navy under the War Emergency Programme. Known by her builders as No. 809, her hull was laid down in the Laird yards on 12 March 1914 and she was in service within a year under the command of Captain Edward Reeves.

The cruiser *Birkenhead* served right through the bitter war years and although her record of service does not contain any outstanding or memorable engagements

The *Birkenhead* Centenary Memorial Service held at the foot of the lighthouse at Danger Point on Sunday, 24 January 1952. About 300 people attended the service conducted by the Revd. R. L. Stuart, M.C., Chaplain of the Missions to Seamen, and among those present were Captain J. Selby, R.N., representing the Royal Navy at Simonstown, photographed laying a wreath, and Mrs. William Whitelaw who represented the Russell family and laid a wreath in memory of Ensign Russell.

After the service three buglers sounded the Last Post, and Reveille, and the congregation than sang 'Die Stem van Zuid Afrika', the South African national anthem, followed by 'God Save the Queen'.

Before leaving everyone signed the books which are kept in the lighthouse and when this had been done, one of the books was put into safe custody, to be brought out again only at the next memorial service, one hundred years later in the year 2052.

she did, however, fight at Jutland, giving a good account of herself and gaining this battle honour.

At the end of the war, with Captain R. H. Candman in command, the *Birkenhead* formed part of the 3rd Light Cruiser Squadron and was in the spectacular line up of 142 British warships at Scapa Flow on 21 November 1918 which took the surrender of 71 ships of the German Grand Fleet. Eighteen months later, on 20 May 1920, she was paid off at Portsmouth and the following year sold for scrap and eventually broken up at the Newport yards of Messrs. John Cashmore Ltd.

The sea breaking over the nearly submerged rock on which the *Birkenhead* struck. Photographs by courtesy of the Williamson Art Gallery, Birkenhead.

During the Second World War, when the battle fleet of the Royal Navy was again enlarged to war numbers, the name *Birkenhead* was regretfully not so honoured and no other ship in the Royal Navy has borne this name since.

It is now almost a century and a half since the disaster yet, in spite of this length of time and the turbulence of the years between, a surprisingly large number of people are aware of the story, or at least a broad outline of it. References to the event have occasionally been made in the press and on television and from time to time feature articles appear in papers and magazines. This is good of course because the story of the *Birkenhead* should never be forgotten. The world today would be a far, far better place if the simple dignity and amazing grace of the manner of their behaviour that night, existed now.

A really constant reminder of what happened one hundred and thirty odd years ago has been provided by the regiments themselves. Their written histories all proudly cover the story, as if it were a revered battle honour, and the museums which are open to the public each offer a display devoted to the wreck. In particular, there are three Hemy oil paintings, one in each of three Scottish regiments, in Glasgow, Perth and Stirling Castle. The paintings are huge and impressive, capturing beautifully the atmosphere of the moment, and they are well worth a visit.

In South Africa too, especially in Cape Town, mention of the name *Birkenhead* is sufficient to get a well informed conversation going which will lead eventually to a heated argument on the 'ifs' and 'buts' of the cause of the disaster.

In recent years (late nineteen eighties) the story of the *Birkenhead* has come very much to the fore, having been highlighted by the publicity and controversy surrounding the quests to find the shipment of gold coins she was reputed to have been carrying. It has gradually emerged that we now have an intriguing mystery

H.M.S. *Birkenhead*. A light cruiser of the First World War. After a distinguished record of service she was broken up in 1921 by Messrs. John Cashmore Ltd. of Newport, Monmouthshire.

on our hands. Was she, or was she not, carrying 250,000 Gold Sovereigns? And if she was, and they are found, who is the rightful owner of this enormous fortune? In re-publishing this book an additional chapter has been added to cover in broad outline the efforts made to find this treasure, and to make known the aspects of the controversy that has arisen.

However, gold or no gold, several hundred men enacted a scene that night in 1852 that, whilst not perhaps changing the course of history, certainly added to it.

Had they not perished with the *Birkenhead* the soldiers would have gone on to join their respective Regiments and they would have fought in the Kaffir wars that

raged in southern Africa from 1846 to roughly 1853. Both the Kaffirs and the Zulus were part of the Bantu race of African people. The taller and more regimented Zulus settled in the northern parts of South Africa, in Natal, whilst the smaller built, but equally war-like, Kaffirs settled in the southern region, in what was later to become Cape Colony.

The first recorded white Europeans to set foot on South African soil were led in 1487 by the great Portuguese explorer, Bartholomew Diaz. Then, from the late 16th Century onwards, adventurous seamen and traders travelling to India broke their journey at the Cape to rest and to take on fresh supplies of water and fruit. In the main they were Dutch and the fore-runners of the great traders who, in their business with the East used vessels that were called East Indiamen.

By 1652 a small settlement had been established (later to become Cape Town) under the shadow of Table Mountain. The settlement grew fast, with new generations of Dutch citizens, leaving the wars and turmoil of Europe, coming to South Africa and regarding their new land as their own. They called themselves *Boers* which is the Dutch word for farmers.

The British started to use the Cape as a staging post in maintaining a sea route to their Indian Empire and, although at one point for tactical reasons, they withdrew their garrisons to England, the army returned again in strength to the Cape in the early 1800's after England paid the Dutch Government six million pounds for various Dutch possessions including the Cape.

After England had fought and won Waterloo, attention was paid to the acquired possession of the Cape and British emigrants, with financial assistance, were sent out to start working and farming in the colony. An English aristocrat was made Governor and the rich and idle from fashionable London society soon began to dominate life in Cape Town.

The Boers, now calling themselves Afrikaners, naturally resented this intrusion. Trouble flared and there were many skirmishes. In the late 1830's the vast majority of the Boers decided to break with British authority and interference. They had had enough. It was their land but they were totally dominated by British rule. Moving northwards, over the Drakensburg Mountains, the Boers in their long wagon trains, and known as Voortrekkers, dragged their belongings across the Orange River into the Highveld to establish the Orange Free State. Others went further, into Natal and the land of the Zulus.

Over the years the Boers, in their 'treks' from the British rule they hated and despised, amazingly enough remained under the protection of the British flag while they were still in the region of the colony and, when the Kaffir wars started in earnest in 1846, both Boer and British soldier fought side by side against a common enemy. The Kaffirs were quick, specialising in guerilla tactics and laying ambushes, where their assegais and knob-kerries could be used with great effect at close quarter. See the illustration of unknown origin across pages 146 and 147.

In 1842 a British fleet sailed up the coast and troops occupied the province of Natal where Zulu and Boer lived in uneasy company of each other. The arrival of the British in this region did nothing in the long term to improve the situation. For a decade there was a peace of sorts between Zulu, Boer and British but events were to move in a manner that precipitated the Zulu wars and eventually the Boer wars later in the century. But this, of course, is another story.

7. The *Birkenhead* regiments

It's a far, far cry from Wellington's immortal and indignant words, 'Certainly not, sir. Officers have better things to do than to shoot at one another', in reply to a suggestion from one of his staff that a shot be taken at Napoleon who was galloping openly up and down the ranks of his troops prior to the start of hostilities. Since those glorious days the British Army has experienced a good many upheavals, not the least of which has been the loss of the image of the gentlemanly approach to warfare.

As the wheels of progress have conveyed us through the twentieth century a vast number of changes have taken place all around us, some of which we have only slowly come to accept, and not the most insignificant of these changes has been the continual reorganization of our armed forces. Even the business of making war is different. It's now more sophisticated, with each phase creating the need for a new concept of what the structure of a modern army should be, and although at present, to fit its role of today our army is smaller and more compact than it has ever been before, by no means is it any less efficient or its standard even a fraction lower.

The old numbered regiments went long ago, giving way to the famous names with which we are all so familiar. Then, more recently, some of the names began to disappear as the units were disbanded or amalgamated into new formations. Sad perhaps, in many ways, but necessary to keep pace with progress. The ten '*Birkenhead* regiments' are still with us though and very much a part of this new army. They no longer answer to the 43rd or the 91st any more, it's the Royal Greenjackets, or the Argylls now, but they are still there in the same proud traditions and *esprit de corps* of the old units, which have lived on and can be found in the descendant regiments. And it's a funny thing, even the old identity is still there too. Like old soldiers, it just won't die.

No story of the *Birkenhead* would have been complete without including a mention of the regiments involved in that inspiring display of courage 120 years ago, as not only does its addition make interesting and truly absorbing reading, it also provides a colourful and tremendously exciting contribution to this book, and on reading some of the never ending acts of courage that are part and parcel of the British Army, the actions of those men on the *Birkenhead* will be better understood. However, students and those in authority on military matters are asked to forgive the omissions which have been made in recounting these histories, for they will obviously appreciate that to present a full and precise account of ten crack regiments of the British Army would take volumes. It is only the intention of this book, as an added mark of respect, and a tribute to the regiments of which the 'Men of the *Birkenhead*' were part, to offer a brief and extremely condensed summary of these units.

2nd Foot

Prior to the restoration of the monarchy in the mid seventeenth century, there was no regular standing army, apart from a small force of cavalry and infantry who were known as Yeoman of the Guard. Right from Anglo-Saxon times any trouble would be met by raising men specifically to deal with the particular crisis in hand, the great majority of men being banded together by the fedual lords and landowners, who then commanded their own units. These trained bands, or militia, were the only troops available when the civil war of 1642–52 started, and the two sides used units from areas under their respective control. However, they were soon superseded by volunteers who joined either for adventure, the pay, or the loot that went with soldiering if you were on the winning side, and, as events were to show, although the militia continued to exist, a paid regular army had come to stay.

By 1659 the country's rule by the iron fist of Cromwell had ended, and under the leadership of General Monk, the Restoration came into being in 1660 when Charles II ascended to the throne of England. Within a year of his return from France he announced to the Houses of Parliament his intention to marry the young Catherine of Braganza, the Infanta of Portugal. As part of the marriage settlement Charles received a sum in the region of half a million pounds, together with the ports of Bombay and Tangier, the latter being a port of high potential and, '. . . a place likely to be of great benefit and security to the trade of England', as the Portuguese

Ambassador in London told the King. However, the Moors, a Mohammedan race of North-west Africa, considered Tangier to be their property and they continually had the place under siege, thus creating the necessity for it to be garrisoned. In September 1661 the Earl of Peterborough was made Governor of Tangier and he was given authority to raise a regiment of troops for the specific purpose of defending the port. Cromwell's army had been disbanded so there were sufficient men available for recruitment who were accustomed to military life and, on 14 October of the same year, a thousand men of the Tangier Regiment of Foot, or 1st 'Tangerines' as they were sometimes called, mustered on Putney Heath under their founder and first colonel, the Earl of Peterborough.

In January 1662 the regiment sailed for Tangier and there they were to remain, under a succession of commanding officers for forty-two years, until 1684 when Tangier was finally relinquished by England. The history of the regiment's almost half a century of service in Tangier is one of extreme hardship and virtually non-stop battles and skirmishes with the Moors. There were clashes with Spain too, as she was far from happy at Tangier being handed over to England, and it was not uncommon for the harbour to be blocked by Spanish warships for long periods.

The conditions the English troops existed in were often appalling, with scarcely enough fresh food and meat to go round, and pay that was frequently months in arrears. Leave was never granted and men served until they became ill and were lucky enough to be sent home, or they simply died in Tangier and were quickly forgotten. Discipline was ruthless, casualties suffered at the hands of the fierce and deadly Moors great, and morale never very high.

One of the most successful commanding officers was Piercy Kirke who became Governor of Tangier and colonel of the regiment in 1682, and the reputation of his success, together with the regiment's badge of a Paschal Lamb, the symbol of the House of Braganza, gave rise at this time to their nickname of Kirke's Lambs!

In 1684, after their return to England, their official style was changed to the Queen's Regiment, an honour bestowed by Charles for their service in protecting part of his Queen's dowry. 'Tangier' was also the regiment's first battle honour, and the oldest in the British Army, but it was not awarded until 1909, 221 years after the event.

On Charles II's death in February 1685, his brother, the Roman Catholic Duke of York, became James II and the style of the regiment changed again, to the Queen Dowager's Regiment, by which name they were known until 1703 when the prefix 'Royal' was granted in recognition of their magnificent display of courage at Tongres. Here, in this small town near Liege in Belgium, the Queen's, and a Dutch battalion, held off for nearly thirty hours a massive army of 40,000 Frenchmen, before being finally overcome, and by their heroism saved the Allied armies, under the Duke of Marlborough, from being taken by surprise.

Between 1685 and 1703 the regiment was involved in the internal struggles of England and Ireland; against the French on the continent; and then, with the Dutch and Austrians as allies, against France and Spain at the commencement of the War of the Spanish Succession (1701–13), involving most of the countries of Europe. When embarking at Portsmouth for this campaign the Queen's were accompanied by a detachment of 'Villier's Marines', who later became the 'East Surrey's' and with whom the Queen's were to eventually merge almost 250 years later.

May 1705 saw the regiment actively engaged in the fierce battle for Valencia and in the attack on the fortress of Albuquerque. They also fought at Madrid, Ciudad Rodrigo, and Almanza.

Hostilities with France started again in 1793, at the beginning of the Napoleonic Wars, and the Queen's found themselves in a new role, that of Marines aboard warships of the Royal Navy. The regiment was split into six detachments, to serve on Lord Howe's flagship *Queen Charlotte*, and *Royal George, Defence, Majestic*, and *Russell*. The sixth detachment served on the *Barfleur* in the West Indies, taking part in the action at Martinique. Serving as Marines was the start for the Queen's of a long and close association with the Royal Navy in which they were to fight in many of England's great naval battles as 'sea-soldiers', their most notable being Lord Howe's outstanding victory on the 1 June 1794 (the Glorious First of June) over the French in the first decisive engagement between the fleets of the two countries.

Between 1794 and 1797 a 2nd Battalion was raised and stationed initially in Guernsey. Meanwhile, out in the West Indies, the 1st Battalion was reduced to such a low level of numbers, through illness and disease, that they had to be reinforced by the 2nd Battalion. The two battalions eventually merged, but the terrible disease continued its heavy toll and when the regiment was brought back to England in October 1797 its strength was less than a hundred, out of over one thousand men of the combined battalions. The 1st Battalion was reformed to full strength within six months but the 2nd Battalion was not raised again until 1857.

Throughout the nineteenth century the Queen's was represented in almost every major campaign in which England was involved and they fought with the highest credit in places as far apart as Spain and China. Their battle honours include Corunna, Salamanca, Vittoria, Peninsular, Afghanistan 1839, South Africa 1851-2-3, Pekin 1860, Burma 1885-7, the Relief of Ladysmith, and South Africa 1899–1902 (the Boer War). At various times between the major engagements they served in Ireland and the West Indies. The 1800s also saw a further change in their title. Earlier, in 1727, they had been officially known as the Queen's Own Regiment, until 1751 when their style became the Queen's (Second) Royal Regiment of Foot, and then in 1881, with the introduction of the Cardwell Reform,[1] they became the Queen's (Royal West Surrey) Regiment.

At the outbreak of the First World War the two regular battalions of the Queen's were at full strength, the 1st Battalion at home in England and the 2nd Battalion in South Africa. However, before the end of the year (1914) both battalions found themselves in the mud and slaughter of the battlefields of Europe. The loss in terms of human lives from both sides was horrifying. By the end of October there were less than 40 men left from the 1st Battalion and by the following month the 2nd Battalion had suffered nearly 700 casualties.

Into the illustrious shoes of the men who had already laid down their lives stepped the soldiers of the Territorial battalions, men whose courage and discipline was to match that of their professional comrades. But the price of victory was high and men died in their thousands. In Holy Trinity Church, Guildford, the regimental war memorial records the fact that 8,000 officers, warrant officers, N.C.O.s, and men were killed in action in Flanders, France, Italy, Gallipoli, Salonika, Mesopotamia, Palestine, Egypt, India, Africa, and Germany.

In 1939 the storm clouds of war gathered once more over Europe and yet again the Regular and Territorial battalions of the Queen's were to be seen on the very same battlefields where twenty-five years earlier their forefathers had fought and died. Known since 1921, by another change of title, as the Queen's Royal Regiment (West Surrey), they fought on all major fronts against the Germans and Japanese.

During the years following the war the regiment served with its usual honour and distinction in the Far East, Germany, and Malaya, with a detachment also in Korea. In 1950 the 1st Battalion (then the only regular battalion of the regiment) had been paraded on the square at their barracks in Iserlohn, Germany, where the commanding officer called for 135 volunteers to step forward for service in Korea, as rein-

---

1. From about 1870 onwards a good number of important changes were made in the weapons system and the structure of the British Army, culminating in 1881 with the Cardwell System. In 1870, for example, the War Office Act was passed which involved better barracks, more pay and improved food. It also brought to an end the system whereby commissions could be purchased, even up to the senior ranks, which had been going on since 1720. Then in 1871 a very big advance was made in the efficiency of the weapons used by the infantry when the Snider rifle, used since 1866, was superseded by the Martini-Henry. Sighted to 1,000 yards and firing a heavy bullet with a great stopping power, it was a hammerless single-loader with an ejector worked by a lever behind the trigger guard.

However, the most notable changes, certainly the ones with the most far-reaching effects, were those of 1881. Pairs of regiments were united to form one regiment of two battalions so that one battalion could serve abroad and be reinforced by the other which would remain at home. (Where this had not already been done.) Districts were allotted to regiments for recruiting purposes and men were no longer required to enlist for life or until they were too old to be of any further use. Together with other changes, the Cardwell System provided for a vast reorganization of the Army which, although provoking some dissatisfaction, was on the whole a good thing.

forcements for the Middlesex Regiment. At the end of the commanding officer's request the whole battalion, with no hesitation at all and as one man, took a pace forward. Such was the Queen's.

However, progress has succeeded in achieving what a score of enemies failed to do when, on 14 October 1959, the Queen's and the East Surrey Regiment amalgamated to form the Queen's Royal Surrey Regiment, and the old 'Queen's', this magnificent regiment who had served their country so well, and for so long, ceased to exist as a separate unit. The Territorial battalions had already gone, and so too had the Regular 2nd Battalion. And now, on that cold and wet day in Germany, the last remaining battalion of one of England's finest regiments disappeared into the annals of military history.

6th Foot

Later to become the Royal Warwickshire Regiment, the 6th is one of England's oldest county regiments, having existed for some fourteen years before being granted the title of the 6th Foot. They had previously been part of a large force of

The 6th Foot at the battle of Corunna from a print in the possession of the regiment by whose permission it is reproduced here.

English troops, originally under Sir Walter Vane, who had fought the French in Holland and France. The force was eventually split into four smaller units, two English, one Irish and one Scots, with command of one of the English units (the future 6th) given to an officer named Lillingston. They landed in England in 1685 at which time Lillingston's old unit, now commanded by Sir Henry Bellassis, officially became the 6th. They returned to Holland a few months later and came back finally with William of Orange in 1688.

It was this connection with William that gave the regiment their colours of blue and orange, the colours of the House of Nassau to which William belonged. The spell of duty in Holland was also the origin of the nickname, 'the Dutch Guards', by which they were most popularly known. Later in life other nicknames included 'the Warwickshire Lads', and 'the Saucy Sixth'.

In July 1690 the Regiment fought at the battle of the Boyne, and five years later in 1695 they were in Flanders in action against the French, here gaining their first battle honour, at Namur. In 1707 they were one of the regiments which, together with the Dutch Army, suffered heavy losses at the hands of the French in the fierce battle of Almanza during the War of the Spanish Succession. Again, at Saragossa in 1710, the British, this time with an Austrian army, were engaged in another bitter encounter also against the French, but this time resulting in a decisive victory for the British/Austrian forces, the 6th having played a prominent part in the success of the action. Under their commanding officer, Colonel Harrison, the 6th were in the forefront of the charge which finally broke the enemy's ranks and in doing so they swept on to capture twenty-two big guns and more than thirty colours and standards belonging to a Moorish regiment. Colonel Harrison, as a gesture of honour to his regiment, was sent back to England with the standards, to lay them before the sovereign. One of the standards bore the design of the ancient royal badge of the antelope, and although no evidence actually exists to support it, there is a legend that Queen Anne, in recognition of the bravery shown, bestowed this badge upon the regiment, and the antelope design has been part of the regiment's cap-badge ever since. Also, for the last hundred years or so the 6th have had a live antelope or Indian buck as its regimental mascot, being one of only five British regiments officially authorized to have a live animal as a mascot.

In 1745 the regiment took part in the suppression of the rebellion in Scotland, and during the march north a recruit named James Gray enlisted at Coventry. His service was short-lived, however, as at Carlisle he got into trouble and was sentenced to 500 lashes. Before the punishment could be carried out he managed to escape and it was later learnt he made for Portsmouth where he joined the Marines and sailed to the West Indies. He saw plenty of action, including, in 1748, the Siege of Pondicherry where he received twelve shot wounds, eleven in the legs, and one in the groin which he removed himself two days later. Gray recovered and eventually returned to England, when, to everyone's amazement, he revealed the secret incredibly kept for over five years. 'He' was really Miss Hannah Snell, a 27-year-old Worcester girl with an obvious urge to don a uniform and fight for her country. She received a pardon, and an annuity for her services, and lived a more peaceful life until 1792 when she died in London.

In 1782 the regiments of the British Army were affiliated to various counties for recruiting purposes and it was at this time that the 6th began its connection with the county of Warwickshire, becoming known as 'the 6th or 1st Warwickshire Regiment'. It was also in this year that the song 'The Warwickshire Lads' was adopted as the regimental march.

On the regiment's return from the West Indies in 1795, where they had taken part in the capture of Martinique and gained their second battle honour, Prince William Frederick, Duke of Gloucester, was appointed colonel and to mark the occasion the regiment received the right to change their badge to an antelope within a crowned garter and the motto 'Honi soit qui mal y pense' ('Evil be to them who evil think').

After a period of seven years in Canada, the regiment embarked for Spain in 1808, here adding Rolica, Vimiera, and Corunna to their battle honours. After a short spell back in England they returned to Spain again in 1812, and took part in the Peninsular War under Wellington, gaining great fame during the following years. In one action, at Echalar in the Pyrenees, their conduct was described by the Iron Duke, who was not often given to pass compliments, as '. . . the most gallant and finest thing I have ever witnessed'. More battle honours, including Vittoria, Pyrenees, and Nivella, were added to their colours.

Later years saw the regiment in active service in Canada again in 1814 for the war against America where they became one of the few regiments to win the battle honour, Niagara; India in 1832 where, in recognition of their service they were granted the prefix 'Royal' by William IV, and their facings accordingly changed to blue; South Africa, 1846–53, for the Kaffir War; and in 1898, the campaign in the Sudan during which the Royal Warwickshire Regiment (as they had become in 1881) marched with Kitchener to Khartoum.

At the time of the First World War there were two regular battalions of the regiment but when the war ended this had been increased to thirty-one and the regiment had been represented in most of the campaigns, losing in all nearly 600 officers and almost 11,000 other ranks. Lord Montgomery and Sir William Slim were amongst those who served with the regiment and have since become famous military leaders.

The Second World War saw battalions of the Royal Warwicks in action in all the theatres of war in Europe (except Italy), and as far away as India and Burma. After the war, between 1945 and 1968, the regiment continued on active service in

Korea, Cyprus, and Borneo and also helped to keep the peace in the trouble spots of Egypt, Hong Kong, and Aden.

In 1963 the regiment was brigaded with three fusilier regiments: the Northumberland Fusiliers (5th), the Royal Fusiliers (7th), and the Lancashire Fusiliers (20th), and consequently their title was changed in May that year to the Royal Warwickshire Fusiliers. Five years later, in 1968, a further reorganization took place and these four regiments were merged together to form the Royal Regiment of Fusiliers. Thus, on 23 April 1968, the 6th, or Royal Warwickshire Fusiliers, ceased to exist as such, but its famous history and fine traditions go on, perhaps in even greater strength than before.

12th Royal Lancers

On 11 September 1960, two famous lancer regiments, who had already enjoyed a close association with one another through over 250 years of history, were merged together at Tidworth, Hampshire. On that day, the 9th Queen's Royal Lancers, formed in 1715 by Major-General Owen Wynne, and the 12th Royal Lancers (Prince of Wales's), formed by Brigadier Phineas Bowles in the same year, marched through Tidworth for the last time as separate regiments. After a simple church ceremony the 9th/12th Royal Lancers was born and a few months later, in 1961, history was to repeat itself when, for its first spell of duty, the new regiment embarked for Ireland where two and a half centuries earlier both the 9th and the 12th had started their independent careers. The 12th, in fact, originally served continuously in Ireland for seventy-five years, until the war with France in 1793.

As was the custom in the British Army in those early days of referring to the regiments by the name of their colonel, the 12th was at first known as Bowles's Dragoons, being officially styled the 12th Dragoons in 1751. Seventeen years later, George III conferred on the regiment the honour of bearing the title 'the 12th or Prince of Wales's Regiment of Light Dragoons', and simultaneously they became a corps of light cavalry.

Prior to its departure to the Mediterranean during the hostilities with France, one of the most notable officers to join the regiment in Ireland was a young lieutenant named the Hon. Arthur Wellesley, who served from 1789 to 1791. Later in life he was to become better known as the Iron Duke.

Whilst in the Mediterranean area part of the regiment moved to Italy and here they served with such exceptionally good conduct and behaviour in the papal states, and so impressed Pope Pius VI that he received some of the officers at the Vatican and presented them with gold medals. There is also a legend that his Holiness gave to the regiment three hymns that have since become the official regimental hymns and which are still played by the 9th/12th Royal Lancers. A less honourable version of this legend is that the hymns were given to the regiment to be played every night at tattoo as a punishment for breaking into a monastery during the Peninsular War, the punishment to last for a hundred years. However, on the strength of the regiment's splendid record and history, it would be safe to assume that if either of the two versions is true, it would be the former.

Over the next few years, until 1815, the regiment saw service in Portugal; Egypt, where they were awarded their first battle honour and the right to bear, on their guidons (dove-tailed standards) and appointments, the Sphinx; the Walcheren Expedition of 1809; the Spanish Peninsular, including in 1812 the battle of Salamanca, at which they earned the nickname, 'the Supple 12th', for their dash and rapidity of movement in action, and a year later, in 1813, they were heavily engaged in the great victory of Vittoria. Then, in 1815, the 12th were sent to the Netherlands to form part of the Allied army commanded by the Duke of Wellington, and at Waterloo they executed a brilliant charge in support of the Union Brigade, suffering heavy losses in the withdrawal and losing one third of their men inside ten minutes.

It was due mainly to the effectiveness of the French cavalry at Waterloo, with the lance, that an order was made directing certain regiments including the 12th to be armed with this weapon. This change was carried out and they were restyled, '12th or Prince of Wales's Royal Regiment of Lancers'.

Following a fairly quiet period the 12th were engaged, first in 1852 in the South African wars, then India, and later in 1855, they embarked for the Crimea to reinforce the Light Cavalry Brigade. They returned to serve in South Africa at the turn of the century and took part in the relief of Kimberley and in the capture of Pretoria.

Throughout the First World War, the regiment served on the Western Front and, to this day, Mons/Moy Day is celebrated each August to commemorate the last occasion on which the regiment charged with a lance.

Between the two world wars the 12th served in Germany, Egypt, Cyprus, Ireland, and home in England, and in 1928, while in Egypt, the 12th gave up their horses and became a cavalry armoured car regiment. In the Second World War, the 12th was the first British unit to cross the Belgian frontier, and later during the retreat they held a front of 40 miles between Ypres and Nieuport, covering the withdrawal of the British Army to Dunkirk. Of this event, Lord Gort wrote, 'Without the 12th Lancers, only a small part of the army would have reached Dunkirk.' Later in 1941 the regiment sailed for Africa and fought with the famed 8th Army in the North African Desert campaigns under Lord Montgomery. They were the first British troops to link up with the Americans in Tunisia in April 1943.

Since the war the regiment has served on security duties in Malaya, Aden, and Germany, and at Osnabruck in the British Rhine Army they were converted to an armoured tank regiment which is their role now as the 9th/12th Royal Lancers.

12th Foot

Of all the duties of a serving soldier probably the least acknowledged, yet one of the most arduous and dangerous, is that of policeman in the world's trouble spots and one of the most successful regiments to have performed this duty, almost continuously since their inception, has been the 12th Foot, subsequently the Suffolk Regiment. While other regiments were making a name for themselves under Marlborough, Moore, Wellington, and so on, and reaping battle honour after battle honour, the Suffolks were quietly and unobtrusively going about their difficult and often thankless business of keeping the peace in far-flung corners of the globe, and the experience gained then, two and a half centuries ago, and in later terrorist campaigns and operations through the years, laid the foundations for a special brand of *esprit de corps* and a unique quality of strength, endurance, and discipline which showed itself so well in more recent years in places like Malaya and Cyprus. Although the Suffolks were not one of the best-known or 'popular' regiments, nor one that immediately springs to mind when mentally recapping on some of England's great battles from the past, they were nevertheless, as their distinguished and honourable record of service has proved, one of our army's truly great regiments.

In actual fact they did win some of the glory. At Dettingen in 1743 during the war of the Austrian succession, for example, which is the last occasion in history that a British king has led his troops into battle. The 12th under their colonel, Scipio Duroure, were positioned in the centre of the forward line and George II, in an inspiring gesture of confidence, dismounted from his horse and placed himself at the head of the infantry, leading his army to eventual victory over the French. Serving in the regiment at this time was a 16-year-old officer named James Wolfe, later famous as Wolfe of Quebec, who, in a letter home to his father, commented on the appalling state of the country around Dettingen and the terrible conditions of the men enduring a long forced march on virtually no rations.

Another famous battle, in which the 12th were prominently engaged, is that fought at Minden sixteen years later in 1759. Here, with the morning sun glistening on cold British steel, six infantry regiments, including the Suffolks, engaged the French cavalry with devastating effect and defeated overwhelming odds after a fiercely contested action. Prior to this remarkable feat the regiments had passed through gardens of roses in full bloom where the soldiers had picked the blossoms and worn them in their headdress, perhaps to symbolize the English rose. After the battle, the Duke of Brunswick who commanded the British troops said of them, 'It is here this day that the British infantry has gained immortal glory.'

The regiment also played a vital part in the defence of Gibraltar, 1782–99, during the great siege, and for its services was granted the crest of the 'Castle and Key' which became part of the design of the cap badge. However, the Suffolks' main contribution in the service of their country, and that in which they earned their high reputation, was destined to be in the involvement of guerrilla warfare and the subsequent maintaining of law and order that followed these actions.

In the year 1685, and only months after his accession to the throne of England, James II found himself faced with an armed rebellion in the form of the Duke of Monmouth, illegitimate son of Charles II, and one of his mistresses, a certain Miss Lucy Waters. Monmouth and his army of supporters landed in Dorset in the summer of 1685 to lay claim to the throne, and to meet this threat James immediately ordered a number of cavalry and infantry units to be formed, one of which, that raised by Henry Howard, 7th Duke of Norfolk, eventually evolved into the 12th Regiment of Foot. Initially there was no connection with the county of Suffolk, but almost one hundred years later, in 1783, the regiment was styled the 12th (East Suffolk) Regiment, and then, after a further hundred years, the number was dropped in 1881 and the regiment received its new title of the Suffolk Regiment. There were no more changes in name until 1959 when the regiment amalgamated with the Royal Norfolk Regiment to become the 1st East Anglian Regiment (Royal Norfolk and Suffolk), and five years later further reorganization of regiments into larger formations necessitated the 1st East Anglians being incorporated into the Royal Anglian Regiment.

In common with other units of the British Army, the 12th in its early years was known by the name of the colonel who commanded it and its character, even its policy sometimes, was very much this officer's creation. Also, until 1855, the colonel of the regiment was responsible for all the equipment and clothing of the men under his command, receiving a fixed allowance for each man, and uniform design was the colonel's choice up to the 1740s when a standard regulation style dress was introduced throughout the Army. At this time, too, around 1742, the flintlock, which was a gun discharged by a spark from the mechanism, had become the infantry weapon in general use, replacing the old musket that required a match to ignite the charge.

The changes in the 1740s, as far as the 12th were concerned, coincided with a new colonel being appointed to command the regiment. A colourful and brilliant professional soldier, of French descent, by the name of Scipio Duroure, and under the dynamic personality and drive of this remarkable man the regiment developed an even stronger character than before and became one of the best trained and most efficient regiments of that period.

Up to the First World War battalions of the regiment had served in Ireland, the West Indies, Gibraltar, the Low Countries, India, Africa, and also New Zealand, in the Maori War of 1860–7. In the latter part of the nineteenth century the regiment was represented in Afghanistan and the Boer War. And then, in 1914, these placid countrymen of Suffolk found themselves in the trenches and battlefields of Europe, and in this holocaust, which became the worst war in living memory, the Suffolk men, like their comrades in arms, gave of their best.

Twenty-five years of uneasy peace followed the Armistice of 1918 and during this period the Suffolks, reduced in battalions, reverted to its familiar role of policemen, serving in Ireland, India, Gallipoli, and the Far East. Then, in 1939, the countries of Europe trembled beneath the ruthless crunch of Nazi jackboots, and like a bolt of lightning, the Second World War began. In common with other regiments, the strength of the Suffolks was increased and more Territorial battalions were formed in 1940, and moved to France and Belgium a year later where they were actively engaged in the battles which ranged to and fro. In 1941 two battalions of the Suffolks, the 4th and 5th, sailed via North America to Singapore, arriving only a matter of days before the island's capitulation to the Japanese. The Suffolks had gone straight into action and were deep in the thick of heavy fighting before the surrender came. The next three and a half years for the captured British Army were three and a half years of indescribable hell, and the savage and diabolical conditions of the men in captivity, including the infamous Burma–Siam Railway (the Railway of Death), are now a matter of history. Six hundred of the Suffolk Regiment alone were to find eternal peace in the jungles and swamps of the East. That any survived at all is indeed a miracle.

The end of the war eventually came and 1945 brought peace and final victory. But at what a tremendous price.

43rd Light Infantry and the 60th Rifles

The foundations for the eventual merger of these two regiments were laid well over two centuries ago, when in 1759, under General Wolfe in the Quebec campaign, they fought side by side in the front of many battles they were to see together through the years. The original 60th were in fact raised on the American continent, in New York in 1755, primarily to engage the American Indians and the French in the frontier forests. Their title then was the 60th Royal Americans and initially they wore scarlet uniforms with blue facings. They changed in 1797 to green uniforms and were the first in the British Army to wear this colour, quickly earning the obvious nickname, 'the Greenjackets'; a name that was to stick, and eventually, with the addition of the word 'Royal', become the official title of the descendant regiment. Close on a hundred years later they also became affectionately known as 'the Kaiser's Own', not through any particular attachment to this gentleman, but simply because their badge of a Maltese cross so closely resembled the German Iron Cross.

A scene showing a small part of the dreadful battleground of Passchendale which was one of the bloodiest of the First World War. Countless hundreds of thousands of men died here, in an action in which nearly every regiment in the British Army was represented. By courtesy of the Imperial War Museum.

Under Colonel Bouquet, a Swiss and their first commanding officer, the 60th successfully took Fort Duquesne (Fort Pitt and now Pittsburgh), and garrisoned the frontier and later, in 1765, they were engaged in what was described as '. . . the best contested action ever fought between White Man and Red', when they defeated Chief Pontiac at Bushy Run. Another notable battle in which they fought was the Siege of Savannah during the American War of Independence where they captured the Colours of the Carolina Regiment.

The 43rd were raised in 1741 and almost at once dispatched on active service, serving in Canada, Martinique, and Havana as well as the War of Independence. Later in its life, the 43rd together with the 52nd Regiment, and the Rifle Corps, which had been raised in 1800 by Colonel Coote Manningham as the 'Experimental Corps of Riflemen', were formed into the Light Infantry Brigade. This in turn grew into the now famous Light Division whose most notable mark in history is their fine record during the Peninsular War under Wellington and General Sir John Moore.

In 1830 the 60th became the King's Royal Rifle Corps, fighting in almost every campaign up to the turn of the century, adding to their already impressive list of battle honours the names of Mooltan, Goojerat, Punjab, South Africa 1851–2–3, Delhi 1857, Taku Forts, Pekin 1860, Egypt 1882, and many more.

The 43rd and the 52nd who had already shared a close association were brought together in 1908, being styled the Oxfordshire and Buckinghamshire Light Infantry, a name by which they will always be remembered. And as this new regiment they continued, through two world wars, to live up to the high standard of skill and courage set by their illustrious predecessors. In the First World War the regiment's bravery and devotion to duty go hand in hand with names like Ypres, the Somme, and Passchendale, as is amply evidenced by the Roll of Honour in Winchester Cathedral and at Oxford. Twenty years later the regiment again answered the call of duty and its battalions distinguished themselves in most theatres of the war with their traditional skill and courage.

The 60th Rifles too, saw bitter action in both world wars, becoming founder members of the 'Desert Rats' in the Second World War in their newly applied role of motorized infantry attached to the armoured divisions. Possibly one of this regiment's most notable achievements in the early days of the war was their participation in the defence of Calais whilst protecting the flank of the Dunkirk evacuation. The British commander had declined the German offer of surrender within one hour, and for four days of intense street fighting, with two additional German Panzer divisions brought in against them, Calais was held before being finally overcome. Simultaneously, a battalion (4th) of the Oxfordshire and Buckinghamshire Light Infantry held a key point a few miles away at Cassel, adding yet another glorious page to the history of that regiment.

Since their formation both the 60th Rifles and the 43rd Light Infantry have had a variety of changes in title, until finally, on 1 January 1966, they emerged as part of the reorganized Royal Greenjackets. Of the three battalions in this regiment, the 43rd form the 1st Battalion and the 60th Rifles the 2nd Battalion.

The Royal Greenjackets

1st Battalion (43rd and 52nd)

1741   The 43rd Regiment
1755   The 52nd Regiment
1782   The 43rd (Monmouthshire) Regiment and 52nd (Oxfordshire) Regiment
1803   The 43rd Light Infantry and 52nd Light Infantry
1881   The Oxfordshire Light Infantry
1908   The Oxfordshire and Buckinghamshire Light Infantry

2nd Battalion (the King's Royal Rifle Corps)

1755   The 60th Royal Americans
1824   The Duke of York's Rifle Corps
1830   The King's Royal Rifle Corps (often shortened to 60th Rifles)

3rd Battalion (the Rifle Brigade)

1800   The Experimental Corps of Riflemen
1803   The 95th or Rifle Corps
1816   The Rifle Brigade

These unique fighting men in their green dress and their green berets have proved beyond doubt their worth as light infantrymen, with their own particular brand of skill and marksmanship with the rifle, whose use they pioneered, and their skirmishing tactics, incorporating a faster marching step than conventional infantry regiments and their control by bugle call, all used so effectively against the American Indians, the French, and a host of other enemies.

Although the concept of light infantry regiments was born earlier, the pattern that emerged in the early 1900s and which can still be seen today in the Light Division, was the result of the efforts and contributions made by Sir John Moore a hundred years before, at the birth of the Light Infantry Brigade at Shorncliffe in Kent. His vision of what an army should be was clear in his mind and he set to work then, to mould in his troops at Shorncliffe the model by which the British Army might in the future shape itself upon. History has shown that Moore's formula was a success and the high esteem and respect the Light Division earned in its first victories has not tarnished to the present day. What was said of them then by General Napier over one hundred years ago still applies.

Moore's ideal [wrote Napier] was the thinking fighting man and the troops he trained to be such, grew into the famous Light Division which, under his successor, Wellington, was the Corps d'elite of the Peninsula Army that broke the legend of Napoleonic invincibility. Six years of warfare could not detect a flaw in their system nor were they ever matched in courage or skill.

Finally, another compliment, unintentional as it happens, came from the French marshal, Soult, who wrote in a special despatch to explain his high loss of officers:

The loss in prominent and superior Officers sustained for some time past by the Army, is so disproportionate to that of the rank and file that I have been at pains to discover the reason; and have acquired the following information, which of course explains the cause of so extraordinary a circumstance. There is in the English army a battalion of the 60th consisting of ten companies. This battalion is never concentrated, but has a company attached to each Infantry Division. It is armed with a short rifle; the men are selected for their marksmanship; they perform the duties of scouts, and in action are expressly ordered to pick off the officers, especially Field and General Officers. Thus it has been observed that whenever a superior officer goes to the front during an action, either for purposes of observation or to lead and encourage his men, he is usually hit.

45th Foot

Were it not for the fact Robin Hood and his Merry Men are colourful characters of fiction, the legends that the origins of the old 45th lie with the famed outlaws of Sherwood Forest could well have been true.

Nevertheless, the connections between the regiment and the county of Nottingham, which at least embraces the famous forest of Sherwood, are very strong and it was to commemorate this association that the melody 'The Young May Moon', used by William Shield in his comic opera *Robin Hood* of 1784, was selected to be one of the regimental marches.

Raised in 1741 by a Colonel Daniel Houghton, and as was the custom known as Houghton's Regiment, it was originally the 56th but re-numbered the 45th soon afterwards, until, in 1881, the number was abolished and it became the 1st Battalion the Sherwood Foresters. During this period it had been a one battalion regiment but in 1881 when taking their new name they were merged with the 95th Foot who then formed the 2nd Battalion. The 3rd and 4th Battalions were also formed from the old militia, which had been maintained in Nottinghamshire and Derbyshire since ancient times.

The 45th's first major action, and its first battle honour, came in 1758 when it formed part of the British Army that captured Louisburg in Canada, a coast defence fortress which the French used to seal the entrance to the St. Lawrence River. Later, two companies of the 45th joined up with General Wolfe for the successful storming of Quebec, the prelude to Canada becoming a British dominion. Almost twenty years later the 45th found themselves again on the American continent, in the campaign in which the colonists of what is now the United States gained their independence. In spite of the eventual outcome in the American War of Independence, the men of the 45th and their comrades in the other regiments involved had nothing to be ashamed of and they did well, fighting many successful battles. But they were up against something quite new in the guerrilla tactics of the Americans, and the red-coated British soldier was obviously at a distinct disadvantage when he could only move, or fire, on the word of command, whereas his irregular American opponents could move about, take cover or fire, at will. And this was not their only adversity. A high rate of sickness and disease among the men took a terrible toll and in 1778, when the 45th returned to England their strength was less than 100.

A private soldier of the
45th Foot, in 1742. By
courtesy of the
Worcestershire and
Sherwood Foresters
Regiment.

Meanwhile the bad state of the country generally, in particular its foreign rela-
tions, was causing a certain mount of alarm to the dignitaries and others in authority
who were aware of the need for some action to rectify the situation. In Nottingham,
for instance, the local leaders called a meeting of the gentry of the country to discuss
the position, the outcome of which was a request to the Secretary of War for a
regiment of the Regular Army to be assigned to the county for recruitment purposes,
thus assisting in the needed build-up of the Army. The request was complied with
and the 4th Foot were selected to be the regiment and dispatched from their
quarters at Chatham to Nottingham. A bounty of 6 guineas was paid from county
funds to each recruit and soon the target of 300 men had been reached and passed,
many of them from the existing county militia, and the 45th from this time on were
permitted to use the style 'Nottinghamshire Regiment' after their number.

A | The British troops under Gen.l Picton Escalading and taking the Castle.
B | The British bravely storming the large breach in the Walls.
C | Attacking the two lesser breaches.
D | The Glacis or outer Wall.

A VIEW OF THE STORMING AND TAKING OF

This City the capital of the province of Estremadrura was Stormed and its Castle taken by General Earl Wellington when after an obstinate and bloody contest the place was taken an[d] the British and allies were 1035 Killed and 3787 Wounded.

Published May 11 1812 by G. Thom[…]

A reproduction of a print showing the storming of Badajoz in Spain, 1812. Reproduced by kind permission of the Worcestershire and Sherwood Foresters Regiment who, as the 45th Foot, took a prominent part in this battle.

JOZ IN SPAIN ON APRIL 6 1812

y the gallant British troops assisted by the Portuguese and commanded
lled and wounded the Governor Gen. Philipon and 4000 Men prisoners: the loss of

E	Gen. Earl of Wellington.
F	British Mortar and Gun Battery.
G	A Mine sprung near the walls.
H	Our brave fellows blown up in the ladders
I	Explosions of shells on the ramparts
K	Signal Rockets

Until 1808 the 45th were either in garrison at home or abroad, or on active service with the Royal Navy. Their longest period away being in the West Indies, where they served almost continuously from 1786 to 1801, but there was such a high rate of casualties from the enemy and so many fatalities from disease and sickness, that despite reinforcements having been received at various intervals, they were forced to return home to England for full-scale recruitment. The remnants of the regiment, just 76 officers and men, landed at Portsmouth on 28 July 1794 and a month later proceeded to the Isle of Wight, where they remained until December, their strength in the meantime being increased to nearly 700, and in this healthy state they returned to the West Indies for a further six years. In 1801 the regiment came home again, their second stay having been fairly uneventful except for the continued sickness, and after staying in various camps in southern England they were eventually garrisoned in Ireland.

In October 1804, a 2nd Battalion was raised and billeted at Chelmsford, Essex, while the 1st Battalion was moved, first to Portsmouth, then to Falmouth from where they embarked for their ultimate destination, Brazil. For three years the regiment was actively engaged against the Spanish in South America, returning home in 1807. Their stay in England was short-lived, however, as after being brought up to full strength they were dispatched to Portugal early in 1808, as part of the Peninsular Army under the command of Sir Arthur Wellesley (Wellington), where they became one of the three regiments to serve continuously throughout the Peninsular War, from 1808 to 1814. They fought in all the major engagements, adding no less than fourteen battle honours to their colours, and on account of their magnificent work, and particularly their doggedness shown at Talavera, they earned the nickname, 'the Old Stubborns'. Early in 1810 the famed General Picton joined the Peninsular Army and was given command of the 3rd Division (the Fighting 3rd) of which the 45th formed part. The regiment also excelled itself at the fiercely contested battle of Salamanca and there is an incident related that, in one of the first advances on the enemy it was only with great difficulty that the officers were able to hold back and restrain the men until the order finally came, 'Let 'em loose', when they rushed like madmen on to the bayonets of the opposing French 7th Division who broke ranks and scattered in confusion under the onslaught. It then appears that one private soldier, with bayonet fixed, chased a Frenchman who, as a last resort, threw away his musket and tried to escape the screaming Englishman by climbing a tree. However, the classic result was that he received a taste of British steel in that part of his anatomy that should never be exposed to either friend or foe. Later, when occupying Madrid, the order was made that for the march of the British Army through the streets of the city the 45th should be given the place of honour of marching at the head of the army.

Simultaneously to the regiment's return to Ireland from the Peninsular in 1814, the 2nd Battalion, which had never as a whole left England, was disbanded and the men transferred to the 1st Battalion.

The 45th were not present at the battle of Waterloo but soon after it they went to India and Burma. They were also represented in South Africa and in 1868 they were involved in the short but arduous campaign in Abyssinia before returning yet again to India, this time for a ten-year spell of duty.

In October 1899 the 1st Battalion, stationed at the time in Malta, was ordered to Africa for the Boer War and for thirty-three months they marched and fought in twenty-eight engagements in which skill with the rifle counted above all. They gained many awards for gallantry including two V.C.s.

At the outbreak of the First World War the regiment consisted of eight battalions, all of whom were at once put on a war footing. Before the war ended the strength of the regiment had been increased to thirty-three battalions through whose ranks 150,000 men had served so gloriously and, as in the case of the nine regiments mentioned in this chapter, it is impossible to do proper justice to the deeds of heroism and the magnificent endurance of the men who fought and died in both this war and the Second World War which followed twenty-five years later. There are so many places that could be brought to mind: the Somme, Ypres, Flanders, and so on in 1914–18, and Singapore, Dunkirk, El Alamein, Tunis, Salerno, and the Anzio beachhead of 1939–45. The list, like the deeds of the men of the 45th who fought there, is great and almost endless.

During the immediate post-war years the regiment served in Egypt, Cyrenaica, Palestine, Malaya, and Cyprus and since 1955, when the 1st and 2nd Battalions merged, they were known as 1st Battalion the Sherwood Foresters (45th and 95th). In 1970 a further amalgamation took place between the Worcestershire Regiment and the Foresters, resulting in the birth of the Worcestershire and Sherwood Foresters Regiment, a regiment which has so much to look back on and so very much to be proud of.

73rd Regiment

There are few countries in the world that can offer a history as colourful and as turbulent as Scotland, and whilst the claims of many historians that she became a home for lost causes may be true, it is also fair to say that much of value has been retained. Events have shown, too, that some of the old causes, defended with an inborn strength and determination, were not entirely lost and that in defending them, Scottish nationality was born.

Of all Scotland's struggles, perhaps the longest-standing and most bitter has been against England, in the conflicts of her refusal to accept the conquest and domination by the kingdom of England.

At the turn of the seventeenth century most Catholics in both England and

Scotland claimed the rightful heir to the English throne was not Elizabeth I, daughter of Anne Boleyn, who ruled, but the Catholic Mary Stuart (Queen of Scots), the grandaughter of Margaret Tudor who was Henry VIII's sister. Mary, however, was destined never to become Queen of England. Her life, so full of violence, deceit and murder, culminated in her captivity in England and finally in her death by execution in 1587.

Sixteen years later, in 1603, Elizabeth died, and Mary's son, James VI of Scotland, next in line, succeeded to the throne of England as James I. A hundred years of bitter conflict and bloodshed passed which saw the reign of Charles I (1625–49); the great Civil War; Cromwell; Charles II (1660–85) and the Restoration; James II (1685–8); William and Mary (1689–1702); and Queen Anne, the last of the Stuarts (1702–14); until in 1707 the Act of Union was made between England and Scotland.

In 1701, thirteen years after his abdication, James II died in exile in St. Germain and the events of the following years, for almost half a century, were to prove to be no exception to Scotland's violent history. The disregard of Scottish affairs by English statesmen, particularly of her economic depression, was one of the main causes of discontent and of the bloody and disastrous Jacobite risings. By 1714 the succession to the throne had passed to the Hanovarian line, and although this eventuality had been covered by the earlier Act of Union, many of the Highland clans were opposed to George I, whom they referred to as 'th' wee German lairdie'. The Jacobites voiced their support of the House of Stuart and to the late King James's son, the young Prince James, who had been born in 1688, and exploiting the opposition to the Union they successfully roused the rebel clans to open rebellion against the British Government and Hanovarian dynasty.

In 1725, the British military commander in Scotland was General George Wade and amongst his measures to establish law and order in the Highlands he formed independent companies of loyal Highlanders into trained organized units to assist the regular troops in policing, or watching, the area. Similar groups had in fact been used before, as early as 1624, but had been intermittently disbanded, sometimes through corruption. The independent companies of Wade's, however, did their work firmly and well.

To distinguish themselves they wore a standard form of dark tartan which belonged to no particular clan or district, being unique to these men, and because of this tartan and their duties in 'watching' the Highlands, they became known as 'Am Freiceadan Dubh' or Black Watch, in contrast to 'Saighdearan Dearg', the redcoats of the regular British Army.

In 1740 the first regular Highland regiment was formed at Aberfeldy, using as a nucleus these independent companies who wore the dark tartan. Their official style then was the 43rd Highland Regiment of Foot, more popularly known as the Black Watch. (They became the 42nd in 1751.) They remained in Scotland for three years, before embarking in May 1743 for Germany and Flanders receiving their baptism of fire two years later at the fiercely contested battle of Fontenoy in France, fought against the French by the British, Dutch, and Austrians. It was here at Fontenoy that the enemy first received a taste of a peculiar technique of fighting perfected by the Scots in their own country. Assembled in a battle line facing the French the Black Watch loaded their arms and then, waiting until just seconds before the enemy fired, the whole line would suddenly fall flat on the ground. If this was timed exactly, as it often was, the volley of shots would pass over their heads. They would then stand up quickly, fire a volley into the enemy ranks, sling their muskets over their shoulders and with claymore in hand charge the surprised and confused French troops before they had time to reorganize themselves and load. And from that battle onwards, through 226 years of fame and glory, 162 battle honours and 21 V.C.s, the history of the Black Watch is the history of the wars of England.

The outbreak of the Seven Years' War in 1756 took the regiment to the American continent where the most outstanding event of their period of service was undoubtedly the action of Ticonderoga. This was a fort held by the French, defended by entrenchments and covered by a thick abatis of large trees. The British, who had no artillery to break a way, failed to penetrate the obstacle at the first assault. The Highlanders who had been posted in reserve, impatient at being left in the rear, could not be restrained and, rushing forward, were soon in front endeavouring to cut their way through the trees with their broadswords. Many fell, yet when they had won through it was in vain. No ladders had been provided for scaling the breastwork. The soldiers climbed on each other's shoulders and fixed their feet in holes made with sword and bayonet in the face of the work, but so well were the defenders prepared, that the instant a man reached the top he was thrown down. The casualties of the regiment exceeded 600. This battle on 8 July 1758, known since as Ticonderoga Day, is kept in remembrance by Scotsmen in the United States and Canada to this day.

At home in England, previous to the arrival of the news of the regiment's action at Ticonderoga, two events of special interest took place. A Royal Warrant was promulgated in July 1758 conferring the title 'Royal' on the regiment as a testimony of 'His Majesty's satisfaction and approbation of the extraordinary courage, loyalty and exemplary conduct of the Highland Regiment'. The facings were then changed from buff to royal blue. Also, a 2nd Battalion was raised but after several campaigns it was later absorbed with the 1st Battalion. However, it was formed again in 1779 at Perth for service in the American Rebellion and remained as the 2nd Battalion until 1786 when it separated to become the 73rd Highland Regiment of Foot. Then in 1809 the style 'Highland' was dropped from the name and they became the 73rd Regiment of Foot and, for seventy-two years, until 1881, during this separate existence, Highland dress was not worn, even though in 1862 the name was changed yet again, to the 73rd (Perthshire) Regiment.

After a period of peace both regiments, the 42nd and the 73rd, again found themselves in the thick of the fighting, first in the Peninsular War, where the 42nd gained nine battle honours, and then in the Waterloo campaign. In the famous retreat to Corunna, in the Peninsula, the Black Watch (42nd) took part in the final battle which saved the situation, advancing in a counter-attack to Sir John Moore's stirring words, 'Highlanders, remember Egypt'. This was a reference to 1801, and the regiment's outstanding part at the Battle of Alexandria, in which the British Commander-in-Chief, Sir Ralph Abercromby, was killed.

The Crimea followed, then the Indian Mutiny of 1857–9, during which the Black Watch won eight V.C.s. In 1881 the 73rd Regiment was linked with the 42nd to form one regiment and their separate numbers were dropped. A year later saw the 1st Battalion, originally the 42nd Regiment, in Egypt where they were engaged in the Nile expedition gaining battle honours at Tel-el-Kebir and Kirkbekan, the enemy position in both battles being carried at the point of a bayonet. The century closed with the South African War and the 2nd Battalion, the old 73rd Regiment, went out with the Highland Brigade, commanded by an old Black Watch officer, Major-General 'Andy' Wauchope. The disaster of Magersfontein where the battalion suffered 300 casualties is still remembered in Scotland. They subsequently took part in the battle of Paardeberg which brought about the surrender of Cronje and the capture of some thousands of Boers.

Ten battalions of the Black Watch served with distinction in the First World War and of the 50,000 men to wear the 'Red Hackle', over 10,000 were never to see their beloved Highlands again. A quarter of a century later the swirl of the Black Watch bagpipes was once more heard over the battlefields of Europe, with the regiment represented in every major campaign of the Second World War except for Norway and Malaya.

The connections between the 73rd and the 42nd Regiments, and their numerous changes of name, are rather complex and tend to confuse. The following 'family tree', however, should make it a lot clearer.

The Black Watch
(Royal Highland Regiment)

42nd Regiment

1725–39	Independent Companies (Am Freiceadan Dubh) the Black Watch
1739–51	The Highland Regiment of Foot, 43rd, also by the colonel's name
1751–8	The 42nd Foot
1758–1861	42nd (the Royal Highland) Regiment of Foot
1861–81	42nd (the Royal Highland) Regiment of Foot (the Black Watch)

73rd Regiment

1758–62 ⎫
1779–86 ⎭   The 2nd Battalion, 42nd (the Royal Highland) Regiment of Foot
1786–1809   The 73rd Highland Regiment of Foot
1809–62   The 73rd Regiment of Foot
1862–81   The 73rd (Perthshire) Regiment

In 1881 the two regiments became, respectively, the 1st and 2nd Battalions the Black Watch (Royal Highlanders). In 1934 the title was changed to the Black Watch (Royal Highland Regiment). The 2nd Battalion was disbanded in 1948, re-raised, and in 1956 again disbanded.

74th Foot

'My Fighting Regiment', was how Wellington once described the 74th Highland Regiment of Foot and never was a description more fitting. Later in its life as the 2nd Battalion of the famed Highland Light Infantry, having linked with the 71st Regiment in 1881 to form the new regiment, the 74th have been involved since their inception in nearly every campaign in which England has been engaged, and they share with the 71st the distinction of having won between them more battle

An officer of the 74th
Highlanders, showing the dress
of the 1852 period.

honours during the period from 1777, when the 71st was raised, up to the outbreak
of the First World War, than any other regiment in the British Army. In addition,
the 74th have the unique honour of a third colour which was awarded to the regiment in recognition of their unsurpassed conduct in the Battle of Assaye fought in
India in September 1803. The regiment, and indeed the British Army, can well be
proud of the example of strength, courage, and devotion to duty shown that day.

In the battle, the British, numbering approximately 5,000 men under Major-
General Arthur Wellesley (Wellington) faced an army of nearly 40,000 well-trained
and mainly French-officered Mahratta warriors who had threatened the territories of
the Nizam of Hyderabad, our most faithful friend and ally. Wellington had been
ordered to deal with the situation, and, after some preliminary skirmishes, eventually
made his position, with the 74th on his right flank, by the River Kaitna, near the
village of Assaye. The Mahrattas opened fire with their heavy artillery, cutting
great swathes through the British ranks. When the big guns finally stopped the
Mahratta horsemen charged in their thousands against Wellington's lines with most
of the weight being concentrated against the 74th who, although cut to pieces and
losing all their officers, withstood the murderous onslaught and held firm. In the
fierce struggle that followed the 74th suffered 11 officers and 145 men dead and 7
officers and nearly 300 men wounded. Their incredible stand, however, enabled
Wellington to advance his centre and left flank. A cavalry charge by the 19th Light
Dragoons sent the Mahratta infantry into a confused and hasty retreat and the main
advance of the British forces overran the enemy guns. It was Wellington's day and
the first of his many great victories.

As Wellington's troops moved forward following his order for a general advance,
he rode swiftly over to the right flank, to the 74th to find no more than
40-odd men standing where there should have been 500. Puzzled and confused he
moved slowly among the bodies, stopping when he saw the regiment's commanding
officer lying in a pool of blood and propped up against the side of his slain horse.
'Get the 74th forward, Swinton. Where the devil are the rest of 'em?' shouted
Wellington. The wounded officer's reply was choked and barely audible: 'They are
all down, sir'.

This incident is said to have affected the Duke of Wellington so much that he spent
the night after the battle sleepless, crouched in his tent with his head in his hands.
At any rate he didn't forget the debt owed to the 74th for their part in the battle.
One of the punishments carried out for plundering was death by hanging and
Wellington was as ruthless as any commander in ordering its use, but he would not,
from that day on, permit any soldier of the 74th to suffer the rope.

> I think it very desirable to avoid punishing with death a soldier belonging to
> the 74th Regiment, [he wrote]. I therefore propose to offer to the man to com-
> mute his punishment to transportation for life to Botany Bay.

The 74th at the taking of the Tanga Pass, India, on 7 January 1898.
From a sketch drawn by an officer of the Highland Light Infantry
and reproduced here by courtesy of the regiment.

In the battle for the Pass the British force, commanded by Sir
Bindon Blood, stormed the heights with the Royal West Kents on
the right of the advance, the 21st Punjabis in the centre, and the
74th Highlanders on the left. The Buffs brought up in the rear;
the 20th Punjabis attacked from along the ridge on the enemy's
right flank, and the whole operation had the support of covering
fire from field battery units.

The opposing Pathan tribesmen poured down a continuous hail
of bullets, but the British eventually scrambled to the top. And
not for a moment did the pipers of the 74th cease their playing of
'The Campbells are Coming'.

To commemorate the battle and the splendid victory, the 74th received in addition to the third colour, the royal authority to incorporate in their badge an Indian elephant superscribed Assaye.

Initially the regiment spent its first sixteen years in service in India, but so great had been their losses in the arduous campaigns fought almost continuously, that they were eventually returned to England in 1806 to recruit and rebuild to their active strength. They had been raised in 1787 under Major-General Sir Archibald Campbell of Inverneil, for the express purpose of reinforcing the army in India. A treaty had been agreed between Holland and France under which the Dutch possessions in India were to be garrisoned by the French, and, although this move pleased the enemies of England, it naturally alarmed the East India Company who immediately requested more British troops, and the 74th was one of four regiments formed and consequently sent to India.

During the Peninsular War the 74th were present at the storming of Badajoz which was a vital fortress on the Portuguese-Spanish frontier. Under the singularly picturesque character, General Picton, the 3rd or 'Fighting Division', of which the 74th were part, scaled the walls of the castle. They were beaten back at first, many were bayoneted as they reached the top, and the ladders were hurled back to the ground. Picton, who had been wounded in the leg, hobbled to the front of his men, swearing and cursing in his happiest state, and seeing a part of the wall which had not been tried, ordered the 74th back up the walls. One of the first men to gain the top was Piper John MacLauchlan who, once on the ramparts, paraded up and down playing 'The Campbells are coming', the ancient march of the clan and stirring battle-tune of the 74th. A bullet through the bag of the pipes brought the music to an abrupt end, but not for long. Sitting nonchalantly on a gun carriage and completely oblivious to the turmoil around him, he mended the hole and continued playing above the walls of Badajoz. Several months later the brave piper was to meet his untimely death, with his beloved pipes to his lips as perhaps he would have wished. At a stage in the brilliant and decisive Battle of Vittoria, the 74th reduced in numbers to under 300, advanced forward with their colours in the centre being constantly waved and exposed, to enable the regiment to keep its formation. Piper MacLauchlan, who was playing behind the colours, was struck by a volley of cannonball that had been directed at the colours. He fell to the ground with his legs smashed to pulp but refused to give in. His pipes were handed back to him and he went on playing until he died. At the close of battle when the bodies of the dead were being recovered it was seen that the piper's body had been untouched by the local peasants who normally went amongst the dead and dying, taking their clothes, valuables, and weapons. MacLauchlan's body alone had been respected, and his pipes, sword, and dirk still lay beside him.

Both as the 74th Regiment and, after 1881, as the 2nd Battalion Highland Light

Men of the 10th Battalion Highland Light Infantry near Tilbury, Holland, during the Second World War. Tanks of the 6th Guards are behind them. By courtesy of the Imperial War Museum.

Infantry, they continued to reap honour after honour, distinguishing themselves particularly in the two world wars with an outstanding record of gallantry and self-sacrifice. In the First World War alone, seventeen battalions of the Highland Light Infantry took part in sixty-four major engagements in France, Belgium, the Dardanelles, Egypt, Palestine, and Mesopotamia, and lost in deaths 598 officers and 9,428 other ranks.

The regiment's association with the city of Glasgow, from where most of its recruits had come, was rewarded in 1923 by the added title, 'City of Glasgow Regiment', and again in 1943 when they were granted the freedom of the city.

In 1947 the 2nd Battalion Highland Light Infantry, the old 74th, was disbanded and twelve years later the remaining 1st Battalion was merged with the Royal Scots Fusiliers to form the Royal Highland Fusiliers, the present regiment.

91st Foot

Twice in their colourful history, at Balaclava in 1854, and a century later in Aden in 1967, the Argyll and Sutherland Highlanders have had world-wide attention focused on them, and no regiment has captured the public imagination more fully.

Due to the tremendous coverage by the press and television, the campaign of the regiment in Aden, especially the spectacular entry into the Crater district on 3–5 July 1967, and then its domination against terrorists through the following few months, is now well known to almost everyone, and nothing new can be added here. Shortly after their return to England, possibly as the most efficient and highly trained unit in the British Army, they were stunned to learned of the decision taken to have them disbanded. Further defence cuts were necessary and the Argylls had been selected to be one of the regiments that should fall under the axe.

The public outcry was quite fantastic. Representations were made on the regiment's behalf to Parliament, literally over a million people signed a petition calling on the Government to reverse its decision, and stickers appeared everywhere bearing the words, 'Save the Argylls'. Until just recently, the regiment had not actually been disbanded but it had been reduced in strength to company size and its future was still uncertain. But like in all its battles through the centuries, it refused to accept defeat and just carried on fighting, no matter what the odds. And now, the grand news (October 1971) that the regiment has been saved. The threat of disbandment has been lifted and they are to be built back up to full battalion strength.

The Argyll and Sutherland Highlanders were born in 1881 when the Cardwell System came into operation, being formed by a merger of the 91st Argyllshire Highlanders, raised in 1794 by Duncan Campbell of Lochnell, and the 93rd Sutherland Highlanders, formed by Major-General William Wemyss in 1799.

In 1794, the Duke of Argyll was one of four nobles instructed by George III to each form an additional regiment, as the King had decided this was necessary to meet the threat of war with France, but through the poor state of health of his Grace, Campbell of Luchnell was deputized in his place. Within a matter of months nearly 800 officers and men had been raised for service in Campbell's regiment and on their first review they presented an impressive sight.

The men wore: 'Full highland dress, facings yellow, lace black and white, yellow oval shoe-buckles, the kilt and plaid green tartan with black stripes.'

The officers wore: 'Field dress jackets or Frocks, hooked at the top through the shirt. Cloth or Cassimere vests, Kilts or Belted Plaids. Black Velvet stocks (buttoned behind) with false collars; hair cut close and clubbed, well powdered at all parades, with rosettes on the clubs. The colour of the Epaulette white, with facings yellow.'

Their arms consisted of claymore and pistols for the officers and sergeants, and flintlocks, with bayonets, for the men. After an initial training period on the island of Guernsey, the regiment, known in these early days as the 98th Foot, proceeded to South Africa where they were garrisoned for seven years.

They saw very little action during this posting, but whilst at the Cape, there were two notable events in the regiment's history. They lost their Highland dress, including the kilt, and were ordered instead to wear a red jacket, white trousers, half-gaiters, and a round felt hat. And a few months later their designation was changed to 91st Foot.

On 28 May 1802, the Treaty of Amiens was signed which resulted in the Cape being handed back to the Dutch. Shortly afterwards the regiment returned to England and there is a fascinating story about the journey home. The ship carrying the 91st was menaced by a giant swordfish which, in repeatedly attacking the vessel, broke its ivory sword, leaving a piece 33½ in. long sticking out from the side of the wooden hull.

It was taken by a Sergeant-Major Andrew MacLean who used it as a walking stick and had it with him right through the Peninsular War. It later became the property of the regiment which still has it to this day, but now it has eight solid gold plates fixed to it, each plate being inscribed with one of the battle honours of the Peninsular.

Following a period at home after their return from South Africa, a 2nd Battalion was raised, primarily to ensure there would always be a source of ready-trained men available to feed the 1st Battalion which was being gradually built up to strength. During 1805, when this happened, the kilt was restored to the regiment and they became known as the 91st Argyllshire Regiment.

In 1808 the 1st Battalion and a draft of the 2nd Battalion, left for the Peninsular War in which they were to give a good account for themselves, particularly in a rear-guard action during the retreat to Corunna when they were in the thick of the fighting. Prior to this battle, they had suffered heavily from illness and disease. In fact, for the first few months of their arrival, whilst forming part of the Reserve Division, their casualties were greater from disease than at the hands of the enemy.

The regiment returned home in early 1808, their strength reduced to less than 400 men who could be considered fit for duty, and on 7 April of that year, for the second time they lost the right to wear the kilt. During the preceding few years, the Highlands of Scotland had supplied the British Army with over 70,000 men, and had finally reached saturation point. There were simply no more men left eligible for military service and the Highland regiments were having to take into their ranks Englishmen and Irishmen to keep up to strength. The appropriate order was issued from the Adjutant-General's office with the following text:

As the population of the Highlands of Scotland is found insufficient to supply recruits for the whole of the Highland corps on the establishment of His Majesty's Army, and as some of these corps, laying aside their distinguishing dress, which is objectionable to the native of South Britain, would in great measure tend to the facilitating of the completing of the establishment, as it would be an inducement to the men of the English Militia to extend their services in greater numbers to these regiments: it is in consequence most humbly submitted for the approbation of His Majesty, that His Majesty's 72nd, 73rd, 74th, 75th, 91st and 94th Regiments should discontinue to wear in future the dress by which His Majesty's Regiments of Highlanders are distinguished: and that the above corps should no longer be considered as on that establishment.

However, the 91st retained their designation as the Argyllshire Regiment, and not even for one day has it ever really lost its true Scottish traditions. Non-kilted Highland dress instead, trews of the Campbell tartan, was eventually restored to the regiment in 1865.

In 1812, the regiment, once more at full strength, sailed again for the Peninsular and took part in the crushing defeats of Napoleon's armies, on the Pyrenees, at Orthes, the Nivelle, the Nive, and finally Toulouse, adding these names to a growing list of battle honours. Ten days after Toulouse the Peninsular War ended, and by Christmas Napoleon had abdicated and was safely on the island of Elba.

During the uneasy peace in Europe that followed the devastation of the Peninsular campaign, the 91st were sent to Ireland, and here they remained until 1815, when, on the news that Napoleon had escaped to France to reform his army, they were embarked immediately for Belgium to join Wellington's forces at Waterloo. Being positioned on the extreme right of the line at Waterloo, they were not fully engaged in the actual battle, but they took part in the pursuit which followed, and in the fiercely contested siege of Cambrai.

Between 1822 and 1879, the regiment served in Jamaica (1822–31), St. Helena (1836–40), South Africa (1842–5), the Kaffir War (1846–8), India (1858–68), and the Zulu War (1879).

While garrisoned on St. Helena the 1st Battalion took part in an interesting ceremony when, in 1840, a party of French officials, under Prince de Joinville, arrived on the island to claim the remains of Napoleon who had been buried there on his death in 1821. The Emperor had expressed a wish to be laid to rest in his beloved France, and now, nineteen years later, this wish was at last to be carried out. The exhumation took place on a cold and wet night, and while an officer's guard of the 91st was mounted over the tomb, workmen toiled by the light of lanterns for more than five hours, digging their way through a solid mass of first clay, then stones, and finally masonry, to reach the coffin. The great Emperor's body had been enclosed inside a complex of five containers, and was in a state of perfect preservation. There were four coffins inside one another, one of tin, one of lead, and two of mahogany, and these were enclosed in a watertight cell. A few years later, the regiment was presented with a large bronze medal by the French, as a memento of their services.

During the South African campaign of 1842–5, the 2nd Battalion was also posted to the Cape, and there they helped to garrison the colony against the continual aggressiveness of the Kaffir, which finally culminated in open war in 1846. It did not last for long and within two years the trouble had been quelled, for the time being anyway.

The 2nd Battalion remained in South Africa until 1855, and was heavily engaged in the bitter fighting against the Kaffirs which broke out again in 1850 and lasted until 1853. The 1st Battalion had been sent home in 1848 but were constantly called upon to ship reinforcements to the Cape, one such draft being on board the *Birkenhead* when she sank in 1852.

At home, the 1st Battalion was being kept up to strength, but the recruits were not coming from Scotland. And yet another link with their rightful place of birth went in 1853, when, by order of the Adjutant to the Forces, they lost one of the last symbols of the regiment's origins, their right to the bagpipes. The pipes were, however, regained in 1865.

In 1854 the 1st Battalion went to Greece and were part of the force there with which it was hoped to discourage the Greeks from forming too close an alliance with Russia. Four years later, they were in India where they were garrisoned in Jubbulpore and Calcutta, and, for four years, in a remote area of the north frontier of the Central Province, called Kamptee. In India their commanding officer was Lieutenant-Colonel Bertei Gordon, who took over the regiment from Lieutenant-Colonel Glencairn Campbell, now promoted to command a brigade. And both these officers are considered to be two of the best commanding officers in the history of the regiment. They were brilliant soldiers and each one possessed the unique quality, for those days anyway, of having the true interests and welfare of their men close at heart. In an age when the welfare and well-being of the private soldier was almost an unconsidered subject, both colonels far exceeded, in that direction, what was expected of them. In return, they each in turn commanded a disciplined regiment, giving of its best, which was second to none. Lieutenant-Colonel Gordon, also, was one of the main instigators in obtaining for the 91st the right to wear Highland dress again in 1865.

On 21 March 1871, H.R.H. Princess Louise, and the Marquis of Lorne, son of the Duke of Argyll, were married at Windsor Castle, and a guard of honour was provided by the 91st. To mark the occasion Queen Victoria was pleased to approve, '. . . of the 91st Regiment (The Argyllshire Highlanders) being in future styled the

"Princess Louise's Argyllshire Highlanders", and of its being permitted to bear on its Regimental Colours the Boar's Head (the Campbell's crest) as a device surrounded with the motto "Ne obliciscaris" with the Princess Louise's coronet and cypher in the three corners'.

Between 1871 and 1879, the regiment was garrisoned in Scotland, at Inverness and Stirling, and in Ireland, and then, in 1879 was sent again to South Africa, this time for the Zulu War. Their most notable action here was undoubtedly at Ginginhlovo, where they bore the brunt of an attack by 10,000 Zulu warriors. The 91st lost 1 killed and 8 wounded, against the bodies of 500 dead Zulus left on the field of battle.

Whilst in Africa, the 1881 reorganization of the British Army took place and the 91st were merged with the 93rd to form Princess Louise's Argyllshire and Sutherland Highlanders.

Although the 93rd were not officially formed until 1799, their origins can be traced back forty years earlier. Since the Scottish uprising of 1745, the trust of the Scots, by the English, was almost nonexistent, and it was not considered advisable by London to have a large number of units of well-trained Scottish troops which, in effect, would have been a standing Scots army.

Instead, in times of national emergency, units were raised in Scotland for home defence purposes only, and immediately the crisis was over they were disbanded. The first such unit in Sutherland was raised by Lord Sutherland in 1759, it was active for four years until the war with France ended in 1763, and then disbanded. Six years later another similar unit was ordered to be formed, but as both the Earl and Countess of Sutherland had died, the instruction was directed to their 13-years old daughter. The little girl replied that, whilst having no objection to raising a Sutherland regiment, '. . . I am only sorry I cannot command it myself'. The unit was subsequently formed, and disbanded in 1783.

Yet a third such defensive unit was raised again, in 1793, by a relative of the Sutherlands, Lieutenant-Colonel Wemyss (later major-general) and three months after their disbandment in 1799, it was decided that Wemyss should form a regular regiment from Sutherland, the majority of men coming from the earlier unit. And thus was born the 93rd Sutherland Highlanders.

Between 1799 and 1881, the regiment served with distinction in most of the countries with which England was involved, including South Africa, America, Ireland, West Indies, Canada, and India, adding battle honour after battle honour to an already illustrious record. But their greatest moment of all came in the Crimea War, at an inconspicuous, dirty little town called Balaclava.

A month before Balaclava, the 93rd together with the 42nd and the 79th formed the Highland Brigade whose commander was the popular and much respected Sir Colin Campbell, and under this officer's inspiring leadership the Brigade successfully stormed the heights of Alma. They had to push their way through beautiful vineyards, and wade, waist-deep in places, through the muddy waters of the Alma River, which flowed along a deep gorge separating the Allied armies from the Russians who were positioned on the hills opposite. The Highlanders, under constant heavy fire the whole time, finally reached their objective, and once on the hill they swept irresistibly forward, shouting and cheering wildly. Men were falling like

Sir Colin Campbell leading his Highland Brigade on the Heights of Alma. Following their commanding officer's stirring cry, 'We'll hae nane but Hieland bonnets here', the Highlanders routed the Russians and won a resounding victory.

skittles from the Russian musket shot, and Campbell's horse was hit and fell from under him, but the charge of the 93rd was not checked and the Russians scattered and fled defeated.

Four weeks later, by October 1854, the Allies had advanced as far as Balaclava and had taken over the town for military purposes. On the morning of the 25th it was learned that a large force of about 25,000 Russians were approaching, but before they had actually been sighted, the 93rd and a battalion of Turkish troops, took up defensive positions outside the town. The 93rd were in the centre, formed into two long lines, and the Turks were on each flank.

'The Thin Red Line.' From a print in the author's possession.

As the Russians crowned the hill across the valley, the columns halted. The cavalry, the élite Cossacks of the Russian army, on the extreme left, trotted slowly forward with squadron after squadron coming up in the rear. The Highlanders, tensed and waiting, could hear the shouts of Russian orders in the distance, but the dust kicked up by the horses' hooves hid from them the sight of the cavalry being formed into one grand line. Then, with the orders now given and carried out, the

shouting stopped. The dust settled and, just for a moment it seemed, the line of cavalry stood motionless.

On the word of command they moved forward. Slowly at first, breaking into a canter. And then, with swords and lances pointed towards Balaclava, and gaining speed with every stride, they broke into a gallop and thundered across the plain, the ground trembling under the feet of over a thousand horses. As they got to within 800 yards of the thin red streak tipped with steel, those of the Turks who had not already fled in fear fired a volley, turned, and ran, leaving but 500 men of the 93rd to face the onslaught bearing down on them.

Sir Colin Campbell, astride his charger, sped down the ranks of Highlanders, his voice carrying above the noise about him. 'There is no retreat from here, men. You must die where you stand.'

The Russian cavalry were now within 600 yards and the volley of shot fired by the 93rd fell short. Some of the horsemen, here and there, were hit by shot from the British batteries behind the Highlanders, but it did not check the charge, and they continued to sweep furiously forward. In seconds they were within 250 yards, and the Scotsmen could now see quite clearly the determined eyes and bearded faces of the Russians.

Closer and closer came the wave of death, but the 93rd stood firm, and another volley of shot flashed from their rifles. The Russians were unable to rein up, or slacken speed to swerve away from the murderous hail of lead, and the leading horsemen tumbled from their horses. Those that were not hit '. . . wheeled about and fled faster than they came. "Bravo Highlanders", "Well done", shouted the excited spectators', as a *Times* correspondent on the spot put it.

The British heavy cavalry, waiting at the rear, now advanced and gave chase to the Russians who were scattering in all directions, in absolute panic and confusion.

Not only is this incident one of the most glorious in the 93rd's history, it is also one of the most spectacular in the British Army. It has been immortalized in books, and on the screen, and over the years many painters have depicted the event in oils, the most famous being the one by Robert Gibb called 'The Thin Red Line', painted in 1881.

As a matter of interest, one of the 'spectators' of the 93rd's brilliant stand against the Russians was Colour-Sergeant John Drake of the Royal Marines. This came about when Drake was posted to the Crimea and found himself one of a detachment of Marines detailed for shore duty and stationed near the hospital on the heights above Balaclava harbour. Their job was to act in support of Campbell's 'Thin Red Line', and from their vantage point were able to witness the whole event.

The battle at Balaclava was followed by Inkerman in November, and Sevastopol the following year. Then, after a few more months in the Crimea, during which the Armistice was signed, the regiment returned home in mid 1856.

In 1857, the regiment was posted to India. And even the journey out was not without its moments. The S.S. *Mauritius*, on which they travelled, suffered a mutiny by the crew, and had it not been for so many soldiers with experience of the sea, and able to assist in sailing the ship, the Captain would have been forced to turn back. However, they eventually reached Calcutta and were surprised and delighted to find their new commander in India was to be Sir Colin Campbell, who had led them so well in the Crimea.

This was the time of the infamous Indian Mutiny, and by November of 1857 the regiment was at Lucknow as part of a force of about 4,000 men, under Sir Colin, whose objective was to storm the city and free the British community of men, women, and children besieged there by the rebels.

Before reaching Lucknow the troops passed through the township of Cawnpore, which had been devastated by rebel forces, and the Highlanders witnessed the aftermath of what had been the scene of a terrible slaughter of innocent people, including women and children, many of whom had been hideously tortured and their bodies mutilated. It was not necessary for Campbell to impress upon his troops the need to free the Britons trapped in Lucknow. If they fell into the hands of the rebels, they would suffer the same fate, and the troops, sickened by what they saw, became determined this would not happen.

It was now a matter of history that, against overwhelming odds, the Relief of Lucknow was accomplished successfully. But only at a great cost in lives, and not for five days in all was the city finally breached and cleared of rebels. First, the British troops had to fight their way across the outer defences, then the main fortifications had to be overcome. It was solid fighting all the way through. In one instance the Highlanders charged a breach in one of the walls to the stirring sounds of, 'On wi' the Tartan', the battle charge of the great Montrose played above the noise of gunfire by the pipers of the regiment.

On the fifth day, the troops finally reached the buildings housing the civilians, who included about 600 women and children, and then it took three more days to evacuate all the people. Eventually nearly sixteen hundred in all were brought out to safety, and this in itself is a remarkable feat, as under the superb direction and leadership of Sir Colin Campbell not one single civilian was exposed to rifle fire from the enemy.

That seven V.C.s were awarded to men of the 93rd for individual acts of heroism is proud testimony of the prominent part played by the regiment in this action.

After the mutiny was put down in 1859, the 93rd spent another ten years in India before returning to Scotland in 1870. There then followed an uneventful period of time and eleven years later, in 1881, they became the 2nd Battalion of Princess Louise's Argyllshire and Sutherland Highlanders.

The Sutherland tartan was adopted by the new regiment and a badge was specially designed by H.R.H. Princess Louise. This consisted of the Campbell's boar's head, and the Sutherland wild cat, linked together by the Princess's cyphers.

From 1881 onwards, there have been few conflicts in which the Argyll and Sutherland Highlanders have not been involved. They fought through the Boer War; Le Cateaux in 1914 where, side by side with the Suffolks, and grossly outnumbered, they fought to the last and held back the German army for nine hours in some of the worst fighting of the entire war; Sudan (1924–5); China (1929–32);

India and the Mohmand operations (1934), and the Waziristan operations in (1937) where they were heavily engaged in mountain warfare on the troubled North-west Frontier; Palestine (1939); the Second World War, where their conduct and courage in so many battles and campaigns is beyond any form of praise, in particular the 2nd Battalion who were wiped out in their rearguard action during the terrible march out of Malaya and the subsequent fall of Singapore into the hands of the Japanese; Palestine in 1945 for three years; then Hong Kong, Korea, the Suez operation, Cyprus, Borneo, and finally Aden, which is where this magnificent story of a great regiment began.

> *Ye may talk aboot yer Gordons and yer gallant Forty-Twa,*
> *Yer Silver-Streakit Seaforths and yer Camerons sae Braw,*
> *But gi's me the Tartan o' the lads who look sae fine,*
> *The Argyll and Sutherland Highlanders o' The Thin Red Line.*

8. The search for the gold

In the immediate months following the disaster British naval divers made attempts to explore the wreck and locate a shipment of gold and silver put aboard at Portsmouth. The equipment however, in use at that time was very primitive and cumbersome and did not enable the divers to carry out their task satisfactorily. Repeated dives were made while weather permitted but, on each occasion, the men would come up empty handed, and exhausted.

The movements of the divers on the wreck were very restricted and they would only be down for a short amount of time. One of two methods was used for the supply of air to the divers. In one, two men on the deck of the surface ship would be frantically operating a giant bellows by hand, pushing air down the pipe to the diver, and it was essential their arms maintained the same regular momentum otherwise the poor man below would have either too much, or too little air. The other method involved a pump machine which was fractionally more reliable.

In the end the Admiralty gave up and abandoned the operation but, having failed to find any coins by their own means, they imposed a claim to one third of any gold or silver that might be recovered in later years. This move being the first official action to acknowledge the presence of a shipment of money, however big or small it might be.

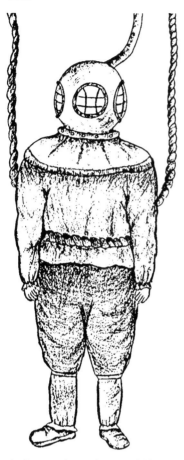

A diver in the 1850's would have looked something like this.

The first independent attempt was made in 1854 after the wreck was sold by the Admiralty at a public auction to a South African businessman named H. Adams. The equipment available to Mr Adams was of no great improvement to that used by the navy earlier but divers employed by this gentleman did in fact bring a number of artifacts to the surface. Amongst the items found were some of Colonel Seton's personal belongings including a cabinet he had used as a writing desk and some silver on which was engraved the Seton family crest.

But, of the gold, there was no trace.

Nearly forty years elapsed and it was not until 1893 that another expedition was made to the wreck. The broken remains of the ship had deteriorated badly and the currents had moved many sections and pieces away from the site. Everything was now spread over a bigger area making the operation even more difficult and arduous. The instigator this time was a man who had actually been on the *Birkenhead* on its last fateful voyage and had survived the disaster. His name was Lucas, ex-Ensign Lucas of the 73rd Regiment of Foot. After the disaster he settled in South Africa, taking up the study of law and, over the years, had become one of the Cape's most prominent Magistrates.

It could be reasoned that, of all people, Lucas was in an ideal position not only to know about the gold shipment but perhaps even its exact position on the ship. The diving equipment too, was much improved from that of forty years earlier. His explorations however, were no more successful than the first. Plenty of artifacts, but no gold. But Lucas did not lose financially over his enterprise because, shrewdly, he had taken the precaution of selling shares in the diving operation at £10 each, so he came out of it very well.

The years rolled gently by, and the fast deteriorating wreck of the *Birkenhead* lay like a ghost, undisturbed fifteen fathoms down at the bottom of the sea, shrouded by the mists of rumours and weird stories. And guarded, say the locals of Gansbaai even today, by giant octupi.

Then, in 1936, a quite remarkable man became interested in the narrative of the *Birkenhead* and the enigma of its gold. His colourful name was matched only by his equally colourful career. In his time, Tromp van Diggelen had been an engineer, a big game hunter, a circus strong man, a racing driver, and a sea salvage expert. He secured the rights to all the hundreds of wrecks lying off the South African coastline, including that of the ship that intrigued him the most. But it was not until 1958 that he was able to organise his first dive to the *Birkenhead* and, over the next few years, this was to be the first of many to the ship that had gradually become an obsession with him.

Obviously it was the gold that was the greatest lure but the story of the actual disaster, and the behaviour of the troops on board, deeply affected him and he was once quoted as saying that if ever he found the ship's bell it would be his wish to present it to England where he felt it rightly belonged.

When the salvage rights to the *Birkenhead* changed in 1936 to Mr van Diggelen he was granted a permit to '... search for and operate on abandoned vessels along the coast of the Union and to take possession of all articles or things of value which he may find.' His programme initially consisted of diving for the precious cargoes of the old Dutch East India Company ships that had foundered around the Cape. Using all the latest equipment and diving gear, including electronic devices for locating underwater metal, this colourful and popular personality's team operated extremely efficiently and successfully on these old wrecks.

He then turned his attentions to the *Birkenhead* and the first dive to the wreck was made in June 1958. The water was very murky and the first diver who went down had difficulty in exploring the vessel because the decks had collapsed and he could not recognise nor visualize the ship as she had been. When she sank, the *Birkenhead* had broken into three – the bow, the section amidships with the paddle wheels and engine room, and the stern. The two forward sections were located with some large pieces of the hull plating still intact, but scattered over a wide area. Of the stern though, there was no trace. It could have been in deeper water within a reasonable distance or, as was imagined at the time, it could have been carried by the currents in any direction over some distance. It had been reasoned too, that the stern of the ship was where the gold would have been stored.

van Diggelen devoted much time and money to the project but, despite comprehensive and detailed diving expeditions onto the wreck, both the gold and the bell eluded him. A great number of artifacts were recovered together with numerous pieces of non-ferrous metals, copper and brass which provided some return for his investment.

It is interesting to note that one of van Diggelen's chief divers, a South African named Nick Dekker fared incredibly well during his time spent diving onto the *Birkenhead*. He became a very rich man, returning to England and settling in the west country with his wealth – but not, he hastens to say, because of any coins found on the wreck.

Is the gold simply a myth, as many claim? Or is there really a treasure far beyond anyone's wildest dreams lying a hundred feet down in the shattered wreck of the *Birkenhead*?

According to legend a shipment of 250,000 gold coins was put on board at Portsmouth, the general theory being that it was to pay the troops at the Cape, some of whom had not been paid for over a year. The Author is deeply indebted to a Mr Peter Humphries of Sea Point, South Africa, for all the help he has so freely given, but Peter is somewhat sceptical about the gold and quite correctly points out that any money required by the army could have been drawn from the Bank of Africa's branches at Port Elizabeth or Grahamstown. Also, like many others, he states this was too vast a sum of money for this purpose – it would have been sufficient to have paid the entire British army in South Africa for about fourteen years. However, the army serving abroad, whilst perhaps having the facilities to draw money locally, often transported specie, the term used to distinguish coins of gold and silver from paper money, to pay the soldiers. It is possible that over the years the amount shipped has been grossly enlarged and that, in actual fact, a smaller sum of gold sovereigns and silver coins of lower denominations, enough in total to pay the troops, *was* transported.

The British Government, through the Ministry of Defence, have always chosen to remain silent, neither admitting nor denying the presence of a shipment of gold and silver. Nevertheless, apart from the act of the Admiralty in 1852 of staking a claim to one third of any specie found, and surely they would not make a claim to non existent money, there is other evidence which cannot be ignored, and other reasons, that does suggest there was a fairly substantial movement of gold and silver from England to the Cape on the *Birkenhead*.

The Treasury Chambers in London are helpful but cannot provide any records to support a claim that gold was transported on the *Birkenhead*. They point out that in 1852 a department called the Commissariat Department provided all the funds for the army and there are indeed various files available at the Public Records Office, Kew, which show all financial transactions that took place. None of these papers make any mention of a shipment at that time. The Royal Mint also, have no knowledge of any gold being transported to the Cape in 1852.

However, it should be noted the Treasury do not deny a shipment of gold and silver was transported on the *Birkenhead*, and there is one Treasury file on this vessel which has not yet been made available for public scrutiny. It would be most interesting to read the contents. Additionally, it is admitted by the Treasury that some of the relevant files on the Cape of Good Hope were destroyed before 1893.

During the Court Martial of the surviving crew members in 1852, after the pertinent questions were asked and the findings of the Court announced, Mr Richard Richards, master's Assistant, was recalled and specific questions concerning the ship's cargo were put to him. It should be mentioned here perhaps, that when enquiries are made at the public records Office for the transcript of the Court Martial, the bundle of papers relating to this do not contain any reference to the recall. Without further searching one would not be aware of the recall of witnesses. On pages 196 and 197, a copy of the transcript of the recall is shown in which it can be seen Mr Richards quite clearly states the Birkenhead was carrying a large quantity of specie. (The under-lining is on the original transcript.)

On page 198 is a copy of a letter dated 8th April 1902 to the War Office, written by Bernard Kilkeary, a Paymaster Sergeant of the 73rd Foot, who had been one of the troops on the Birkenhead's ill fated voyage; referring to the specie carried. A letter from the War Office, dated 19th April 1902, to the Secretary of the Treasury is shown on page 199 referring to Kilkeary's letter and written in a manner which does not throw any doubt on the suggestion there was specie carried on the ship.

Perhaps it was not army money that was being taken to South Africa. At that time there was a tremendous British influence at the Cape. This was the period in England's history when the ruling class, those with the power and the wealth, were the landed gentry. It was general practice in the army for commissions to be purchased, and promotion thereafter was frequently more by the ability to pay rather than by experience or competence. Since the late 17th Century the aristocracy had seen enough of Cromwell's model army and were constantly terrified of military dictatorship. They were so determined that professional soldiers should not be allowed to dominate the nation that they bought their way into service, even buying control of whole regiments, to maintain their high positions with the knowledge the army could not interfere. Despite England's great military victories, the men who won them, in the majority were nothing more than Dandies in uniform, more used to lounging and gambling in the clubs of St. James's, fishing, hunting and shooting, and doing the London season, rather than fighting for Queen and country. There was more devoted attention to the fit of their military dress than the workings of their muskets.

This set was well established at the Cape and with the long periods spent there it is possible they would want their wealth with them. These families were in possession of large amounts of readily accessible gold and silver which they would want available in South Africa to enable them to continue to buy power and maintain their lifestyle in the Colony.

CM 7ᵗ May 1852

Report on Court-martial (Continued)

11 - 27 -
16⅓

By the Judge Advocate.

Mr Richard Bevan Richards
masters assistant, was again
recalled. ——

Q. Was there any leadsman in the chains
previous to the ship sinking

a. Yes. Stone one of the prisoners.

Q. Did you hear him give any soundings

a. Yes, but I did not take any particular notice.

Q. Where were you when the Birkenhead struck

a. I was below

Q. When did the ship strike

a. a little before two oclock

Q. when were you sensible to this fact

a. When the impact took place, I looked at the
cabin clock, it may have been a minute after
she struck.

Q. Was she under sail or steam or both.

a. she was under steam alone

Q. Do you know what the Birkenhead was
carrying

carrying

a. Yes. Troops, Government stores and specie

2. Do you know how many troops

a. Not exactly without looking at the records

2 Do you know what stores she had on board

a. Yes but not the quantity without the manifest

2. Do you know what specie she carried

a. Yes, there were 120 boxes of specie but I cannot say except from the manifest what each or all the boxes contained.

2. What did they contain

a. Some 10000 some 5000 and some less in pounds some gold and some silver

2 Did the boats stay by the wreck till daylight

a No, but nearly till dawn

2. Was there any attempt made to save anything

a. No the vessel foundered too quickly

2. Did you see Mr Brodie at any time

a No, but I heard his voice

2. Do you know the names of the look out men

Copy

The Square, Dungannon
Coy.Tyrone.
8th April 1902

Sir,

Re Wreck of the Berkinhead.

I beg respectfully to enclose for the perusal
of the Rt.Honbio the Secretary of State for War a Newspaper
containing Narrative Supplied by me in connexion with this
Wreck from which I have purposely omitted any reference to
the "Specie" on Board which I understand was very considerable.

The information which I possess upon this subject
I shall place at the disposal of the proper Government
Department upon request being made to me.

I am Sir
Your obedient servant
(Sd) Bernard Kilkeary
formerly Paymr.Sergt.73 Regt.
late Mid.Ulster Artillery.

The Under Secretary of State for War
War Office Pall Mall
London.S.W.

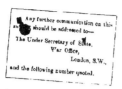

114/Misc:/1336. (F.1.).

TREASURY

6626

21 APR 1902

War Office,

London, S.W.

14 April, 1902.

Sir,

I am directed by the Secretary of State for
War to forward for the information of the Lords Commissioners of His Majesty's Treasury, the enclosed letter received from Mr. B. Kilkeary, formerly Paymaster Sergeant
73rd Regiment, respecting the Specie which was on board
the Birkenhead, at the time that vessel was wrecked in
February 1852, together with the enclosure which
accompanied his letter.

I am,

Sir,

Your obedient Servant,

The Secretary,

The Treasury.

The shipment on the *Birkenhead* therefore, could have been private funds and would account for the fact there are no official records. Obviously some of the rank and file, and crew, on the ship would have been aware of the shipment, hence the letters referred to in the previous paragraphs, but they might not have known whether it was official army money or the combined resources of these landowners turned military who commanded them.

It could even have been money in transit to India, either military or commercial.

A rational conclusion, forgetting even there is generally no smoke without fire, and ignoring too the surmise that any ship under water for more than fifty years or so automatically becomes a treasure ship, must be that for whatever purpose the *Birkenhead* was carrying a fairly substantial shipment of gold and silver on her last journey.

In the early nineteen eighties, to resolve what now had become one of the great mysteries of the sea, two of South Africa's most prolific salvage companies combined their individual skills and resources to mount an operation costing hundreds of thousands of pounds to challenge the elements and take from the reluctant ocean a secret it had retained for over one hundred and thirty years.

The Depth Recovery Unit (pty) Ltd., of Johannesburg, led by Doctor Allen Kayle, took their high technological equipment and expertise to Cape Town and joined forces with Aqua Explorations, a team of skilled divers whose assets included courage, endurance and dedication. It was an obvious partnership with the men of both organisations sharing one impulse and one preoccupation. A preoccupation with a ship built in England a century and a half ago and which now lay battered and broken one hundred feet down in the Indian Ocean just three miles off an appropriately named place called Danger Point.

Portable stanchion and portions of wood binnacle and rings, salvaged from the wreck.

This and the next photograph are shown by courtesy of the Williamson Art Gallery, Birkenhead.

This reminder of an honourable and chivalrous age long gone, this heroic and inspiring legend, this that is so much a part of England's great heritage, had now attracted the attentions of men who possessed the knowhow and the determination to succeed and solve once and for all the question of the gold.

In 1983, Doctor Kayle successfully applied to the South African National Monuments Council for a permit to perform salvage work on the wreck of the *Birkenhead*. In being granted the permit it was required that the work be conducted in a scientific and proper archeological manner, with due cognisance of the historical and cultural aspects.

Additionally, to preserve the site, and protect it from 'pirate' divers, the wreck and an area of 500 metres around it was declared a National Monument.

The salvage work on the *Birkenhead* was to be conducted under the supervision of the National Maritime Museum, the South African Cultural History Museum being the parent body. All such marine salvage work on historically important wrecks must be done under the supervision of a recognised academic institution such as a national or provincial museum, or the department of oceanography or archeology of a University. One of the conditions is that the museum receives a percentage of all artifacts recovered, not necessarily by monetary value, rather by historical importance.

After a year's work in bringing massive equipment down from Johannesburg to Cape Town, and undertaking preliminary exploratory dives to the wreck, the main operation commenced in the African summer of 1986, January, February and March. The broken remains of the stern of the ship having been located this was where the search was concentrated. Following the earlier pattern set by van

Bronze stanchion, deck light, frame and glass with bull's eye and lead scupper, salvaged from the wreck of the *Birkenhead*.

Diver Erik Lombard with a mustard container brought up from the *Birkenhead* wreck,
cork intact — it stinks horribly.
(Reproduced by courtesy and permission of *The Argus*, Cape Town)

Diggelen it was again reasoned that as the stern section contained the officer's quarters and stores rooms it was there the gold and silver would have been stored.

It had been the intention of Depth Recovery Unit and Aqua Explorations to use a diving bell, employing saturation diving techniques but this proved to be impossible. The salvage vessel was anchored dangerously close to the *Birkenhead* rock and was riding huge sea swells, suffering up and down movements beyond the safety limits for using a diving bell.

Divers like Charlie Shapiro, who led Aqua Explorations, went over the side with gas cylinders on their backs and spent long periods on the sea-bed before surfacing to use the de-compression chamber on the surface vessel. The weather was certainly no friend to these men and the sea swells and high winds constantly hindered and delayed operations. Conditions on the wreck too, made even the most simple of tasks an effort, with visibility sometimes no more than two metres. The divers would meticulously sift through the sand and silt, labouriously clearing small areas at a time and then return later to find the sand had swept back and covered where they had previously cleared. It became soul destroying repetition.

Conglomerate, which is a mass of rock hard substance caused by chemical reactions over the years was also a major problem, as was the fact that all the levels of the ship occupied only one plane. The wooden decks had rotted decades ago and the broken and twisted sheets of hull plating lay scattered over a wide area, totally distorting any recognisable shape and making orientation virtually impossible. Nevertheless, diagrams were constructed showing various parts of the ship as she now lay and calculations were made enabling it to be possible to pin-point, accurately, where any particular section of the ship would be.

But still .... no gold.

Many times the team were near to total despair in their search for the elusive gold but they were still convinced of its existence. They found encouragement in the condition of some of the metals brought to the surface. For instance, copper that had been located in certain areas was uncorroded, yet copper taken from other parts of the sea bed was seen to be heavily corroded which could have been caused by a process of electrolysis, indicating the presence close by of a more noble metal. The transference of electrons when two different metals interact produces corrosion in the 'weaker' metal. Thus, steel will sacrifice itself to copper and in turn copper sacrifices itself to silver or gold. They felt this was in their favour. It helped to spur them on and, with an inexplicable premonition, tension mounted.

And then, on Thursday 27th February 1986, just one day following the anniversary of the sinking of the *Birkenhead*, it looked as though the team's faith and resolution was about to he rewarded. Jubilant divers recovered 24 gold coins from the wreck. They could hardly believe it and one or two even cried for joy. All hearts beat a little faster but: regrettably however, it had to be acknowledged that rather then being part of a large consignment, they probably represented a private cache belonging to one of the officers. The excitement naturally dimmed a little.

Nevertheless, numismatists who examined the coins claimed they could easily be among the best examples of gold sovereigns anywhere in the world, in particular the following four:

1821 George IV with Laureated Head;
1850 Victorian with Unicorn;
1837 William IV;
1820 George III with St. George and the Dragon on the reverse.
This last coin was designed by Benvenuto Pistrucci, an Italian of French nationality who worked for the Royal Mint.

The finding of these gold coins had quite a startling effect on the British Government who suddenly came to life in the matter and, whilst still not conceding there had been a shipment of gold on the *Birkenhead*, became locked with South Africa over the ownership of the wreck and its contents.

South Africa's stand was that, apart from England relinquishing any rights to the ship because of the sale by auction in 1852, under the terms of South Africa's Sea Shore Act anything lying in their territorial waters belonged to them.

England, on the other hand, ignoring the question of the auction, quite bluntly stated that a British Ship with British crew and soldiers aboard could belong to no-one but England. It was also a War Grave, they said, and should be left as such.

A spokesman for the British Embassy in Cape Town exclaimed indignantly, 'We have never abandoned the wreck.' And to leave not the slightest doubts in the minds of the South African authorities he added for good measure, 'A British bottom is a British bottom no matter where it might be.'

A classic statement of some brilliance but one that has not stopped the South Africans. 'What does England want the gold for anyway?' they ask with a wry smile. 'To use in their national budget, perhaps!'

Oblivious to the controversy Depth Recovery and Aqua Explorations pressed on and, late in 1986, preparations and plans were put under way for the forthcoming dive in 1987. Charlie Shapiro came to London and the Author had the privilege and the pleasure of assisting him in detailed research into the possible whereabouts of the gold on the ship.

To Charlie, and the others, it was not really a question of whether there was gold or not, it was a question of *where was it?*

His confidence was totally infectious.

Divers with gold coins from the *Birkenhead*.
(Reproduced by courtesy and permission of *The Argus*, Cape Town)

Row brews over who owns the wreck off the SA coast

Britain wants the Birkenhead treasure trove

Weekend Argus Foreign Service

A STORM is brewing between South Africa and Britain over the right to the Birkenhead treasure.

The British Foreign Office maintains that the HMS Birkenhead wreck and everything on it — including the gold coins found by South African divers last week — belongs to Britain.

But the South African Government says that in terms of the Sea Shore Act, anything lying within South African territorial waters belongs to South Africa.

A British Foreign Office spokesman said the two governments had locked horns over the Birkenhead as recently as this year and that contact was continuing.

"We maintain that we own the ship and its contents, which are part of it. We are also concerned about the ship because it is a war grave," he said.

Dr Chris Loedolff, director of the South African National Monuments Council, said while he was aware of the negotiations between the governments, he failed to see how the British could lay claim to the gold.

"The divers will be entitled to 50 percent of whatever they salvage from the wreck and the South African Government will get the other 50 percent.

"The shipwreck had been abandoned for years until our divers received a permit from the National Monuments Council specifying that they had to report back regularly to us and make an inventory of their finds.

Donated to museums

"Material from shipwrecks is usually donated to museums. We will be donating our 50 percent of the salvaged material to museums in South Africa but we are prepared to consider applications from British museums," he said.

Ever since the ship went down off Danger Point in 1852 with the loss of 445 lives, there has been controversy over whether it was carrying gold.

The Ministry of Defence in Britain has said officially that it could not confirm or deny the rumour of gold aboard.

Taken from the South African *Weekend Argus*, March 8th, 1986, to whom acknowledgement is made for their kind permission to reproduce.

In 1987, and the later series of dives of 1988, the team decided to carry out their operations in the area of the armoury room. This was situated on the lower deck of the ship, forward of the engine compartment, more or less midship. For loading purposes at the time there would have been comparatively easy access down through the ship for men carrying the heavy chests. Also, of course, as was the custom, there would have been an armed Royal Marine guard on the arms room. They could then have served a dual purpose, guarding both the weapons and the gold.

The same torturous conditions were endured by the divers as in the previous year. In fact, the weather was reckoned to be even worse and many times the lives of those involved were at great risk.

Needless to say, the *Birkenhead* kept her secret.

Interesting *Birkenhead* relics handed over to the South African Cultural History Museum by the salvors. Will the bulk of the historically-significant items brought to the surface be lost to the South African public because of a three-year secrecy agreement? Happy with what has been received so far are, from left, Tom Graham, curator of the SA Maritime Museum, Mary van Blommestein, museum officer, and Dr. Bruno Werz, marine archæologist. The model is of a ship of the same era as the *Birkenhead*.
(Reproduced by courtesy and permission of *The Argus*, Cape Town)

A selection of artifacts in the author's possession.

The broken bottle, made of thick, dark glass, probably contained port. The two handles are of bone and are all that's left of two knives, the blades of which have totally eroded. There are two small pulleys, and two large copper nails, one of which is still affixed to a piece of wood deck planking. The badge is that of the 43rd Light Infantry, and the two buttons are of the Navy (left), and of the 74th Regiment on which is incorporated an Indian elephant to commemorate the battle of Assaye. The artifacts are in remarkably good condition, having spent so many years under the sea.

After every dive, back to 1986, a constant flow of fascinating artifacts from England's Victorian heyday would be brought to the surface, marvellous pieces of tangible history from which an intriguing picture can he built of the manner and way of life of the soldiers and sailors of that time. A toothbrush made of bone, its bristles had gone but the copper wire by which they had been tied to the shaft remained. A rubber overshoe and a brass padlock. Royal Doulton china. The bone handle of an army issue knife with the name and number, J. Nielsen 3113, carved into it. Ornate door handles. Literally hundreds of items, each one with a story to tell.

The expeditions are now well over and finished. The salvage ship, her crew and the divers have returned home. They are many miles from the scene that became so much a part of their lives. Only the rock, still pointing upwards like an accusing finger, the waves that batter it, and the wreck that lies beneath, remain.

Another year perhaps, for Allen Kayle, Charlie Shapiro and all the others who came to know the *Birkenhead* as well as those who perished in her.

Let us hope they try again, because men like that deserve to succeed. Not just for something to do as simply another job. Not so that England and South Africa can continue to argue over who owns what. Not even for the wealth the finding of the gold would bring — it has gone far beyond that. They need to succeed to prove to themselves their type of faith, blind faith, and courage, which have their own deeply private and satisfying rewards.

Throughout history too, every story has a beginning, a middle, and an end. The story of the wreck of the *Birkenhead* has a beginning and it has a middle. The end will come when they find the gold.